RH
4/30/77

D0332015

A Complete Guide To Therapy:
From Psychoanalysis To Behavior Modification

Also By Joel Kovel

White Racism: A Psychohistory

A
Complete Guide
To Therapy

From Psychoanalysis To Behavior Modification

JOEL KOVEL, M. D.

PANTHEON BOOKS

New York

Copyright © 1976 by André Schiffrin and Virginia Kovel, as Trustees under the Trust Agreement dated May 25, 1973 for the benefit of Jonathan Kovel and Erin Kovel.

All rights reserved under International and Pan American Copyright Conventions. Published in the United States by Pantheon Books, a division of Random House, Inc., New York, and simultaneously in Canada by Random House of Canada Limited, Toronto.

Library of Congress Cataloging in Publication Data

Kovel, Joel, 1936–
  A Complete Guide To Therapy.
  Includes bibliographical references and index.
  1. Psychotherapy. I. Title.
RC480.K67 1976   616.8'914   75-38120
ISBN 0-394-73336-3

Manufactured in the United States of America

First Paperback Edition

To the memories of Simeon Tropp and
Alfred Corvin

Though in many of its aspects this visible world seems formed in love, the invisible spheres were formed in fright.

—Herman Melville, *Moby Dick*

For All Things Exist in the Human Imagination. . . .

—William Blake, *Jerusalem*

CONTENTS

ACKNOWLEDGMENTS

To my wife, who gave me the idea to write this book, and numberless reflections since; to Jean Strouse and André Schiffrin, who guided the development of the manuscript; to Barbara Plumb, who worked with it in the late stages; to Mel Roman, for his advice and critical reading; to Edward Sachar and Jack Wilder, who provided academic support; to Russell Jacoby, Carol Lopate, Stanley Aronowitz, Elizabeth and Stuart Ewen, David Nasaw and Rosalyn Baxandall, for their reflections; to Ken Porter, who helped immeasurably with a course in comparative psychotherapies at the Albert Einstein College of Medicine; and to the residents in psychiatry who participated in the course and the guests who provided its substance; to Marie Mele, who typed heroically in the face of my handwriting; to Benjamin Nelson, Bennett Simon, Fred Sander, Jane and Andy Ferber, Sylvia Davidson and Jane Vern, who provided knowledge and/or materials on one theme or another; and, so the scope of my indebtedness is plain, to my teachers, students, therapists and patients one and all.

INTRODUCTION

What follows is one man's view of the world of therapy. It aims to acquaint the reader with the principal therapeutic approaches to the various forms of emotional difficulty now practiced in the United States; and, more importantly, to enable him or her to make a sound decision when faced with the all-too-common necessity of seeking help for personal distress.

Because such decisions are not technical matters, but stray into the deepest areas of value, I have not hesitated to confront some rather knotty problems in the course of this work. To do so came automatically, as I have long been personally involved—on both sides of the therapeutic relationship—with the very issues the following pages disclose. Thus there was never any chance of Olympian detachment from the matter at hand. If the work may seem opinionated as a result, I hope it makes up in depth and commitment what it lacks in evenhandedness.

Of the impressions I brought with me to this study, one in particular has been reinforced in the writing: that therapeutics necessarily involves ideology and is based upon real practice. Although a rational analysis of the realities of therapy can be made—and I hope that this work meets such a standard—anything approaching the impersonality of experimental science will only succeed in purifying the subject out of its actual existence in the world of human affairs. Like politics, the art of the possible, yet also like religion, the care of souls, therapy seems true to nothing but uncertainty. The proper approach is that of *critique,* by which I mean an inquiry that reveals the hidden inner assumptions of a

phenomenon, grounds it in history and does not pretend that the
observer stands separate from the thing observed.

As to my own immersion, I have been engaged in the practice
and teaching of Freudian psychoanalysis and psychoanalytic psychotherapy for a number of years. Some years before that, I went
through a Reichian phase. The only other approaches with which
I have some direct experience are group and family treatment,
practiced within a basically psychoanalytic framework. Knowledge
of the other approaches has been confined to reading, discussions
with some leading practitioners and general observations gleaned
over the years concerning the curious ways of *Homo therapeuticus*.
Thus there should be no question from the outset that though
the pages ahead present a view of the whole range of therapy, it
is a view from one side—and a side many would regard as
old-fashioned at that. In truth I am something of a therapeutic conservative. I distrust dramatic instant cures and therapeutic breakthroughs. For all the razzle-dazzle, they seem as tedious and
old-fashioned as the tidings of a new messiah or the miracles at
Lourdes. We have enough inflation without adding the promise
of salvation through therapy. Such an ethic betrays the real needs
of people for emotional assistance by promising more than can be
delivered. More, it distracts energy from where it is needed most—
the overhauling of society—to an ultimately individual realm. For
it seems to me that, given the nature of the psyche and present
social relations, a certain amount of neurosis is inevitable, and
any therapy that tries to short-circuit this truth is baying at the
moon. In contrast, a modestly held therapeutic goal, rationally
and ethically applied, can do more real good for the individual—
and leave the way open for authentic social action.

It follows that my therapeutic conservatism is combined with
a rather radical political sensibility, and that I apply political
criteria to the evaluation of therapies. This is because therapy,
being a social relation, has a real, though ambiguous, political
content. I shall try to spell some of this out in the last chapter.
However, the reader should be forewarned that many of the
pages in between are marked with a social and political concern
unusual in writings about therapy, most of which simply assume
neurosis and treatment to be something going on in an isolated
individual or family. I do not, of course, expect every reader to
share the political opinions expressed in what is to come; however
I do hope that a heightened awareness of the hidden political content of therapy will result from the reading.[1]

The tension which underlies this work can be briefly described as that between radical thought and reality. Both Freud and Reich were radical thinkers who developed systems of therapy. Freud's system held out the hope of reconciliation within the self as a means of cure, while Reich moved in the opposite direction and promised breakthrough and transcendence. Both conceptions continue to play a role in the development of therapy. Yet, by being radical—going to the root—Freud and Reich were each deliberately incomplete, and set aside much of the actual world in which the neurotic lives. More, they necessarily tended to ask too much of people. (Indeed, Freud and Reich both failed to come to grips with their own implications for a correspondingly radical social change, although Reich, to be sure, went further than anyone else in that direction, at least for a while.)

But therapy is built out of what is possible and moves on the ground of everyday life. Thus it remains in some tension with radical thought and politics. Indeed there are times when therapy succeeds insofar as it is shallow and conformist. But from another angle there are other times when it succeeds because it is more precisely attuned to the real situation than is classical Freudian or Reichian practice. Thus in my own instance I moved away from Reichian therapy as I came to be of the opinion that it was too remote from psychological reality to be genuinely useful. And while my experiences with Freudian treatment have been considerably more productive, its limits as a therapy, both in a given case and for the whole range of emotional disorders, are quite clear to me.

Given the immensity of emotional suffering, one either extends therapeutics from the original psychoanalytic model or falls victim to nihilism. Whether one rejects the therapeutic ideology from the standpoint of a conservative critic of culture like Philip Rieff[2] or in the interests of political radicalism, the results are unsatisfactory. The questions are, rather, what are the particular varieties of therapeutics, what emotional and ideological needs do they meet, and how are they to be assessed in the infinitely fluid and complex real situation? It is to these questions that the following pages are devoted.

In the system I am proposing, Freudian psychoanalysis retains an important yet limited role as therapy, and a central one as theory. As a theory psychoanalysis is indispensable for an authentically human psychology poised dialectically between biology and society. It will be obvious in what follows that I am no defender of a rigid psychoanalytic orthodoxy. I do believe however that there is a certain nucleus of truth in its method and in its basic notions of repression, the unconscious and infantile sexuality, and to this nucleus I try to remain loyal while modifying other aspects of the theory in accordance with a historically developing reality.

The limitations of psychoanalytic therapy are related to the truth of a theory which sees too much to be readily reassured about human possibilities. Russell Jacoby has put the matter well:

> The acuteness of Freud as bourgeois thinker is here again glimpsed; he unflinchingly articulated contradictions and refrained from blurring them in the name of therapy or harmony. From his early writing to his last no attempt is made to reconcile individual therapy with the metatheory of psychoanalysis; they exist in contradiction. Insofar as civilization was repression, individual therapy was education in repression, albeit conscious repression.[3]

Yet, as stated above, the theory remains incomplete and it cannot allow for all the possibilities of therapeutic change. Meanwhile other theories and therapies have sprung from the varied soil of bourgeois culture, each with its own claim, its own truth, its own ideology. The prospective consumer, emotionally hurt, his judgment often compromised, feels at times like a stroller down the midway of a county fair, surrounded by hawkers shouting a confused jumble of overlapping terminology, quarter-baked claims and polemics.

This study bids to set matters a little straighter. Many works exist in which different exponents of the various schools each sell their wares, while in others one individual attempts to take on some segment—usually the different psychoanalytic schools—of the therapeutic project, but usually from the therapist's standpoint.[4] If the present study offers anything different it is the effort to explore the great majority of main approaches from the standpoint of the *user*.

If it is to be useful, any presentation of the different schools must be set in a unified and general framework of neurosis and therapy. Accordingly I have preceded the actual description of the therapies with two chapters: the first presenting what can go wrong emotionally and how to recognize and assess it; the second taking up in a broad way the possibilities of therapeutic change. Following the main text of each chapter concerning a particular school, I have appended a little catechism entitled "Practical Synopsis" in which questions about the usefulness of the therapy are considered. All these questions are later drawn together and amplified in Chapter 15, titled "Guide For The Perplexed." The last question posed in this chapter, because it extends into matters of social theory on a broader scale than can be encompassed by a practical view of the therapies themselves—indeed, because it calls into question the very practicality of therapy—is accorded a final chapter all its own.

There is no universally recognized way to classify the therapies. I have chosen one that is roughly organized along historical lines and follows a certain thematic progression. Thus the reader who wishes to develop some systematic understanding of the basic issues in therapy should read the chapters in order, since each builds on the ones before. At the same time each chapter on a type of therapy is written to be read independently by those who wish particular information on a given form of treatment.

It should also be stated that with a few minor exceptions I have concentrated on the disturbances and treatment of adults. To include children and adolescents in the presentation would be both unwieldly and outside my competence.

This work does not attempt a scholarly review of the vast literature on neurosis and therapy. Accordingly I have been rather sparing with footnotes. Those that have been used are designed either to orient the reader to a few key works where further study can be pursued, or to amplify an occasional point not directly germane to the text.

The limits of this study go beyond my personal shortcomings and the fact that it is impossible to do justice to all angles of such an immense subject as therapy. They include also the imposition of a view through the lenses of one main body of theory and experience—in the present case, Freudian psychoanalysis. While inevitable if the account is not to become chaotic, this also necessarily imposes some limitations on how effective other approaches may seem. That psychoanalysis is the most general theory is some reassurance, but no guarantee against one-sidedness. Perhaps the present work will stimulate someone to do the same from the standpoint of a different theory.

I have tried to be as fair and comprehensive as I can, and to present each therapy in its own light without undue polemic. But what is or is not "undue" is not exactly an objective category. The fact is, I am a person of strong opinions and it would be hypocritical if not impossible to write otherwise. Moreover, therapy is a serious matter and a fundamentally problematic one. It can touch the human heart and promote freedom; but it can just as likely mechanize, enslave and drive a person crazy. The fact that most real instances lie between the extremes in no way means that a study of the therapies should paper over actual contradictions. For a guide to therapy to be worthwhile it has to be critical. In any event, if Blake was right when he held that "without Contraries is no progression," then in the field of the therapies there exists a ground for something potentially worthwhile.

Part ONE

Neurosis And Therapy

1

The
Contours Of Disorder

The number of ways people can go awry is countless. Many, perhaps most, instances of unhappiness may be the product of ultimately impersonal forces, but more than enough suffering of human origin is left over. And these personal instances are in themselves of bewildering variety. So wide is the range that almost any theory of emotional disturbance—and therapy—will find at least a few examples that make sense according to its terms.

Bearing this in mind, yet with the hope that, if we look closely enough, something of the world can be seen in a grain of sand, let us turn to one example of suffering and try to appreciate its terms.

THE CASE OF MR. A.

William A. was forty-two years old and had lived his life in the great, decaying urban metropolis for whose government he worked as a building inspector. His father had been a contractor, and although his own aspirations to follow in the same role had somehow never materialized, he took comfort in being in a position to check up on the work of other contractors. Meanwhile, he nursed his boyhood dream of doing the job himself someday.

He was once proud of his work. Lately, however, things had not been so good; indeed, seemed to be going to pieces. Some inspectors had been caught taking bribes; others had been assaulted by construction men. Demoralization and foreboding had replaced the sense of prestige which once lay in the work. Several of Mr. A.'s colleagues had already resigned in a tide of anxiety that was lapping at his feet on the day in June, six months before I saw him, when a contractor with whom he had had entirely unremarkable dealings before suddenly turned in the midst of the inspection, cursed him and knocked him down with a violent blow to the chest.

Dazed, Mr. A. struggled to his feet and retreated. He felt no anger at the man, only fear, and would have preferred to let the matter drop. But there were witnesses; charges had to be pressed. He spoke no more to his assailant and saw him only once again, on that day in court when a suspended sentence was handed down. He still felt no hostility toward the man, but despite the absence of any further threat, his fear increased. More troubling yet, it began to take a new form; he now began to be haunted by worry about the exacerbation of an old wound.

Ten years ago he had lain on the edge of death, victim of a trap set by nature. While enjoying fine health, robust and athletic, he had been seized by a sudden excruciating headache. Rushed to the hospital, his life hanging on each minute, he was just barely saved by the neurosurgeon. An aneurysm—a weakness in the wall of a cerebral artery—was discovered, ligated and removed just before it would have fatally burst. A metal clip was left in place to strengthen the ligature, and except for the presence of this foreign body—about which he would jest in lighter moods—he made an uneventful recovery and emerged from the hospital with full use of his faculties.

Still, he was wary. Too wary, said the neurosurgeon after the prescribed recuperative period had passed. No need to worry about the clip, or the vessel opening up. And yet Mr. A. could not shake the fear. He had been too close to death and, always finicky about his health, he now worried more and more. Gone were vigorous athletics. Sex suffered too, through the gradual attrition people are so willing to take for granted. For about a year Mr. A. and his wife had slept apart. He said his wife didn't complain, but I never got to know him well enough to determine what this meant.

In any event, fear that the blow to his chest might have loosened the clip in his head became a ruling idea and no reassurances by physicians helped. He took a leave of absence from his job and planned to move from the city, though without any clear-cut goal. In fact, his behavior was deteriorating altogether, and when finally, at the urging of his family and physician, he sought psychiatric consultation, he looked like a man who had been living with the devil.

Despite a cocky façade, his confidence was only a porous barrier through which swarmed unknown fears. He would try to identify the source of his terror so that corrective action could be taken—maybe the clip would break, maybe his assailant would come back. Each idea corresponded to something real, yet each was swept aside by a fresh surge of nameless dread.

There was more to his story, of course—there always is. But unlike his account of the attack and the aneurysm, he made no spontaneous connection between his unhappiness and these further findings. Oh, yes, he said in response to a question about early illnesses, yes, he had once been sick as a two-year-old. Very sick. Funny, but come to think of it, it also involved the chest. Lung abscess. They had to open the chest wall and put a tube in—for a long time, too. He had been sick like this for six months, then bedridden and sickly much longer. No, he didn't remember much about how this affected his life as a child, except that he recalls being happy. . . . Maybe he got so interested in athletics to compensate. . . . The story trails off; he appears to lose interest.

The topic changes, drifting into other concerns. Children: six of them; the wife and he always wanted children, for reasons that get lost somehow. Fine kids. Healthy, though he doesn't envy young people nowadays. Too much to do, they're spoiled, hang around and watch television or go out in the street and get into trouble. Why, in his day—the eyes shift, glance around hoping to pick up something reassuring—he mentions how hard he worked, then switches back to his children. The oldest, a daughter not quite eighteen, got married a year ago. A little young, perhaps, but of course he was glad. Somehow he doesn't look glad, and launches right away into a tirade on wild kids. One wonders about the circumstances of the marriage, but he becomes positively defensive now and evades everything, the thread of his ideas becoming more disconnected, returning again and again to his bodily fear and the need to move, perhaps to Arizona, while references to past and present family life flit through the maze of associations like fireflies at dusk.

"Well, Mr. A.," I say to him, "it's a good thing you came to our clinic, as you are in need of the help we can give you."

He agrees, then returns to plans about Arizona.

What ails Mr. A.? One knows so little, really, about him. Where can you stop learning about a person and say, "This is enough, now I understand"? The most exhaustive technique can only glean a small fraction of the communicable mental contents of another human being; and while each bit and unit of understanding adds to the image we form of him, the image remains but a reflection of another consciousness no one else can ever share—any more than sparks can be collected as they fly off a wheel. And even this received picture may be grossly devoid of basic detail. I worked with a woman once for two years before she casually mentioned that she had had a baby sister who died in infancy, and that her illness and death had ruined her family for a while, bankrupting her father and driving her mother into a mental hospital—all when my patient was four years old. If I had stopped with her the session before, none of this would have been known as such to me; and yet it must have been with her somehow throughout, lived out in her own special way. Nor did my learning this change things much for her, as the emotional impact had long since been split off and diverted to those "special ways" through which her misery was expressed.

Still, no matter how little we know of another person, we are constantly reasoning about what we do know and forming hypotheses. One must take Mr. A.'s story at some of its face value. His fright has *something* to do with the reasons he gives. Since fear is a response to danger, and since being struck by some brute or having a life-threatening illness are dangers, then there are actual grounds for fear. Talking with Mr. A. for the first five minutes or so left me with no other conclusion to draw, and while what he said later forces us to regard his own level of explanation as seriously incomplete, it remains incomplete rather than insignificant.

This is a general and vast problem. It is so easy to say something partially true about a person, so utterly impossible to encompass the whole. The external, environmental or, shall we say, "real" sources of distress are so palpably there, and common sense is so self-evidently true, that it is not only easy but even unimpeachable to let our understanding come to rest at this level. That's just what it in fact does: comes to rest. Common sense is peaceful and reassuring; and the evident is both what is true and most convenient to see.

The city *is* decaying; its dangers *are* real. To be at the gate of death *is* so frightening that a man doesn't have to be crazy to be uneasy about reassurances against the return of such a threat—one, moreover, emanating from unseen bodily places. There is nothing for psychotherapy to do against such a fear—so long as it remains such a fear.

It turns out that this is not often the case. Things are almost invariably more complicated, as Mr. A. reveals to us by the inconsistencies in his behavior. To begin with, one is perplexed by his lack of hostility toward his assailant. A person does not have to act on it, but the expectable feeling toward someone who knocks him down is anger, which is as "natural" in this setting as fear itself. Now Mr. A. may not have been angry at all; or he may have been angry but chose to forget it; or he may have been angry but chosen not to speak of it to the interviewer. In each instance something is out of place and calls for explanation.

One wonders not only about omissions but also about excesses. Here we sense that the degree of disturbance is simply not accounted for by the realistic threat. It is not just quantitative, not the surplus of anxiety as against the real danger. After all, how can we measure the extent of a threat that belongs in another's experience? No, it is rather qualitative, the way his thoughts wander, the way his own explanations break down and are seized by forces that cannot be named, the way his eyes dart around, looking for something immediate, some external sign of a subjective state.

And one wonders about recurrences, about things which are brought together so forcefully that they stir us into an attempt at explanation. It cannot be without meaning that Mr. A. ends up inspecting the work of those who do what his father did—and what he wanted to do. And what of the connection between the current blow to the chest, the lesion in his head and the childhood lung abscess that led to the opening of his chest wall and the insertion of a foreign object.

It is notable, too, that the omissions intertwine with these recurrences: that it is the figure of the contractor who both suggests his father and toward whom his feelings are so strangely devoid of anger; and that he seems to evade emotional significance exactly at that point—the early illness—where logic would most expect it to occur. Could it be that what he keeps out of awareness at these points of the story will show its effect at others?

But this, too, though it offers a more satisfactory understanding, also falls well short of accounting for even what little we know. For this man lives his life in the present among other people—his family and the community surrounding it. How can we limit our concern to the immediate perimeter of those few focal events and the memories they evoke without comprehending the day-in, day-out fabric within which these events are shaped?

For example, what about his sexuality? He does not seem to recognize this as a problem, but it surely is. No part of life is more easily distorted in the experiencing or telling. Mr. A. reveals to us only that something has gone wrong—notably enough, well *before* the event to which he ascribes his distress. He tends to minimize its significance, thus reducing his wife to a shadow. But simple reflection tells us this cannot be so. He may see her in a dim light, but she is there all the same, living out her own existence, interpenetrated with his. Sex negated is no less critical than sex affirmed; we know it lies there behind Mr. A.'s screen even if we cannot see more of it. No matter for now; what is important will come out in good time. What is told at first, no matter how lavish it may seem, is by and large an official account: what the public face can show, both to itself and others. Further back, closer to the core of experience, lurk phantoms. They may assume some dream guise which is forgotten upon awakening; or they may burst through in some fantasy; or be enacted in some disguised way, then go to rest again. We sense their presence in Mr. A.'s haunted look, but can say no more of what the inner content of his experience tells him.

Meanwhile his actual life goes on. Each instant his consciousness is played upon by a multitude of forces. His wife's effect we wondered about, then set aside. What of those children? How does a man feel who has lived his life on the verge of terror, who senses time gathering up on him, feels age and impotence, sees, however fitfully, his dread in the morning mirror while he shaves, and perhaps shakes off a lingering bad dream—then turns to regard his children. What of the intervening years with their myriad hopes and fears? What of the transient rage he may have stifled long ago when they were babies who took his wife away from him; or the adoration when he sensed a perfection in them and put onto them his frustrated hopes; or the special feeling when the daughter who would later go off with another man sat on his own lap pledging fealty? And what of his keepsakes, mementos, little pleasures, the threads weaving current life with lost childhood? What recapitulations, thwarted hopes, lingering pains must enter into every moment, sum themselves up in his current despair?

Moreover, this, his personal life, has to be grounded in social existence. Mr. A. is part of society, too; he has defined himself and is defined by others by class, race and occupational identity. These memberships give form and structure to his more intimate concerns; they are neither indifferent nor tacked on. What he is becomes defined by the integral of his private and public worlds. Consequently, changes at any one level will affect all the rest. If he is oppressed at one end, it will not be without effect on the other; and the interplay of these effects will enter into his every feeling. His loyalty to the social order enters here just as much as the material resources he can extract from it. His work gave him a sense of being somebody, and it defined and delimited his feelings with respect to others, most notably his father. The status of an official is proof of his life's value. If that is taken away, as by a general deterioration in public confidence, then he is primed for trouble.

Enough has been written by now of the troubles of Mr. A. for us to realize both the difficulty of definition and the need to take a holistic view. In other words, no matter how circumscribed a neurosis may seem, it is in reality embedded in the totality of a person's relationships.

This approach might at first glance appear to make matters more difficult for us. It would be more appealing to select out of the mass of human phenomena some touchstone of disturbance—say, "infantile trauma," or "fixated libido," or faulty "interpersonal relations," or "emotional blocks," or "conditioning"—and lay the blame at its feet. Not only would the task of understanding be simplified, but the strategy for restoring health would be equally clear-cut. The only thing missing would be an appreciation of the richness of human reality.

We are perversely attached to our demons, creating them to be destroyed. Faced with the fright that skulks around the edge of consciousness and with the baffling uncertainties of life, it is reassuring in the extreme to conjure up one goblin or another, fix the blame on it and prepare an incantation to drive the devil out. Illusions of this kind restore a sense of order to the world and thus make people feel better—for reasons we shall have to consider further. As a result our thinking tends to drift into such channels. Furthermore, the need for a therapeutic is so powerful that whatever demonology happens to be fashionable comes to establish a whole psychological climate. People define their problems in terms of whatever it is that puts them in line with prevalent therapeutic dogma—for example, "emotional blockage"—and such being the symbol, the reality begins after a while to appear cast in its mold. This creates a nice self-perpetuating system, and keeps a lot of therapists in business, but it will stand up only so long as it remains unexamined—or until time washes it away.

The fact is that although all people share some profoundly important qualities, no two are ever nearly alike in the crucial details. What we call "emotional disturbance" occurs at the level of self, where the elementary qualities are put together, and thus where differences arise. Mr. A. is completely unique, even at the primitive level of understanding we have managed to achieve about him. There will never be another Mr. A., and Mr. A. will never be the same again as he was on that day I saw him. By now the ceaseless flow of events has thrown him into a different configuration. He would be of course recognizable, and if one looked closely a tremendous amount of repetition could be observed, for people have it in them to keep coming back to the same themes— the same crimes, if you will—as long as they draw breath or have memory. But they are never the same people nor fully definable, and unless we keep this Heraclitean postulate in mind, we will have no grasp of the situation of therapy.

THE NATURE OF NEUROTIC EXPERIENCE

It should be clear from the above that there are no absolute qualities here, only gradations in varying combinations. Still, even as we can look at a continuous spectrum and sort out distinct colors, so does the continuum of distress permit some useful distinctions in seeking some guide to the structure of disturbed behavior.

Most people who consider psychotherapy do so after experiencing some form of misery, whether it is a feeling of dissatisfaction with a life that has failed to meet one's goals, perceived failures of one sort or another in human relationships, sexual unhappiness, or some variety of anxiety and/or depression, such as Mr. A.

was suffering. Of course, it is doubtful that anyone reading these pages has not experienced most of these feelings at one time or another. We may have different names for them, or have trouble pinning the bad feelings down at all, since they tend to shift around, ebb and flow, and change shape with the ceaseless movement of life.

It is nonsense to think immediately of psychotherapy whenever someone is unhappy. That would indeed be a parody on our times. But when the distress takes on enough magnitude to seriously affect the rest of life, then psychotherapy becomes one possibility of change.

The laborer just fired from his job, owing to impersonal social forces, or the person just told of a carcinoma are seriously unhappy people, yet we would not think at first that they were in need of psychotherapy. And by contrast certain individuals who clearly could stand help of some sort are not at all unhappy—one thinks of the manic states here—while others are unhappy in vague, shifting and nonspecific ways.

The surface misleads. Clearly, external symptoms, or consciously experienced feelings, are a poor guide to either the nature of the disturbance or the need for help. When we try to explain behavior from the standpoint of consciousness, we get a partial truth, usually along the lines of a reassurance that we are not the source of our trouble. When the problem is outside ourselves, then no matter how bad, it can be attacked or fled. When it is within, we are stuck, and so the hope is generally to see our troubles as external. Anxiety? What if one is experiencing a real danger? Ideas of persecution? One could, in fact, be being persecuted. Sadness? Who hasn't lost something terribly important at one time or another? Loneliness? Consider how few satisfactory possibilities for good relationships exist. Depersonalization or hallucinations? Perhaps one is undergoing a religious breakthrough. Marital discord? Find a better mate. . . .

Those subjective states which are *prima facie* "psychopathological"—for example, the obsessional, obligatory thinking of an nonsensical idea or the phobic avoidance of a trivial danger—are, in the first place, quite uncommon as leading symptoms and, moreover, almost nonexistent as isolated ones. Mr. A., for example, had an essentially phobic structure to his main complaint: He needed to escape from the city or avoid work in order, so he thought, to forestall damage to his brain. Yet how much further did the problem extend, and how limited would be any attempt to reduce his problem to one symptomatic pattern!

We have to look within the given structure of conscious experience to find a pattern of behavior that can be termed "psychopathological," or "disturbed," or "neurotic," or "crazy," or whatever one chooses to call it. It is important to do this not just to find an underlying pattern to unhappiness but to distinguish between those instances where external troubles seem to be the sole agent and those where the individual is in some way worsening his lot. The worker laid off may only need a better social order, but he may also be responding neurotically to the one he has. Similarly, a person with carcinoma will surely need appropriate medical care, but may need psychotherapeutic attention as well, and we need to know how to determine this.

In doing so we shall have to pretty much skirt the problem of defining emotional health. It is just as well. One shudders at the mass of claptrap written about "mental health," a concept which gets endlessly confused by the mixing up of values and adjustment to social norms with the presence or absence of neurosis.[1] I myself have opinions as to what is to be preferred in life, and these standards—which include the capacity to love, or to act with inner freedom and against outer injustice, or to be steadfast, affirmative and so on—may in some way be affected adversely by neurotic functioning. But it would be a great (if prevalent) error to confuse health with virtue. For present purposes we need do no more than define "emotional health" simply as the absence of neurotic (or psychotic) functioning—which brings us to the problem of just what this sort of functioning may be.

The job is to make some sense out of the often vague feeling that one's life is not being lived as well as it could be. To what extent can we say that this is the result of an emotional disturbance that can be approached therapeutically? The questions before us now are, first, how do we recognize the existence of neurotic qualities; second, how are they constructed; and third, at what point should they be considered treatable? In exploring them, we shall have to touch upon and brush over a number of more general issues which shall reenter when the particular therapies are discussed.

We may begin with one essential fact about neurosis: a loss of the ability to make choices. It could be called a matter of inner freedom. In other words, the outer world permits a range of choice, but some subjective obstacle blocks the way. Complications arise because this fundamental theme can be played out in innumerable variations. But whatever the structure, the hallmark of neurosis is compulsion: something unbidden, forcing itself upon us, turning us away from reality. A student finds he cannot finish the task set before him, no matter how much opportunity he gives himself; a woman breaks out of a marriage only to find that the man she thought she wanted fails now to excite her, while the one who arouses her interest bears an uncanny resemblance to the spouse she just ditched in disgust; a couple attempts again and again to make love, but when he is ready she finds herself inexplicably fatigued, and when she is ardent he discovers something on TV he simply *must* watch; a man about to get a job won't call because "something" tells him he might be rejected, then calls the next day to find the job went elsewhere owing to his lack of interest; another can't leave the house without going back four times to check the lock—and the last time leaves it open anyhow. The list could be multiplied endlessly. No doubt each reader could fill a few pages with bits from his or her experience.

Neurotic phenomena range from the forgetting of a proper name to phobias so severe that a person has to spend his life in bed lest he encounter some dirt on the floor. The compulsive pattern is always there to see, and in every instance, whether laughable or tragic, a few additional elements can also be spotted if one looks closely. For one thing, while the neurosis is often experienced as helpless inability—one can't remember the name, or can't get out of bed—scrutiny reveals the "can't" to be a "won't": I *won't* remember, or move, or love, or whatever. This is usually disguised as helplessness because, first of all, it is generally accompanied by an honest opposing desire to do that which appears impossible, and, second, because this impossible thing, if done, is imagined to be the occasion of great pain and fear, feelings that everyone loves to forget. In other words, a person in the grip of neurotic experience is embroiled in an emotional *conflict* he seems set against understanding, because at least one of its sides would lead to *anxiety* if it were allowed expression. Thus he won't remember, though he wants to, because to remember that one thing might bring other horrid things to mind; so he forgets, and forgets that he forgets, and experiences the whole as a gap, the "can't remember." Or he chooses to not be able to get out of bed, since the occasion of getting out of bed, though *objectively* trivial, brings again certain forbidding things to mind, all of which get crudely, blindly yet powerfully summed up as "dirt."

Further—and this is where dealing with neurosis gets risky and intriguing—the ideas that would be brought to mind if neurotic experience didn't deflect them before they reached awareness, these things that are so horrid and forbidding, are also quite desirable. This stands to reason, since if the ideas were simply unpleasant, we would drop them. The only thing that could hold them in place and keep them hammering away, making their forbidden claim, is the promise of some far, far more intense pleasure than we are granted by everyday, waking life. In fact when we are neurotic, as wretched as we look, we are really much closer to this despised pleasure than when we are more happily engaging in normal, "well-balanced" pursuits. Our very wretchedness is then both the price we pay and a disguise that allows us to carry out that for which we pay the price. At times this so-called *return of the repressed* makes itself clear enough— as when the individual noted above, who couldn't get out of bed for fear of the dirt, eventually soiled himself because, of course, to go to the bathroom would mean exposing himself to the dirty floor. Why soiling oneself should be a pleasure and why it should be forbidden are both interesting facts to explain, but whatever the explanation, they are facts, and the kind that quite invariably get involved in neurosis—the kind, also, that cause what is neurotic to be condemned, and mixed up with moral judgments of all kinds. A neurotic person may, and often does, succeed in being virtuous, but his virtue is won by struggling against real wishes within himself, wishes that he at the same time condemns. Indeed, neurosis is nothing less than an exorbitant price we pay for achieving some degree of control over our own destructiveness.

Often the pattern is not so neat—that is, not so obvious and self-contained. The neurosis may display more subtle and disguised forms, where the same kinds of elements involve a number of people over an extended period of time and in a way that seems to merge imperceptibly into quiet desperation. Consider a family: the mother who wanted, yet hated and feared her own father, and now apportions her feelings among various others, shunning her husband because mature sex stirs up too much in her, fondling her son whom she can manage and set against his father, and persecuting the daughter out of her own guilt—as perhaps her own mother may have done to her. And we have the others playing out their own conflicts as well. Here the *system* of the family is clearly neurotic, no less so than the individuals who make it up, and who may well shift the fray to some other neurotic mode, and appear later on as a case of this or that.

To recapitulate, in neurosis we see that conflict is involved; moreover, a conflict within a person, carried out somewhat in the dark, so that some part of experience is locked in struggle outside consciousness. This means, however, that there is a struggle going on within the mind, between conscious and unconscious levels of fantasy and feeling. In other words, there is a battle in the *subjective* world. But this battle would never reach neurotic intensity if some of the combatants in this subjective world were not stirred up by the person's interactions with the *objective,* external world. Thus the fight is carried out simultaneously on two fronts—between the person and his world and within the person—and it is in some way the tension between these fronts that raises the battle to neurotic proportions.

For example, a man—let us call him Mr. B.—troubled by premature ejaculation, is making love with his wife. All is going well until she, lying on top for the occasion, begins to turn herself head to foot. At this instant the consciously pleasurable thought enters his mind that he is "a hundred percent inside her." The next thing he knows, he has ejaculated, much to their mutual rue.

Here we can see how a subjective event—the conscious thought, "I am a hundred percent inside her"—is stirred up by an objective one—the actual lovemaking—and how it is succeeded by a neurotic act—the premature ejaculation. If we are to make sense out of the event, though, we have to postulate a further subjective state which is *unconscious.* This would consist of a set of fantasies the consequences of which would be devastating were they consciously translated into the reality of being 100 percent inside— i.e., if his physical body (or penis) were completely contained by his wife. It is not difficult to guess that some kind of castration might be included among them. But what counts for the neurosis is that he believes in the fantasy without knowing he has it. He believes in the imaginary. The danger he senses is not in the world of space-time; not, that is, an actual threat to his genitals. It occurs rather in the inner world which represents the outer world, takes off from it yet pursues its own path of development, and, because it is so powerful—and harmful—brings about an objective neurotic event in its wake. In sum, we would not be neurotic were we not so incredibly imaginative. Here the imagination is brought up against reality by the objective lovemaking, and is transformed by an event—the neurosis proper—that "realizes" some part of its unconscious content (leaving his sperm, with 100 percent of his germ plasm, inside, while he acts like a castrated, sexually inadequate male). And yet, by the logic of the inner world, the imagination preserves the physical integrity of his genitals—and, doubtless as well, gets even with his wife, soils her, and represents whatever else is implied in the unconscious fantasy structure. Thus with the assumption of an unconscious state the neurosis becomes intelligible, method in madness; without it, neurosis is simply unreasonableness or bad habits.

This complex interplay of an inner and outer event, with all their layerings, has to be stressed if we are to account for the basic fact that a number of different kinds of therapeutic intervention can be employed to alleviate a neurotic situation. For it is as though each and every neurosis consists, first, of a state of *imbalance* between objective and subjective that allows a previously held-back store of unconscious fear and desire some partial expression; and, second, of a neurotic solution that attempts, fails and attempts again to restore order and harmony. Hence the repetition and the feeling of blindness. It's as though gears that ordinarily mesh were slipping, sending a whole engine out of control; or as if the brakes and the accelerator were applied simultaneously, sending the car lurching forward, stopping it, starting it again, and so on and on.

In everyday life we have an immense repertoire of means for bedding down the unconscious world. In other words, we have our defenses. A lot of our membership in society consists of drawing upon its resources for this purpose. Between social displacements, identifications and discharges on the one hand, and innate biological capacity on the other, most people have ways of extinguishing neurotic distress. The kinds of situations that we call "pathological" are then basically states of sustained imbalance. Either stress gets too strong—as when someone enters puberty or has a child; or the defenses get too weak—as when we become ill or intoxicated; or, most commonly, both change—as after losses of one kind or another. In any event the inner system goes haywire, and with this, its relationship to the outer world also becomes unbalanced.

Looking again a little more closely, we arrive at a model that has a subjective self, with its conscious and unconscious thought, in equilibrium with an objective, outer world that makes varying demands upon it. This outside world includes both nature (most immediately, our body)[2] and society (most immediately, the family and other intimate associations). We cannot understand ourselves—and our neuroses—unless we keep in mind that it is not any one of these factors but all of them acting upon one another that makes us what we are. A neurosis is set going by a serious imbalance between biological need, psychological state and social influence—as when Mr. B.'s sexual needs failed to mesh with the reality of his wife and so induced an eruption of unconscious destructivity. And when neurosis comes into being, it brings about some new, half-stable rebalancing of forces. Thus neurosis becomes not some kind of disease that can be eradicated but a whole way of living, a *process*. Indeed, the most general way of describing how people feel in the grip of neurotic experience is to call it a sense of not living well.

Since the outer world in which we live is a world of people and of nature, of society and the body, the neurotic dialectic can be played out in any or (likely) all of these spheres. It will reveal itself then either as disturbed relations with other people and/or as a disturbed relationship with one's body, manifest in tension, stasis, shallow breathing, flaccidity—ultimately in an organic disease when changes in function turn into changes in structure. Through all this, however, the subjective world, with its unconscious, invisible sphere, is making its claim.

Neurosis cannot be sharply distinguished from ordinary growth and development. At the beginning of life everything seems a oneness to us. As we grow we differentiate ourselves: We develop a sense of an "I," a center of subjectivity, that lives with, but is not the same as, our body and the world of other people. Given a facilitating environment, this development proceeds in a way that we call—somewhat smugly—reasonable and harmonious. The normal person, be he good or bad, experiences a certain integration between self, body and society—or it may be more accurate to say that he takes the unity for granted and goes about his business without a second thought. This does not mean, however, that normal development proceeds without a hitch; on the contrary, there are plenty of struggles, as anyone who observes children can detect right away. What makes it normal, or unneurotic, is only the quantitative factor. The struggles are somehow manageable and rarely get out of hand—which is another way of saying that repression is enabled to work smoothly to keep unconscious layers of terror and desire nicely buried.

In the neurotic, on the other hand, this seamless pattern fails to hold. Fissures appear early in the ground of experience, allowing the lava of the unconscious to break through. Though it may solidify, it remains both a scar and a weakness. Thus neurotic living is experienced as a sense of heightened splitting: We feel estranged from our bodies as well as from other people. In the gaps are alien elements—blocks of unconscious stuff forged long ago stand between the self and the outer world. At the same time, the inner world is sensed as fragmented, confused, seized by inexplicable bursts of mood, involuntary thoughts and fears, all pressing forward with a kind of archimperiousness, a declaration that this has to be so even though a person may judge it non-sensical.

The alienation within neurosis is one of its most essential features. In reality, though we are not all One, we are all interconnected; and the notion of an absolute self, free from deep linkages with the rest of humanity, is but a peculiar fiction. Similarly, though our selves and our bodies are not one (else we would be genuinely lessened when we went to the bathroom or cut our hair, as the child fears), they are deeply interpenetrated with each other in the human organism. These connections are dialectical, not linear, but they are the more real for that, and bind us together.

Not so for the neurotic, who experiences an alienation within himself, and so between himself, society and nature. It may be felt simply by looking in the mirror. The objective person seen there seems strange to the subject doing the perceiving. "Is that body really mine?" he might say, or, "What a strange fellow I see here!" Others may appear equally strange to the self, seeming less fellow humans than creatures from another world. This can be especially felt toward the other sex, whose distinct body plan seems an absolute mystery, whether this is felt as a total split—"There is no part of my self in that other"—or a false sameness—"There is no difference after all between the sexes." But alienation is felt toward all others, too. Its forms are familiar enough, ranging from a paralysis in affirming a sense of community to the inability to love, for one can neither love nor affirm a stranger.

Alienation is certainly not the exclusive preserve of psychopathology. It has a necessary social aspect, which is ultimately the crucial factor, but one that cannot be pursued further here. Whatever its historical roots, neurotic experience is not directly reflective of social reality. Indeed neurosis may be considered a special kind of withdrawal from society; and it has to be approached from the standpoint of what does the turning away. For present purposes, the key point is that what stands between and alienates in neurosis is the intrusion of destructive unconscious experience into the conduct of life. This experience arose in the past and is carried forward in a state of repression until some set of circumstances upsets the balance. Let us then turn to the past.

NEUROSIS AND CHILDHOOD

Our neurotic dispositions follow, as Freud discovered, from the peculiarities of human childhood—its prolonged dependency; its intense narcissism, or self-centeredness; its unbounded yearning; the special character of infantile thought. It would exceed our scope to detail these matters. The reader who wishes more familiarity with them may turn to one of a number of excellent accounts of developmental psychology.[3] We must simply emphasize here that it is our infancy which is immediately implicated in neurosis. Social forces play a necessary enabling role, yet neurosis remains the unfinished madness of childhood carried forward.

Essentially, neuroses arise because the human mind is forced to undergo too many intense and contradictory feelings before it is able to deal with them. Although continuous from one moment to the next, the child's experience undergoes many drastic modifications in a relatively brief period of time. Too often there is no other way to deal with the flood of stimuli and the child's vulnerability to these stimuli than to transform them into neurotic experience. The family exists to provide a buffering world of play and protection against infantile hazards; and to the extent the family does its job, the individual is spared neurotic disturbance. Yet that extent is never complete. Because of the inherent contradictions of the infantile situation and the inevitable shortcomings of a family's adult members (who were infants themselves, and live moreover in a society that demands a certain degree of neurosis), the family can never do more than approximate the goals of developing autonomous, free offspring. And generally speaking it does a lot less.

The fundamental contradiction arises from this: Human infants are creatures of the utmost helplessness and at the same time limitless desire. The two qualities are, moreover, coordinated; the weaker we are, the greater our needs and dependency, and the less we can do about impulse. The little child's need is so great—far in excess of what is biologically required for survival—that real gratifications must often be felt as frustrations. And despite the fact that his power is so inconsequential that he can engage in murderous or incestuous thoughts without worrying about the actual effects of his wishes, the child freely confuses intentions with actual deeds. These wishes are furthermore no mere isolated ideas, but sensuous states of being, experienced by an aroused body. There is probably an autoerotic component to every significant infantile wish. The child knows no other course. Without built-in control, the body is at first a playground over which desire can flit carefree.

Yet even without parental interference—through suppression, unavailability, seduction and so forth—these wishes are bound to founder on their own contradictions. We cannot tolerate the presence of a hate toward those whom we also genuinely love. Yet the child has to deal with just such problems. We all did. No doubt we have forgotten much of this, especially if it was not overwhelming, but one need only observe normal children to appreciate the struggles they go through. Thus nothing is more real than jealousy, or feeling the impossibility of incestuous wishes. If one is to have one's mother, what will become of father? Even if he doesn't retaliate, how can he be gotten rid of, this giant-man whom the boy loves and needs? Can the little girl escape the fear that her genitals will be torn apart by the father she wants, or the little boy that his will be swallowed up within the mother? Can a boy stand his feminine wish toward his father—especially as it might be fueled by a reaction against hate and fear? Can a child stand full realization of its love for the mother—for does not this attraction lead back in memory to a time of undifferentiated union with her, and would not all individual acquisitions and powers be obliterated in the course of reunion?

Thus, while the real trouble sets in if the parents contribute their own disturbance, or if fate somehow intervenes in a destructive way, it is essential that we recognize the great susceptibility of the child-mind to neurotic influence. We may regard this as measured by fear. The course of childhood development contains its measure of reason and its peaks of joy, yet is set round with terror. We cannot give exact names to the forms of terror that sit around our campfires, precisely because it is everyone's wish that those campfires be drawn close, that the naming part of the mind, what we consider our waking consciousness, not be applied to them. In normal, favorable development this is what happens. The child's inherent ambivalence becomes blotted out by the continual reaffirmation of parental regard; fears are put to rest by parental benevolence; and desire is neither squelched nor fanned into uncontrollable flames. There is thus no reinforcement of inevitable fears by the environment. The child's capacity to love is then given sway; and the developing personality is allowed to put things together and to set aside from consciousness what is impermissible. The demons lack sufficient impetus to break down the barrier, while the structuring agencies gain every day from identifications with civilizing influences.

Of course, this can never be complete, owing both to the ever-present contradictions in the child-mind and to environmental imperfection. For one thing, desire never lets up, it simply shifts its terms around to put a more acceptable face on things. And infantile gratification, although an essential condition for later achievement, is incompatible with the mature self. The former demands total discharge and is heedless of the welfare of its object; the latter is differentiated, graded, and regards the other as a separate being whose needs have to be respected. Our deepest, most persistent desires thus expose us to the gravest risks. The trouble we get into on this account is something called a *trauma*. "Trauma" may be defined as a noxious state, of any duration, in which the person feels overwhelmed, flooded with stimuli beyond his capacity to master. Physical injury could be traumatic (pain itself is the most elementary trauma), but more important for our purposes are traumatic situations occurring within human relationships. Here the pain is inflicted by those who have the power to seduce, abandon and retaliate against the growing child, those who may withhold protection against some other blow, or who may simply drive the child mad through incoherent communication within the family system. Ordinarily, it should be added, children have considerable resources for dealing with potentially traumatic situations. But there are many instances where disease or some other weakness lowers resistance to a traumatogenic level (we should remind ourselves of this lest we fall into the infantile habit of blaming everything on bad parents); and there are innumerable instances where things are so bad as to overwhelm the stoutest barrier, so that some traumatic situation, and with it some ingraining of neurosis, affects us all.

What is traumatic to the growing person will make itself felt as a flooding of stimuli beyond his power to integrate. As a result some portion of infantile experience becomes overwhelming and is sealed off from the remainder of the personality by an emergency defense—the way a bulkhead would prevent leaking water from swamping a ship. But just as the water remains behind the bulkhead, so does the unassimilated experience persist out of awareness. What happens along with this is of great importance. That which has been used defensively, even though it corresponds to a weaker, more immature stage of development, is granted great importance owing to the magnitude of the frightful trauma it holds back. As a nation aggrandizes its army for driving out barbarian invaders, then lives off a military mentality and eventually conjures up more barbarians to be repulsed, so does the child-mind overestimate its neurotic structures. And it has to be emphasized that what the neurotic defense protects against is generally but one step removed from our most precious desires. Hence it will not be let go; and if the wish cannot be experienced in pure form, then the neurotically distorted version will draw to it all of the original clamor.

We all have within us partially dissolved lumps of infantile experience, reappearing in strange crystalline forms, inhomogeneous with realistic thought, destructive and tagged with an ineradicable sense of omnipotence. Each traumatic experience is like a particle of bad psychic substance. When enough are lumped together or occur over a long period of time, we have the stuff out of which neuroses are made. One can know as much better as one likes, but these neurotic structures live on, sometimes protruding an irrational idea into consciousness, generally keeping their vast bulk hidden.

Thus Dr. C., a man with overwhelming fears of castration, is quite convinced, though he knows better, that the primary erogenous zone in the female is the uterine cervix. This man practices good medicine, he would not tell any of his patients something of this sort, yet he has to believe it himself, in a kind of double registration. Why? Perhaps because it gives the woman some phallic quality, no doubt also in response to some specific child-hood need; these things always have multiple causes, and it is not to the point now to figure out the details of the fantasy, but only to note its irrationally abiding existence.

Another example is Mrs. D., a woman with diabetes and many hypochondriacal fears and doubts about her femininity. Of good intelligence and education, Mrs. D. believes nonetheless—in the same fashion as Dr. C. believed—that when she took medication for her diabetes and developed vaginal bleeding soon afterward, the blood came directly from the stomach, which was therefore, according to her inner logic, connected to the reproductive tract.

Again, we needn't ferret out the many implications of this fantasy. The point of these two examples is to give some indication of the quality of neurotic thought and of the strange combination of unreality along with blind belief it imposes. For if we grasp this, we shall be in a position to understand some themes of great significance. In each of the examples above the infantile fantasy was both believed in and not believed in. We are usually quite capable of holding some wild conviction without letting on that this is the case. Another part of ourself is equally convinced of a more realistic or official position and generally sees to it that the fantasy is kept in place, quite secure for a life-time. Thus, while logic would have it that a proposition cannot be both true and false, the mind has it that logic is of secondary importance to the maintenance of some kind of equilibrium as a bulwark against unbearable inner pain.

What this means is that most pieces of behavior are compromises between trends that may be quite incompatible, even warring. So long as overall order is maintained, the mind, like a benign despot, will let its separate elements go their various ways.

It should be noted again that the more unrealistic and infantile of fantasies can be clung to for only one reason—the powerful degree of satisfaction they provide (or the powerful degree of pain they ward off). It tends to follow that the less rational or realistic our thoughts are, the more intense the feeling attached to them. Otherwise there would be no motive for holding onto them. We all know how precious our daydreams, or conscious fantasies, are, but even more precious are those that are unconscious. For the fact that they are unconscious means these thoughts are so charged that they must be kept secret from ourselves as well as others.

There is one area where such secrets assume special importance, and that is in the persistence of wishes toward parents. No one can dispute the exceptional significance of the child-parent bond; and yet none of us is fully able to appreciate, in an emotionally vivid sense, the power that these childhood wishes exert in the adult. This is because of the screening function, the double registry alluded to above. The forbidden ancient yearning will be simply kept around in unofficial form. We will deny that it is our wish, and we will deny that we have denied it. Thus the correct posture is maintained, while that which we repudiate rolls along in disguise. Our wishes for a lost parent are usually handled, of course, by having children—that, after all, is how mankind keeps going. But other ways are found, too, whether by substituting pets, plants or other possessions for the children, or by substituting leaders, heroes and, to be sure, therapists for the parents.

Now nothing can be human unless it is paradoxical. Note how hard it is to admit what we want, how the wish for a parent diminishes us—since it strips us of all we have acquired—and yet aggrandizes us—since it restores a time of complete, if illusory, perfection and completeness, a time when it was possible to believe that we and the universe were one. We are dealing here with something called "narcissism"—a dimension of immense importance in human life and, needless to add, in therapy. "Narcissism" refers to all of those attitudes, thoughts and feelings that invest the idea of one's self with importance, value or love. Nothing could be more basic, and nothing is more paradoxical—or troublesome. For narcissistic attitudes combine weakness and strength in amazing illogic: the total helplessness, ignorance and dependency of the infant with the grandeur, omnipotence and omniscience of his wishes. It underlies the questions of pride and value, and much else besides, and it is a safe bet that we will underestimate its influence in anything we do—no doubt because admitting its power hurts our narcissism.

To point out the utter absurdity of such a state is not to disparage it. Narcissism is only too real and cannot be condemned away. More, if we look at those things that make life worthwhile— love, play, art, achievement—we will find them all heavily saturated with a narcissistic charge. In anything valued—in the sense of value itself, worthwhileness—we come upon some expansion of the self, some union between it and that which is beyond it, whether the embrace be with a loved person, with something made, with a piece of beauty or some portion of the truth. Recall that the state of freedom is really a state of harmonic balance between all that is in us; and the narcissistic dimension, though it begins in infancy, can be perpetually re-edited and reharmonized throughout the course of a life, ending up as the quality of wisdom.

So, too, does the wish for the parent, even if it persists only as a decent respect for tradition. More to the present point are those undigested foreign bodies of traumatic experience which figure in neurosis. These traumatic particles invariably arise in the context of human relationships, usually with family members or those who stand for them, and the wish toward the family member remains in all later versions of the original experience. So, too, does the narcissistic element. At the core of each bit of neurotic behavior is a special narcissistic claim: "I"—not the official everyday person, but the magician and superman within—"say this is so; and it must be so because I say it is. I don't care whether the rest of me, or you on the outside, thinks it's crazy or destructive; it must be so because I insist." Such insistence cuts unconscious and neurotic thought off from ordinary correction, while it magnifies fantasied dangers far beyond the scope of any real threat. The degree to which this kind of pathological narcissism takes over is one measure of the misfortunes to which the developing person has been subjected.

If we were to search about for the one feature which most distinguishes those particles of experience that form the nucleus of neurotic structure from those that join in the free development of personality, we would find this: In instances of traumatic development, the person *experiences an overwhelming hatred while in a state of desire toward one who is also loved.* Look closely enough into the heart of any neurotic formation—whether it be a depression, some specific sexual dysfunction, a phobia, an obsessional thought, a hysterical attack, an addiction, even a paranoid delusion—and there, suffused through the particular structure, will be found lurking this same hatred directed in some transformed way toward new objects of the old desires.

WHEN THERAPY IS NEEDED

Up until now we have been describing the heart of the neurotic process and how it is experienced. We have yet to consider the need for treatment. How is this to be assessed? More specifically, how can we tell when things have gone too far?

In general it takes much time and effort before a clear image can be obtained of what has been going on with one's emotional life. Neurosis, remember, comes into being in darkness and remains hidden from the light of day. Vastly more neuroses have gone away on their own or out of some haphazard intervention than have been clearly understood and rationally treated. In any case, the presenting signal is usually a sense of demoralization. One feels that life is out of control, that it is bringing more trouble and pain than happiness, and that it seems to be governed by inexplicable forces that generate a sense of confusion. Put another way, people sense they are unhappy because of something wrong in the conduct of everyday life. They cannot control their misery by means of their ordinary devices, and they are at a loss to account for what really bothers them. So they set about trying to figure out their problems.

As explained earlier, most people, as they attempt to analyze their situation, initially conclude that what is external to them is the main cause of the difficulty. Indeed the great majority never budge much from this point of view. It's not my fault, they seem to say, but rather that of my wife, or school, or men in general, or mother, or Society, or perhaps the weather or phase of the moon.

This, however, is mainly the gnawing of our narcissism due to the fear that we might have to change. One does not minimize the strength of judgments of this sort—all too often they outweigh all the rest. Nonetheless they are usually wrong and should be corrected. Their error lies not in the fact that they introduce external factors, since in truth something objective is always present in every neurosis, but in the way they eliminate the subjective side, thus turning away from responsibility for their lives. For as reflection about what has been stated so far will reveal, the problem is not one of "fault," where the world acts against the person like a bad parent against a helpless child, but of a complex *interaction* between what life brings to us and what we bring to it. Thus while no one is to blame for a neurosis, everybody is responsible. Blame is reserved for injustices; and while plenty of injustices are committed against the growing child in the course of neurotic development, and still more await the neurotic person as he or she enters society, in their neuroses themselves, people are bringing what they have chosen into the picture. A basic part of the choice is made unconsciously, and so is removed from direct moral consideration. Nonetheless it is a choice that the individual makes as he or she interacts with the external situation which appears in the neurotic process.

This point of view obviously won't simplify our job in the way that blaming the world (or oneself, for that is but a tricky reversal of the same theme, not a freedom from it) does. For it means we will have to take into account both our external situation and our inner state of mind, not separately, but as they interplay with each other, in each instance.

It might help to consider a spectrum, at one end of which are cases where external events seem preponderant, while at the other are those problems where it doesn't seem to make much difference what is going on outside in order to bring out a neurotic state of affairs. Depending on the position in the spectrum, one would have to give greater or lesser weight dealing with the inner, subjective or the outer, objective worlds. Some sketchy examples may help clarify this.

An eighteen-year-old girl, Miss E., thought she was "going crazy," and indeed gave a fair impression of being right. It turned out that she had recently begun sleeping with her boy friend and was terrified of her parents' judgment. No doubt unconscious fantasies were stirred up by this and were enacted in her emotional storms. However, as soon as the event was called to her attention by the therapist she had an outburst, wept copiously and ceased her madness. End of case.

. . . Perhaps not. She might come back some years later, sleepless, agitated and wildly anxious. It turns out she has gotten married, a union that is less happy than it could be, as she married someone with whom she shares little, and has had to leave mother to boot. We may surmise that the marital choice, the separation and the inner symptoms are all functionally related and bound up in erupting unconscious fantasies. Now things are tougher. She can't give up either her husband or her mother without major disruption, yet both cause her pain. Maybe now she should look more thoroughly into the subjective side—maybe, but not necessarily. Perhaps the whole family should get together and hash things out. After all, it may only be a "phase." Indeed, leave it alone and she may calm down on her own, may do all right.

. . . For a time, at any rate. She might compensate for the break with her mother by adopting the latter's ways, and protect herself against a sense of guilt through heightened scrupulosity and a kind of self-effacingness that would seem both excessive and irritating to others who were not privy to its inner sources. Then her mother dies, and the terms of the struggle are drastically altered. She grieves and becomes depressed, feels she's no good, that she was a faithless daughter (though she devotedly nursed her mother through the last days), and loses interest in life. Up to a point this need call no special attention to itself. It is part of the inevitable cycle of loss and reclamation without which life would be inconceivable. Ideally we just mourn—i.e., feel, sadly, the absence of those gone, then slowly redirect our love elsewhere. But owing to inevitable conflicts, the mourning process is usually mixed with some depression—i.e., along with feeling the loss, we take out our bad feeling on ourselves, castigate ourselves, feel empty and hollow and in general lose some of the supply of self-regard required for the conduct of life. Since conflict and loss are each ubiquitous, it is safe to say that no one, no matter how "normal," can get through life without spells of depression. And certain losses, such as the death of a parent, are almost sure to induce some of this.

However, if this particular woman kept sliding downhill to the point of functional incapacity; or if she failed to rally after a few months of mourning (and sometimes the *inability* to mourn can signal the potential for serious trouble); and if her symptoms began to include major interferences with sleeping, eating and bowel function; or some break with the sense of reality occurs (so that she begins, for example, to feel persecuted or develops bizarre ideas about her body); or, it goes without saying, if she entertains seriously the thought of suicide—if any or all of these occur, it will then be clear that the living presence of her mother was a patch that held back the kind of major emotional difficulty that clearly calls for intervention.

Or, she could have weathered the storm and returned to her old ways free from neurotic shoals.

. . . Maybe not. The woman and her husband could appear some years later, sexually miserable. Now the problem is chronic and much more involved. Maybe, the marriage having been a neurotic mistake from the start, they have simply grown out of love with each other and are better off apart. There may be complicating issues, such as children, religious values or economics, but these can be approached on their own terms. Pain will be involved, but (so far, at any rate) it is not a neurotic issue, since the current situation dictates that they should go their own ways. To be sure, this reality may harbor a desiccated neurosis—and the neurosis may sprout again as they try to resolve it—but that is another matter.

Other possibilities exist. The neurosis may still be rampant, in which case enough hatred and lack of communication will exist along with sexual incompatibility to demand a full-scale inquiry into the life between them and/or within each one. Or this may not be the case. They may get along rather well except for the sexual unhappiness. Now two main kinds of bases exist for sexual miseries of this' kind, often mixed with each other. One is connected with the fact that in order to preserve peace at the outset of the marriage—that is, in order to defend against a neurotic outburst at that time—a general repression of sexuality took place, since it was in the sexual sphere that the unconscious fantasies were lodged. Of course were this strategy completely successful, they would not be unhappy, since no unfulfilled desire would exist to insinuate itself into their equilibrium. If, however, it is only partial, then a further problem rears its head. To tamper with the localized neurotic inhibition of sex is to risk rousing the demons that plagued her at the beginning of her marriage. Hopefully she is more mature now, and better able to assimilate them, but there is no necessary reason why this should be so.

Let us now examine the second main basis for sexual incompatibility in the face of a reasonably successful marriage. It may also be true that, way back at the beginning of her adult sexual career, she did not so much *repress* sexuality—that is, put it out of mind—as *avoid* it in the interests of managing the anxiety that so plagued her then. In other words she remained subjectively open but kept herself objectively inexperienced and simply never learned the ways of eros—perhaps to maintain the image she wished her parents to have of her: a clean girl, sexually ignorant and innocent. It is amazing how much of this still goes on in so-called advanced civilization. It is also remarkable how much people are able to learn once they have matured enough to do so. And it does not generally require therapy to effect the maturing. Living awhile can do the job.

Thus there is a whole range of patterns that can underlie a given piece of neurotic behavior. In general one could say that, to the extent that a person's subjective world remains rich, plastic and open to experience, the neurotic block should be remediable by mainly objective means—as, in the above instance, by giving the couple sexual counseling. The suitability of this approach would be manifest in the couple's intimacy and ease of communication. And to the extent that the opposite holds—that the subjective life is experienced as deadened, twisted, empty or closed; to the extent, so to speak, that a person remains hungry in the presence of adequate nutriment—the neurosis may be said to be deeper and to require correspondingly deeper attention. This is only a way of restating the central idea that the heart of a neurosis lies in the subjective world, beneath the level of consciousness. Therefore, the closer disturbances revolve about these invisible spheres, the more profoundly neurotic they are; and since our felt subjective experience is closer to the unconscious than is our external activity, it is a more reliable indicator of the depth of the neurosis. No matter how deep it is rooted, however, the neurosis can only be adequately assessed in relation to the balance of forces across the whole of a person's life.

Nevertheless, we should not think that the given social standards of success will do. Many achieve outwardly in order to avoid inner guilt, anxiety or depression. The ordinary material rewards of success may sour in such a situation. Indeed they only increase a sense of hollowness, or magnify a feeling of guilt, or, all too often, only spur one on, like a squirrel on a treadmill, to more false tokens of value. The end result is a "perfect" life—job, family, possessions, pleasures, all in place, yet all just so many bars on a cage. Only subjective misery continues to bear witness to the fundamental contradiction in such a life.

Of course it is one thing to call attention to a situation of this kind, another to say that it is necessarily neurotic. It might instead be the glimmerings of enlightenment. Generally speaking this cannot be told at the outset, since the misery is usually accompanied by an equally intense sense of confusion. But this itself should be a stimulus to seek help. Whether or not the prime problem is neurotic depends on the degree to which unconscious destructive forces have broken through; but if this cannot be determined right away, then a person should begin with a kind of treatment that helps him find out what is going on, and proceed from there. Some further examples:

1. We could not live without anxiety. Given the amount of unfinished business we carry about, this feeling may be expected to

arise from diverse sources, from dangers in the outer world no less than from occasional surfacing of unconscious fears. Only the person who represses his dreams never has a nightmare. However, past a certain point in subjectivity, anxiety can become a problem in its own right, signaling that the forces behind it are calling for particular attention. Up to this point anxiety functions as an alerting device, a sensor that helps us pick a path through our own minefields, or rouses us to special effort. But beyond this point it becomes a source of disorganization, as when we panic at everyday tasks, or fear to sleep lest we dream; or it paralyzes a person like a deer before an oncoming headlight. When this happens it is time to seek help.

2. Then there are the *symptom-neuroses*[4]—the obsessions, compulsions, phobias, hysterical attacks and so forth. We need not go much into them here, both because they are less common than is generally thought and because, when they do occur in full form, they leave little doubt that something is wrong, in that they seem impossible to rationalize away as belonging outside the self. In the grip of *obsessional thinking,* a person is helplessly forced to repeat certain thoughts to himself; while in the *compulsive* neurosis he suffers the need to perform a ritual such as handwashing. In each case rationalizations for the behavior fail to explain it or make it go away; and, unless we are to resort to the occult, the locus of the difficulty must be ascribed to the hidden subjective world.

In the case of the rather more common *phobias,* there is an attempt to turn the difficulty outward. The phobic person projects his anxiety onto some external situation which he then feels has to be avoided. Although phobic people often try to rationalize their fear, it is not usually difficult to convince oneself of the illogic of their beliefs. This is especially so for the more serious instances of phobia, where the tendency of neurotic solutions to collapse becomes evident. For example, a woman who was plagued with unconscious hostility toward her infant, and had this feeling stirred up in a parking lot, thenceforth had to avoid the parking lot. But she could avoid neither her hostility nor this pattern of dealing with it; and so found herself within a shrinking perimeter of forbidden areas until she finally had to remain confined to her bedroom—where she soon became afraid of her impulse to jump out the window.

But the key point is not the symptom; it is rather its severity that determines whether treatment is needed. Grading backward from the severest cases, we come to a zone where neurotic symptoms are manageable, part of the color of life, even cause for amusement. Consider how many minor phobias each of us has—whether about bugs or some kind of food (we rationalize the latter as a matter of "taste"). Consider also how many trivial rituals we observe, long since collapsed into habits and harmless superstitions, like avoiding sidewalk cracks (lest we "break our mothers' backs"); or how many pointless repetitive thoughts murmur through our mental space like the sounds of so many transistor radios at the beach. None of these calls for treatment—though any and all might be very instructive in helping us understand the murkier sides of our natures—because they do not affect the conduct of life, being rather a backdrop to it. The first sign that one of these incubi is about to break loose and amount to something more than a harmless peccadillo is often an increase in free-floating anxiety. Short of that, or of some other functional upheaval that demands attention, our minor neuroses can be left alone.

3. Many people experience nothing so focal in a neurotic way, neither having an identifiable symptom nor being able to pin their difficulties to any one event, such as a death in the family. What usually happens is that a pattern of setbacks adds up until the person feels he's had enough and begins to consider the possibility that the endless series of reverses and the resulting chronic depression might be caused, at least in substantial part, by some force within himself that makes for defeat. At times no apparent setback is necessary. It may just be a landmark—a decadal birthday perhaps, or the anniversary of an earlier event, or passing the age one's parent was when something crucial happened . . . or just the steady current of time casting too many dreams up upon the beach. Whatever, things go beyond the threshold and a self-reevaluation begins.

4. Very often one's troubles merge imperceptibly into the anomie and boredom of middle-class life in late capitalism, so that it may be no easy matter to distinguish between a crisis of meaninglessness and a neurosis. Nor are the effects of social oppression and manipulation easily disengaged from the damage we inflict from within when infantile terrors seize us from the unconscious. It is true that feelings of anomie and oppression often mask neurotic anxieties, but this does not make them any less problems in their own right. If the real world is alienated beyond reclama-

tion, then for those who live in it to feel alienation is only a sign of good judgment. Still, there is no reason why one cannot be neurotically paralyzed as well, nor any reason why objective and subjective sources of distress should not aggravate each other. The burden of deciding upon therapy becomes an especially complicated one when the personal and societal disorders run in parallel grooves. We shall not be able to approach this problem in any depth before the latter part of this study. For now we'll have to rest with the idea that the two levels of conflict are connected but not identical. Therefore they should not be collapsed into each other. A person can be socially alienated *and* neurotic, and should bear in mind both the connection and the difference so that he will seek appropriate remedies for each and not believe that political participation will cure his neurosis, or that his therapy will make one whit of difference in the larger disorder.

5. The same type of complication holds for those people who happen to transgress conventional standards of behavior. Society cannot function without labeling some behavior deviant. And labeling here is only the signpost of an active exclusion.[5] Consequently, anyone who behaves in a deviant way—whether he be a homosexual, a fancier of intercourse with animals, a Holy Roller or a nudist—will be labeled "disturbed." He will then have to struggle against his self-acceptance of that label and its lowered status, will feel pressure to act as though he were disturbed, and will suffer any or all of the many deprivations and stresses accruing to social outcasts. It should be emphasized that no form of behavior in itself indicates very much of the inner state of mind of the person who practices it; indeed, except for extreme and incontestable cases of disorganization, there is no good way to translate how a person behaves into what he feels. Thus, any deviant may or may not be motivated largely by neurotic forces. However, the practice of deviant behavior in itself may be enough to magnify neurotic tendencies that might have remained hidden within a conventional life. In those instances of deviancy—perhaps the majority—where neurotic pressure already lay behind the choice, the result is all too often a severe state of distress.

There is usually another side of the coin in human affairs, and in this case there is the possibility that the person may have chosen his deviancy as a way of *reducing* neurotic pressure—i.e., the deviancy becomes itself a kind of therapy. This effect may be accentuated if the deviant person joins up with a group that proclaims the deviancy as a virtue and holds itself together by getting itself persecuted. A number of gay-rights organizations are of this form. Thus they exert a very powerful emotional hold over their followers, and effectively remove them from the clutches of therapy—which at this level may be regarded as only another kind of group seeking the allegiance of the deviant person. Similarly, many people undergo religious conversion in the flight from some searing emotional problem. This is particularly the case with youths fleeing a tormenting family situation. Such youngsters often join a deviant religious sect, which becomes a kind of good inner family insulated by ostracism from the bad outer world—all of which works to strengthen their belief and reduces the neurotic pressure from within themselves.

We need take these matters no further, as to do so would prematurely anticipate the question of therapy. To summarize: Because society, as it is presently organized, forces a great deal of unpleasure and alienation on everyone, doing the forbidden is mostly pleasurable; and as the neurotic process involves some realization of forbidden unconscious desires that the individual has found both exciting and overwhelming, it tends to infiltrate deviant behavior. The perversion, Freud observed long ago, is the negative of the neurosis. This means that the pervert (or the addict, the criminal and so forth) acts out what the rest of us manifest only in our neuroses, our alienation, our ennui—or even transform in our creative protest. Needless to add, the rest envy him for doing what they've held back. But it further means that we are all of us a pretty mixed bag of goods who have no solid grounds to judge others "sick" and force them into treatment, or force them to give up what is most precious to them as persons.

But neither, on the other hand, should we glorify the deviant for living more intensely than the rest of us. This ignores the actual possibility of his suffering no less than it ignores the destruction he may be wreaking on himself and others. Indeed it is only the projection of our own frustrated desires onto him. Both judgments—the pathologizing and the envy alike—particularize us, falsely dividing the "healthy" from the "sick," when what is needed is present help for those whose emotional patterns call out for it and, basically, social treatment for the general alienation.

The moral may be drawn: There is no sharp boundary between one's neurotic state and the conduct of life; each of us has to survey his or her personal landscape and choose whether or not to define the compulsivity and lack of freedom in it as a treatable neurosis. Accordingly the homosexual is no more *per se* in need of treatment than the heterosexual, or the ascetic than the orgiast. Each can scrutinize his life to see how much inner destructive compulsion is there, how much confused murkiness, and then act as he sees it. Definition here is not a trivial act. A tree is a tree no matter what we call it, but anything human is to some extent brought into existence by being named. And once it becomes identified its further development—which may include a particular form of therapy—is shaped by how we conceive of it.

We should not conclude this account of the forms of emotional disorder without mention of states that are in themselves seriously disturbed. I refer to psychosis and to the state of being suicidal, conditions that are automatically thought to warrant intervention and to be inaccessible to self-evaluation. The latter point is not necessarily true, even though people who are psychotic or suicidal *are* often too upset to ponder their condition in any balanced way. Consequently the remarks that follow are meant more to round out our discussion than as a guide to self-assessment.

SUICIDE

The suicidal and the psychotic person are alike in feeling overwhelmed by an inner feeling that overrides any objective consideration. In brief, the individual is considered "withdrawn"; he seems to be undertaking some private transaction and ignoring, or out of contact with, other people in the environment. This is not strictly so: The environment is registered, and even in the most extreme instances some credence is given to it, but it is swept into submission the way an ocean storm drives surf over a retaining wall.

For those who consider taking their own lives, the feeling is one of hopelessness and despair, combined, according to the circumstances, with a surge of hatred so intense that its only resolution seems to be self-destruction. We should not deny that there are objective situations where one's values are so totally overridden by reality that one may rationally decide to finish the job oneself. But these instances are not at issue here. More commonly, the individual is not capable of making such a considered choice, and this is the case that concerns us. Here it turns out that the suicide is construed by the sufferer in a dual light. From one angle it appears that an end is sought to relieve pain. This is valid enough so long as one focuses on the level of consciousness. However, a close look will discern a peculiar turn of affairs coming from the unconscious side. Here the act becomes the fulfillment of a positive *wish*—a wish, say, to kill someone, or to fuse with someone in a sleep that is death, or to be killed by someone, or to forget, or to revenge oneself, and so on. From this angle, the suicide is not imagined as one's nonexistence so much as a future state in which *someone* is, to be sure, dead, while the self, immortal as only an unconscious wish will have it, is envisioned as there observing the event. The suicidal person, so to speak, imagines himself at his funeral.

If the fantasy of immortality can be grasped by a surviving fragment of self-reflection within a suicidal person, he may permit himself to get help—for no one would like to go out with the idea that his last act was one of self-deception. Indeed the suicide, which seems to be grounded on an utter failure of narcissism, or self-love, is in fact the most profound and ruthless assertion of the undying megalomania within us. And in the sense that it is self-delusive, it cannot be the assertion of freedom that romantic existentialists make of it. True, a morality of freedom has to include some provision to take one's own life, but this has to be done freely if it is to be compatible with that ethic. Instead the suicidal person is governed by his unconscious and in the grip of the greatest inner unfreedom he has ever known. Further, all our rights, it seems to me, are purchased with the obligation to fully explore alternatives and consequences before we act. And it may be argued therefore that suicide is never ethically justified, since it denies and diminishes the only sovereign base of value, the human community, most particularly the lives of others in which we share, but also the universal ground of the principle of community itself. Needless to add, points of this degree of abstraction may not go over too well with an acutely suicidal person, who should not be expected to have much in the way of loving feeling toward the world. Nonetheless it can serve as a basis for practical efforts by others.

PSYCHOSIS

We come now to *psychosis*. I shall not be discussing problems concerning the causes or classification of this phenomenon except to mention that the model of disturbed childhood experience presented earlier, which served to account for the development of the neurotic process, is not sufficient to account for the evidence of psychosis. Instead we have to add a biological factor, partly inherited and possibly fixed into place by very early infantile experience, when our biological system is maturing under the influence of the environment. In any event this creates a predisposition for subsequent forms of psychological disturbance which are brought into being, first, by disturbed family relations and, later, exacerbated by the stresses of living. This barely suggests, of course, the immense amount of effort that is going into the elucidation of the riddle of psychosis.[6] Nor is it possible here to go into the vast question of the wretched social situation of the psychotic person which so aggravates the problem. All we can do here is briefly address ourselves to the psychological, experienced manifestation.

Up until now we have been discussing neurotic and characterological problems. As multifarious as these are, they share a common feature: The self—i.e., the center of the "I" experience—is intact. Ordinarily this self feels nothing of what it is doing; it just goes on and does it, loving, hating, getting easily upset, dominating others, evading and so forth. In the neurosis, the self experiences an intrusion, but it watches this, as it were, from a safe vantage. The sense of reality, that indescribable yet absolute firmament of our life, is preserved. We "know better" than to be afraid, or obsessed, or irrationally despondent, yet feel so nonetheless, and wrestle with the distress.

In madness, however, the firmament of self-experience erodes, crumbles and disintegrates—we don't know better anymore. There is no fixed limit to this. We are all capable of degrees of self-dissolution, as when we fall asleep, or lose ourselves in the act of love. And we are all capable of mixing this in infinitely varying degrees with the distress of psychotic experience. The psychotic person, if we must label him at all, is merely one who goes through worse forms of psychotic experience more of the time, until an entirely arbitrary line is crossed and his reality becomes defined by madness. Now fact and fantasy cease to be distinguished; the subject and object split, merge and recombine; and the integrity of the body—which is, let us note, the one part of the objective world that belongs to the self—loses its boundedness and the sense of its physical organization. In the full-blown state of madness, thoughts are vested in alien parts of the world; the unity of perception and sensation is broken; the laws of causality that govern the physical universe are breached; and the body image, fragmented into smithereens, may become actually experienced as a host of separately willed particles.

And the hate and fear. . . . There is a tendency nowadays, with the loss of faith in technocracy, to romanticize madness. Its relationship to ecstatic states and creative thinking is seized upon, and madness is seen as something we choose to do to escape a humdrum or constraining reality. It is further argued that since the social world is evidently crazy—i.e., its actual structure is a violation of what it professes to be—then to be mad in official terms is really to be sane and true. Two negatives make a positive, right?

Wrong. For the negative in madness is not the blithe reversal of official insanity; nor is it the mystical state of transcendence, though it abuts this in a way that has considerable therapeutic implication, as we shall explore later. No doubt madness can be a breakthrough in some instances; but generally speaking it is unbidden and filled with hate. It entails the release of all the fear and rage that comfortable adjustment to ordinary (crazy) life protects us against. The real state of psychosis is simply a living hell. No greater suicide risk exists than someone who has just become psychotic; and no one else experiences a comparable degree of panic. For neurotic or realistic forms of anxiety have to do with some impending threat to an existing self: Either someone we need will go away, leaving us with anger and longing; or love will be withdrawn, setting up a feeling of depletion and low self-regard; or some valued part of us will be injured; or we will be made to feel guilty or humiliated, or what not. But in each such case there is an "I" to be hurt—and an "I" that can run from or fight the danger.

In madness, however, the "I" falls apart, shattered, and with it go all the defenses against the many summed neurotic dangers. And beyond all this is the unnamable sense of dread stirred up by the feeling that, as the self breaks, so will the world itself disintegrate, for to each person the world only exists through the lenses provided by the structure of the self. The replacement for the lost world—again the contrast with the transcendent experience, with its sense of universal love, is instructive—is a chaotic swarm of broken-off bits of the self diffused in a sea of hatred. This is the core of psychosis, and though the overall picture is often mixed with more intact elements, it is well to keep this nucleus in mind when thinking of madness.

No one knows death—and yet it is the ultimate fear. But is not this fear really the representation of what we all do know latently—that we can go mad, obliterate the ground of our experience, and so in effect die?

In any event, the degree of anxiety unleashed in psychosis is of a higher order of severity. However, in common with other, lesser disturbances, all the bizarre manifestations—the delusions, hallucinations, catatonic trances, the attacks on the world and withdrawal from it—are still elaborated to master this psychotic anxiety. Now, though, in the effort to shore up a sense of reality, the psychotic needs to rebuild a world. There is indeed method in madness. The most illogical and seemingly disorganized delusion thus provides for its sufferer a universe of relationships. At least somebody exists to hate me; and at least there is a location in space-time from whence the voices come.

But by the same token, someone immersed in this form of experience has, for the time being at least, severed the customary communicative links with the human world. The psychotic, who suffers the most intense craving for love, the gravest suspicions as to love's effect and the deepest hostility toward those he needs, is on all these accounts sentenced to a life of exile on a mental island where his idiosyncratic construction of reality proceeds unhindered. The hideous isolation of psychosis may help account for its being the most resistant to influence of all the forms of disorder—even though the person suffering it is himself considered the least stable of men.

If we pause now to survey this landscape, it will be clear why almost any model of therapy will work for somebody, and why no model will work for everybody. The only features common to all manifestations of the neurotic process are, one, a loss of inner freedom and, two, domination by hateful and frightening elements of experience. But these stakes are the product of an innumerable number of disequilibrations between the forces of impulse, of psychological givens and of social influences. Depending on the particular play of things, we will end up with a picture of loneliness or alienation; of failed relationships or self-hatred in the midst of plenty; of some discrete fear or some chronic discontent; of intolerance of success or generalized madness; of vague dissatisfaction or excruciating torment—or of some entirely new combination of unhappiness.

The point is, if the balance can be upset in so many ways, so can it be righted in many ways. And since social and moral questions are everywhere involved in neurotic distress, each of these strategies of change have to be assessed by these standards as well. But first we need some general understanding of how the balance shifts—that is, whether and how people change.

2

On Therapy
And Therapies

CURE VERSUS HELP

Consider the different actions that can affect a neurotic state of affairs. One can

— take a trip and avoid what is stirring up anxiety;
— take a rest and strengthen one's inner defenses;
— yell, scream, cry—"let off steam"—and reduce inner pressure;
— have some sex if it reassures, or
— avoid having sex if it aggravates, or
— learn sexual techniques that one avoided out of anxiety, if the sex one is having is unfulfilling and tension-producing;
— breathe deeply or try a massage to loosen up bodily tension;
— make friends, or join a club if one is not too inhibited;
— work harder and get a reward if one's narcissism is low;
— fail and get punished if one's guilt is high;
— join a religious cult;
— take a drink, or
— be smoother and try tranquilizers;
— attack the ruling class;
— join the ruling class, or work for it;
— be a double agent;
— leave the family;
— make up with one's family;
— commit a crime;
— enlighten oneself, meditate;
— share experience with others in a group and try to work out neurotic patterns in a living way;

41

— go to an analyst and try to obtain insight and mastery over
the unconscious world;

— watch television,

and so on. . . .

Now if any of these maneuvers tips the neurotic balance in such
a way that a person is better able to deal with the intrusion of
unconscious destructivity into his life, it may be called therapeutic.
A sign that the balance has been so tipped might be a subjective
change, such as feeling more inwardly peaceful; or it might be an
objectively determinable change, such as being more flexible in
coping with personal stress; or it might include both subjective
and objective changes.

It cannot be too strongly emphasized that the changes can
never be measured by some absolute standard, but only through
the way a person evaluates his life. In other words, the "better
way" is the way one values. What is one man's inner peace is to
another a zombielike inertia. Flexibility to A may be opportunism
to B; while what B calls his integrity may seem rigidity to A. Try
as one likes, none of these changes can be rinsed clean of likes
and dislikes. And this goes for the means no less than the ends.
There is no reason why a neurosis can't be obliterated by an
odious change in a person's life. Thus some therapeutic means
may resemble putting out a forest fire, and preventing future
fires, by paving over the forest. Indeed the list above—which, of
course, by no means exhausts the possibilities—includes some
strategies that are loathsome, some that are noble, some that seem
good, clean common sense and some that seem conformist nonsense—and all of these in different ways to different people. Yet
each of the strategies can have a "therapeutic" effect in some
circumstances, and whether they "work" or not depends less on
any intrinsic virtue, or even on how well thought out they are,
than on whether they fit or not with a given neurotic situation.

If so much is therapy, then what is a Therapy? The answer
develops out of the fact that no particular strategy can be carried
out in isolation. It has to be justified, organized and fitted into the
rest of life. Therapies then are *organizations of therapeutic
strategies,* a peculiarly Western, post-Enlightenment experiment
in tinkering with lives. And they are carried out by a new class
of people, the *therapists,* who devote themselves to mastering the
technique of this organization, and earn their livelihood by ex-

changing their time and expertise for some remuneration. In consequence the therapist has a relationship to the emotionally troubled person that is—in principle at any rate—highly specialized: intense and yet disinterested, different from personal intimates or the family by virtue of the mediation of the work relation.

Therapies have an ideology, a certain view of the human world, a theory of neurosis and health, a set of practices, a training program, membership qualifications, training centers and so forth. In short, they are institutions that relate to the larger society at one end and to the individuals who partake of them on the other—like the family itself, like schools, political parties and religions. In fact Therapy as a total institution has come to supplant (and in some cases cross-fertilize) religions as the vision of what ails people has passed from a spiritual into a scientific-secular form of explanation. Thus whenever a person enters therapy, he is also entering the stream of history and casting his lot with it one way or another.

We shall have more to say of this in the last chapter. Here we need only acquaint ourselves with some of the fundamental issues of therapy in order to move more intelligently through the discussion of the therapies themselves which is to follow. There we will learn that the therapies have remarkable differences in basic assumptions, techniques and goals. Here we would like to consider what, if anything, they have in common.

The job is greatly complicated by the extreme degree of confusion, semantic and otherwise, that currently prevails. In truth, we now have a babel of therapies. Groups, movements and schools spring up like weeds, often marching behind the flag of some notable healer, and spouting shibboleths like "analysis," "synthesis," "real self," "emotional contact," as they vie for the therapeutic dollar and/or seek the True Cross. This is not true of all approaches, of course; many are modest, focal, some even skeptical and scientific. But the prospect as a whole must look to an initiate like a collection of high-school bands milling noisily about the parade grounds. What, if anything, is each of them playing? And is it what the customer would want?

Confusion may be one of the things that the therapies too often have in common. Another unfortunate and all-too-frequent property is the claim to "cure" neurosis. On countless occasions over the years, I have heard someone state that the form of treatment he practices or the one he has received has cured the neurosis—has, so to speak, obliterated the bad behavior, reduced it to rubble and constructed a New Jerusalem in its place. And as we shall see, some therapeutic ideologies go further, each proclaiming its therapy to be the millennial answer to *all* the problems of neurosis.

Such claims are nothing but the folly imposed on us by our own demand that we be perfect, or that those we believe in be so. It is the urge for God and timelessness in another form. Considering this, we should not expect the desire to be absent in any of us. But we are able to criticize it, and should do so. There are better ends toward which our narcissistic longings can be directed, and much mischief in the therapeutic situation can be avoided by keeping them under rein.

An examination of our model of neurosis will show why cure is literally not in question. For neurotic functioning consists of a set of imbalances—imbalance between the forces within a person and imbalance between the person and his world—such that unconscious spheres take destructive control. There are no foreign bodies here, nothing that exists in isolation from anything else, or that can be removed, like a splinter or a bacillus. More, there is no real standard of health that can be appealed to the way a doctor can, for example, measure the progress of a healing fracture by comparing it to the natural form of the bone. For the body lives within nature, which has its own harmonies; but the self lives between nature and history, two spheres that, as you know, often don't get on too well with each other. We cannot therefore conceive of the health of the individual apart from that of the social whole in which he is imbedded—and for reasons we shall touch upon at the end of this work, there is as yet no therapy that takes more than faltering steps down this path.

But while therapies cannot cure, they can help; and for all that we may yearn for ultimates, we can also learn to prize more down-to-earth improvement. Yet, there are so many ways to shift the balance, and so many different kinds of imbalance.

Many types of emotional disturbance are quite focal and symptomatic, and can be cleared up to all intents and purposes by changing the one factor that is causing the imbalance. As we know, simple drunkenness can be accompanied by marked emotional disorganization, all of which clears as the body cleanses itself of the offending chemical. Similar social situations exist too, as when a youngster goes haywire upon leaving home, then spontaneously adjusts. These instances can become neuroses, however, if one is inwardly primed for trouble, so that the exciting cause sets a whole chain of imbalances in motion. But even within more definite neurotic situations, we often see instances where some relatively simple intervention can grossly alter the state of imbalance and lead to a remarkable change in behavior. There are families, for example, where an enormous amount of disorganizing anxiety is being stirred up by something obvious, such as having a child sleep in the same bed with its parents, and where this can be largely reversed by simply changing the sleeping arrangements. True, there may be "deeper" reasons why such an arrangement was made in the first place, but what was decisive here may have been the extra disorganization imposed by the anxiety. With different bedroom relationships, one may afford to leave matters alone.

Or consider a similar instance of a couple whose sexual incompatibility is (1) stirring up deeper problems by maximizing frustration, (2) grounded in avoidance patterns, hence much was never learned properly, and (3) is, in consequence, enabled to get unstuck through a relatively direct learning experience of proper technique. Here again, all sorts of deeper issues may recede once the immediate one is set straight.

Finally, we have all seen people who seem neurotic wretches in a bad marriage, but bloom upon divorce; or those whose loneliness brings out the worst in them and who do just fine with a mate.

Yet, we would scarcely apply the term "cure" to instances of this sort. All we have said is that people are, after all, complicated, and that their imbalances can be approached in many ways. In order to propound a theory of cure, on the other hand, the therapeutic ideologue would have to first of all redefine the neurotic situation—and the human situation itself—in a simplistic way. He would have to demonize, finding hobgoblins in bad parents; or finding something held back like an emotional pus within a boil that could be lanced by *his* technique; and he would have to ignore the social reality that imposes suffering, both real and neurotic, from every angle. In short he would be setting up a little religion in therapeutic drag. And he might find customers and actually make them feel better, too, since for many of us the illusion of narcissistic perfection, with certainty and promise of reunion, is worth more than all the real goals that can only be laboriously attained. But he would not be curing neurosis, only promoting illusions. And his treatment, whatever it professed, would reside in a special category of therapeutic processes, those that attempt to seal off neurotic self-alienation with a narcissistic illusion.

"Process" is the term that applies to the therapies, just as it did to neurosis. In each case we have a system of forces in some kind of balance in time. The system is carried forward from the past, meets a current influence (whether from nature or society, the body or people), is altered thereby and is carried forward into the next moment, for which it becomes a past. In neurosis our attention is drawn to the pressure from the unconscious within as it affects the process. In therapy we think of some kind of controlled intervention from without that introduces a countervailing influence into the neurotic state of imbalance. For a therapy to be doing anything, then, a person must experience it as a pressure within his life: It has to make things seem a little topsy-turvy, bring up new feelings or make one see things in a new light, or bring into question the assumption one had always lived by—and suffered under. Thus, a good therapy should not be seen as a smooth, steady addition, but rather as a grappling with a hitherto unseen antagonist—who is part of one's own self. And in the course of this struggle new skills are acquired.

The model for therapy is not the cure of a disease but the growth—more specifically, the education—of a person. In contrast to education as it is usually conceived, therapy takes into account emotional and subjective need and assumes an imbalance that has to be righted. Thus it works toward the removing of unwanted modes of behavior rather than the adding on of new skills, and hence involves struggle. But this is only a *tendency;* some therapies work directly by teaching new kinds of behavior, while all therapies work with a set of instructions, some new rules of conduct with a more or less implicit set of values attached to them—just like education. True, some therapies use drugs as a primary part of their methods, but one would have to be an utter fool to ignore the social matrix in which this is necessarily fixed. Drugs in therapy never simply act on the nerve ending toward which their molecules are targeted, but always on the whole, thinking, feeling, socially defined person.

Without straining the comparison, we can say that therapy, like education, can be of use to everyone who needs it. Education primarily fills in gaps caused by ignorance, while therapy addresses the person in conflict; but each, applied correctly, has a certain legitimate potential for help—and each has limits beyond which its usefulness becomes more problematic.

Therapy properly conducted can always be of benefit in the following ways:

1. It can apply a needed emotional cushion at times of emotional crisis. Because the therapeutic relationship is ideally both intense and disinterested, the therapist can allow a troubled person (or family) to let go of feelings that get bottled up in everyday life, without fear of reprisal. This is bound to have a helpful, balancing effect. The very least that can be demanded of therapy is that it provide a person with someone who pays attention to and accepts him without responding in the ways others close to him have always responded. In fact, it has been argued that this is the base of all therapy, the rest—the particulars of each school, the infinite variations in stance, technique, goals, etc.—being but a superstructure resting on this base.

2. By the same process, therapy can give virtually everyone some clarification and understanding of his position. As we observed in the previous chapter, one of the most striking features of almost all neurotic situations is a sense of confusion. This can usually be alleviated to some extent by skilled guidance. Indeed, in many instances, a proper therapeutic consultation may conclude with the advice that no further therapy is required.

3. Therapies can address themselves to and to some degree remove the external aggravation of a neurotic imbalance. Even when this reality is intractable—as, for example, when a person becomes permanently blinded or disabled—a good therapist can usually help him to become better able to bear the impact of the loss. At this end there is no boundary between therapy and social work or rehabilitation. Each of these approaches is best carried out with an eye to the interplay between emotional factors and the impact of the environment. Each person, well or sick, is always at a given phase of development when some issues are critical. Therapy can address itself to these issues and, by resolving them in a progressive way, help the overall state of balance. Thus a mentally retarded youngster who is psychologically out of control may be best helped by being taught some manageable and useful skill, thereby increasing self-regard and using it as a bulwark against emotional disorganization. Similarly, an impulse-ridden youth can be stabilized by the opportunity to find some activity

which allows him to identify with helping parental figures. Just so are many chronically psychotic people best treated by the combination of a "sheltered workshop" setting along with some structured social environment. And finally, an elderly person in the grip of chronic depression owing to the reality of loss can be at times substantially helped by an altered reality of useful work and new associations.

Obviously matters are generally not so simple, but just as obviously is there almost always some room to be of help by changing the external situation. We are describing here what is called "counseling." A good counselor is one who provides emotional support, intellectual clarification and some attention to concrete environmental problems.

Therapy gets more ambitious as it attempts to go beyond the limits of counseling into the incursions made by the unconscious, and it also gets more problematic, more liable to bog down, or even to harm. However far it goes though, therapy retains some of its base in counseling. It often proves the case, for instance, that a treatment makes rapid initial progress but then enters a phase of confusion and repetition. What has happened is that the first phase has been a kind of counseling; the patient lets go of feelings, feels supported, draws some conclusions that tend to clarify matters and even acts upon this basis with good effect. All looks well—for a while. Then, the initial thrust gets exhausted, and a counterattack begins from the more deeply entrenched forces that maintain the neurosis. Had the therapy stopped after a few weeks or months, it might have been able to claim remarkable results. But this would have been at the expense of deeper knowledge, and without the gains of really trying to come to grips with the full problem. Not that such additional goals are unalloyed boons; on the contrary, they can stir up as much if not more trouble than they're worth. It's just that they are different, providing the patient with special skills for special needs, the way different educational programs do.[1]

THE THERAPEUTIC RELATIONSHIP AND TRANSFERENCE

Essential to all therapies and counseling is the effect of the relationship with the therapist. Try to imagine what treatment would be like without this relationship—if, for example, interpretations of behavior were transmitted by computer print-out instead of a human dialogue. I am told that something of the sort took place in England, and that the subjects liked it! But this development is more of a comment on where our civilization may be heading than on the present state of therapy within it. For now, most of us could not conceive of altering the neurotic balance without some human influence. This, however, calls attention to a problem vaster than the scope of this study. Some of the themes have been touched upon already; others will be dealt with more fully below. Here let us just introduce a few key concepts.

Try as we may to think of ourselves as separate individuals, human reality will have it otherwise. Each person exists in fact, as the center point of an enormous web of human relations, and these relations extend in several dimensions at once. They extend backward in time so that each relationship continues the unfinished business left over from all previous relationships; and they extend outward into society so that each human contact tugs at the whole social order. In other words, whenever someone enters therapy a main portion of what is going on will have to do with the personal relationships he forms; and these will reflect something of the society to which he now belongs, and something of the family from which he came—all tinged with the influence of the neurosis for which he seeks help.

As we have seen, neurosis is self-estrangement felt as a state of imbalance. But since the self lives with other selves in society, a sense of balance can be restored by attachments to others. We thereby replace estrangement with community. All therapies offer some sense of community, mainly with the therapist, but also just by knowing others are undergoing the same kind of experience. Indeed a kind of communal feeling is established with the entire ideology and institution of the therapy, its way of life. What distinguishes a therapy from the isolated therapeutic actions listed at the beginning of this chapter is the kind of organized personal force with which the patient can join. Whoever undertakes therapy then should recognize that he is going to experience a powerful pull toward joining up with its community, and that the kinds of feelings he is likely to find himself having toward the therapist and the therapeutic ideology are going to play a large role in what happens to him.

Because there is so much self-alienation and frustrated longing in neurosis, therapy can most readily alleviate neurotic suffering by allowing some means of gratification. For this, two things are necessary: There must be an object who can satisfy the wish; and there must be some source of permission, assurance that it is all right to do so, since the desire would not have entered into the neurosis had the person not experienced it as destructive and forbidden. Often these two functions can both be performed by one person, the therapist. Hence the therapist who offers himself as a love object to the patient, and who permits this love, will be off to a flying start in his profession. By the same token, therapy can swiftly make some people feel less neurotic by setting itself up as a moral authority. By specifying what is right and wrong, the therapy takes over the condemning power that had plagued the individual in neurotic conflict, and so relieves the pressure from within. But it does more, for therapy of this sort also realigns the person with the larger community, since it is society that in the last instance holds the power to make legal tender out of moral currency.

We can also extract a broader point, which is that therapy has to work by creating a new whole, i.e., restoring a state of order that has been sundered. And these wholes need not conform to any natural pattern, or be adjudged the good. They only have to be relatively more unified than the state of neurosis had been. As Lévi-Strauss observed for primitive healers,[2] the "cure" need not succeed by objectively working with the truth of the patient's situation, but by supplying a missing piece of a myth, acceptance of which serves to reunite the sufferer and his community. Or we can call it a language, or symbolic code, that retranslates the individual life into the life of the whole. In the case of our society, "advanced" to the point of fragmentation, there is no given whole, hence no unique language, hence a plethora of therapies, choosing among which will be a matter of value no less than rational selection.

Bewildering as this may be where society is concerned, there is a unifying thread at the individual end, for the history of each life becomes simpler and more powerfully emotional as we trace it back into childhood. The language of the therapy will thus derive a substantial part of its vocabulary from this end of things. And the effect that childhood exerts on the therapeutic relationship we sum up in the concept of *transference*.

From the earliest eighteenth-century ventures into psychotherapy, it had been observed that the relationship between therapist and patient—more precisely, its trusting quality, or rapport—played a key role in the outcome.[3] Not until Freud, however, was more exacting attention paid to what had previously been a rather nonspecific concept. He observed after a while that his patients began to treat him in ways approximating earlier relationships—usually, though not always, as a parent. This was at first considered an impedance, a *resistance,* to the treatment, because the attitudes revealed were often hostile and always irrational. Even the loving feelings, though they could spur on much work, soon enough became obstacles to change in depth, insofar as giving up the neurosis also meant giving up the wish for the analyst's love.

Freud eventually came around to a more balanced view. Transference was a resistance, true, but it was also the living, breathing actualization of the neurosis. If one wanted to grapple with the real beast, then the transference had to be carefully nurtured and just as carefully dissolved. The means of doing this would be, roughly speaking, twofold: (1) Do not gratify the transference wishes directly; and (2) resolve them through interpretation, or telling the truth about the meaning of what was transpiring. In this way transference feelings would gradually grow into a new edition of the infantile neurotic text. It would take on an intense reality, yet one that was always recognizably artificial—i.e., a reality that could be isolated from the total self and its values.

Psychoanalytic therapy may in fact be defined as one that systematically proceeds with the transference in this manner. The details of its workings do not concern us here; but we do need to inquire as to the general importance of transference in therapy and of its particular influence on the values of the patient—more exactly, on the autonomy of those values, his right to hold them on his own.

The answer is that it is potentially enormous. Recall that every neurosis involves the special claims of infantile wishes; that these wishes generally are directed toward parents; and that they make their strongest demand outside the range of consciousness. Now such desires would not be in a position to be gratified unless the essential qualities of the infantile relationship were reproduced. Here, of course, therapy can provide a ready model of the child-parent bond. And since one invariable quality of this relationship is the child's lack of autonomy, manifested in the adult as a passive acceptance of the parent's values, the way is prepared for a flourishing loss of freedom in the therapeutic relationship.

The infantile authority with which the therapist is endowed is the root of the authority he picks up by virtue of representing a society to the patient. This follows from the fact that society, too, is in some measure cemented together by childhood desire. Transference is therefore the deep link between therapy and society, which is something we shall bear in mind while considering the link between cure and conformism.

Transference wishes are stirred up willy-nilly, whether the therapist cultivates them or not, but the form they assume depends greatly upon what the therapist does. Along with specifically addressing himself for transference, as the psychoanalyst does, a therapist has numerous options: He can use the parental authority he is given as a kind of benign engine of change without further exploring it or drawing on it; he can explore the transference a little, perhaps emphasizing its less seamy and inaccessible sides; or he can exploit the depths of transference, set himself up as a kind of god and establish awesome control over the patient's life. There is an amazing degree of susceptibility to this kind of manipulation. We all have something of the sucker—literally— in us, and we bring our need to deify into the therapist's office. That shall interest us at length below; just now we need only recognize that the nature of therapy is such—because the nature of neurosis is such—that transference is always a factor.

SOME PARADOXES AND EXAMPLES

Indeed, therapy is full of "factors," not all of which mesh smoothly with each other. Because of this, whenever a therapy ventures beyond the stage where it can provide counseling and emotional support, something will have to be given up if gains are to be made. When one is shattered or overwhelmed, or simply confused, there is not much question about what sort of help is needed, or about its limits. But what if one is not simply confused, but *wills* confusion as a way of avoiding a painful realization? Or suppose one *needs*[5] to create catastrophes and punishments as a means of expiating unconscious guilt feelings?

In other words, suppose what is the case in all of the major neuroses: that one is locked in conflict between forces that are all part of the self, and none of which is about to be surrendered. In these cases any new balance will have to include all the elements of the old, hopefully rearranged, perhaps defanged—but still present. People say they want to change and they may mean it and work seriously at it. But this has to be taken advisedly. Change can mean forgetting, or self-knowledge, or finding new relationships, discharging bottled-up feelings, or working toward a new social order. It does not, however, mean a new self—change of this magnitude is only done this side of the grave by extremes of brainwashing and behavior control. To call these "therapeutic" is to endorse such anxiety and loss as could only be associated with the grimmest totalitarianism. Hence, the best one could hope for in therapies that promise total transformation of the self is that they are inept—and fortunately this generally proves to be the case. Indeed, such therapies are in the same category as those that promise "cure." What they are usually offering is a new, fancied-up version of an infantile relationship, what is called a "transference cure."

In any event, if anyone is determined to find a new self, he will do so with or without therapy. For the rest of us, change will have to come more gradually, or, to be more precise, dialectically, through some praxis that re-creates the terms of the basic dilemma and permits some reworking of them, thus yielding new levels of contradiction which can in turn be confronted. Though one may dearly hope to discover a new life in the therapist's office, what happens in fact is that the terms of the old one are re-arrayed and set out in a new manner so that one may grapple with them. Every contradiction that has been in the neurosis is at least potentially reclaimable in its treatment. People who hate authority, yet can't leave it in the "real world," will do the same in the therapy. Those who abuse themselves to frustrate others will experience the same pattern in treatment, where they will have to contend with a need to ruin their therapy in order to "get back" at the therapist. Those who compulsively need to dominate relations outside will find themselves struggling with the same problem within therapy—and so on. These intrusions are not a distraction from therapy; they are its essential condition. All therapies work by this model. They differ essentially in the direction the contradictions are taken and how far change is pursued. And since they attempt change through contradiction, they always have to weigh one side or another and leave some kind of hole behind. Therapies are thus like a somewhat complaisant customs inspector who checks passage from one land to the next, while allowing enough illegal (neurotic) goods to be smuggled in to keep an exchange going. What goods? How complaisant? What kind of exchange? These are the questions on which therapies turn. Let us consider a couple of examples.

A young woman complained of chronically depressed and tense feelings that led her to compulsively seek dangerous sexual contacts in which she would more or less provoke rape, then end up performing fellatio. Following this her bad feelings would return, forcing a repetition of the dangerous behavior. This continued unabated for several weeks until the therapist recollected that she had told him, in the first session, that she had been born with a serious deformity—a communication, or fistula, between the trachea and esophagus, which made it impossible to eat without aspirating some food into the respiratory tract. As this would have been fatal if uncorrected, she had to undergo many operations as an infant to repair the defect, during which time she had to be fed directly into her stomach. Consequently, she lost the opportunity to gain any kind of adequate use of her mouth. In addition to this trauma, which also involved repeated separations from her parents while she was in the hospital and other family-related emotional distress, she had to bear the stigma of her operative scars. The significance of all this had been denied, or had otherwise been kept from her awareness, until the therapist realized the connection and communicated it to her through an interpretation that said, in effect, your compulsive and unhappy sexual experiences of today are continuations of old struggles; they are attempts to master your infantile sense of deprivation and injury by gaining pleasure and the esteem of being desirable, yet they must continually fail, indeed repeat the past surgical trauma in the guise of undoing it.

Following this interpretation her compulsive sexuality abated. She lost the restless craving for fellatio, and ceased placing herself in jeopardy.

Now this is indisputably a therapeutic event, and there can be little doubt that the giving of knowledge was the effective agent of change. Something that had been so all her life, but which she was enacting blindly, became *true* to her. This is the function of an interpretation, to make an empirical statement that explains some pattern of behavior that had hitherto been out of the patient's awareness. Interpretation is the specific instrument of all analytic therapy, the means to enlarge awareness in a way that counts. The same terms could be reflected upon with all her capacities as had been blindly discharged in activity. With the restoration of a split-off part of her life, she was able to apply a maturer judgment. From another angle, her infantile way could only flourish in darkness; the eye of truth sapped its power and caused it to wither away.

So knowledge can play a role. If one were doing a "scientific" study of symptom relief, a success could be chalked up here. But consider its limits. The neurotic current was temporarily deflected and she gained the self-regard that comes from controlling oneself. This made up for the loss of immediate gratification—but only for a little while. How could a lifetime go away with one positive turnabout based upon a few therapeutic words? Can a few events compensate for the years of pain, the absent formative experience of using her mouth, the turning inward of hatred and the embedding of unsatisfiable longing? Only the most puerile view of human nature would take these warpings lightly enough to pretend that a bit of intellectual truth and a momentary behavioral change based upon it would be compensation.

We might expect instead that the brief remission would be followed by a new outbreak of her disorder, calling for protracted work on her part as well as new, tougher, sustained interventions by the therapist. And with each step she will be further drawn into the struggle.

Looking back a little, it was hasty to say that the new knowledge, in and of itself, did the trick. Reflect for a moment on whether the same result would have obtained if the information had been typed out and mailed to her. Obviously the fact that it was being told to her by another person, and by somebody who was there to help, who was a doctor (to be contrasted with the other doctors in her life), who was male (to be contrasted with her pickups) and who was older and in a role of authority (to be contrasted with parents)—all this lent weight to the knowledge and gave it emotional force. And we can be sure that this force will not grow less complicated with the passage of time. Indeed it is not hard to imagine the circumstances under which the influence of the therapist would be such that any communication from him that carried a sense of conviction and had an air of novel insight would do the trick, whether or not it was true. Further, there are times when a deliberately false interpretation may succeed where the truth fails, precisely because it feeds the wish to forget and permits a spurious yet powerful sense of unity with the authority of the therapist *cum* parent *cum* leader.

Still, in this instance the patient suffered from a lack of correct knowledge, which could only have been imparted to her verbally. Moreover, this knowledge was in some measure antithetical to what she had been doing—it replaced those activities and pushed them aside. And it may be hoped that further advances, perhaps even an eventual mastery of her neurosis, could come by similar verbal means. Often, however, the pattern is not so one-sided, as the following example indicates.

A young man handled intense feelings of anxiety—which had germinated in relationship to his parents—by becoming a ski bum. His mother was intrusive, seductive and hypercritical (hence the self-image of bum), his father remote, ungiving and never protective against the mother. The patient's feelings of helplessness and passivity could be both represented and mastered in action by skiing. This he pursued compulsively and to the exclusion of any other sustained interest or personal relationship—until he passed the age of thirty and sustained a severe depression about not doing anything else. What perpetuated the depression, gripping it, so to speak, in a neurotic vise, was a set of actions in which his self-destructive and infantile tendencies were allowed full sway. One, he fractured a leg on the last day of the season just as he was about to win a race from a hated rival (he recognized that there was no special hazard causing him to fall when he did); and two, lacking the means of independence, he moved back in with his parents to recuperate, thus setting up a vicious cycle of recrimination, mutual hatred and covert gratification between himself and his mother. By the time he came to therapy the level to which he had fallen back, or regressed, was indicated by the rages he would fly into because his mother would not keep the refrigerator stocked with his favorite flavor of ice cream.

In any event he arrived at the therapist's office in a state of virtual paralysis, fearing that he would never ski again, or indeed ever undertake any other sustained productive endeavor.

Despite the severe symptomatology, the therapy was brief and, from the patient's standpoint, highly successful. The therapist mainly listened sympathetically and made some truthful but not very far-reaching remarks pertaining to the patient's loss of self-esteem, how hard it was to deal with a mother like that, etc. Within a couple of months the patient's mood lightened and he began to get itchy to move again. Since treatment began in September, it was by now once again the skiing season. At the first whiff of snow off he went to the mountains, with effusive thanks for his remarkable recovery. He did concede the existence of deeper problems that led up to the recent disturbance, and he resolved to return in the spring to clear them up, yet was adamant in his fidelity to the slopes. That was the last of him.

The therapist was cognizant of the intrinsic appeal of skiing. And though he might speculate here that the slopes represented mother's body, the snow being the ice cream and milk that was to come from her, and the skiing an attitude of active movement over mother's body as against passive, hateful wallowing inside it, he could not conduct therapy on the basis of so tenuous and deep a root meaning. Of greater practical significance was a grasp of the immediate surface of the patient's situation. Undoubtedly the young man chose the joyous activity of skiing as a way out of his passivity (why this way and not another could be speculated but not determined in so brief a contact). And this worked until his conflicts about aggression led to the accident which, closing off this path of resolution, led to the further regression of the depressive neurosis. Just as clearly, the therapeutic work here consisted, for this phase at least, of doing for him what his father couldn't— namely, providing a buffer against the pull to his mother. The therapist did this just by being there, on his side, letting him know he understood some of the problem.

But the key to the matter lies in the limits of understanding the patient would tolerate. Here action conquered knowledge. For it was certain that the patient did not want to know too much, either about the inner nature of his wishes toward his parents, or about the emerging transfer of those wishes onto the therapist. To know more would have entailed the risk of an anxiety greater than he was willing to gamble on. So the universal temptation of the mountains became an irresistible lure, and he left, returned to motion, feeling better but still shy of any solid grasp of the roots of his predicament and thus more or less at the mercy of fate.

Was this a successful treatment? Who is to say no without equivocation? The patient feels better; being in the hands of fate means that chance may as easily be on his side as against him;

age may sober him; new relationships may provide adequate buffers against relapse. Is it not better, he feels, to ski gloriously for a few years than to slide safely into the mediocre life of work in modern industrial society, or into some entrapping bourgeois marriage hatched out of unconscious fidelity to his parents? Would protracted treatment guarantee any better lot, with therapy's inherent uncertainty, probability of inducing anxiety along the way and extensive commitment in time and money—which in turn forces a certain way of life upon the patient?

The answer is that there is no answer. Nothing unequivocal, in any event, nothing that does not take into account the vagaries of value and choice. The fact (assuming it *is* a fact) that this person runs from self-knowledge into an action that is compulsive tells us nothing about whether he should stay and risk the pitfalls along the path to greater self-mastery (which would certainly not take from him the pleasure of skiing, only put it in some self-selected organization of means and ends), or leave and risk the pitfalls of the hills. We might draw up a list of probabilities as to the outcome of one decision or another, but he is going to have to choose. Without the freedom of that choice, no therapy based upon self-mastery could, by the most elementary logic, ever hope to succeed.

In the preceding example, the patient's ordinary mode of adaptation, skiing, was infiltrated by the neurotic process. For him, skiing was not simply done for itself; it became as well an obligatory means to ward off neurotic suffering. By the dialectic that reigns in these matters, it was marked by what it defended against. If the neurotic process is seen as the imposition of an inner compulsion upon human potential, then what made him feel good—skiing—was also an attenuation of what he could become, and it could be used by the defensive, conservative part of him to resist a therapy that bid to open up a new range of possibilities.

Such a pattern is, in one form or another, exceedingly common, and a good part of ordinary life is shot through with rationalized neurotic limitation. But it should not be thought because of this that any therapy presents the other end of the spectrum—complete inner freedom. Although therapy promises a greater range of inner freedom than that which exists in ordinary adaptation, it can achieve this only in a relative way. All a therapy can offer is to relieve neurotic distress. It can do so either by dulling the pain or by shifting the person in a less neurotic direction. The former, dulling of pain—with drugs, simple suggestion or various distractions—can never promise greater freedom. But even a technique that bids to attack the neurotic problem at its source can only provide hope for greater freedom; it cannot promise absolute freedom for the simple reason that no such thing exists. Freedom is hewn out of limitations, and each program to increase freedom contains the germ of a new set of limits.

The analytic strategy of inner truthfulness and self-mastery entails one of these limits in a glaring way: It requires that action be suspended so that inner truth be put in verbal terms. The two examples above demonstrated the dialectic between doing and verbal knowing in a way that suggested the primacy of knowing. The story does not end here, however. What was being compared was a false state of acting to a relatively truer one of knowledge that could develop from the suspension of action. But verbal knowledge has its limits, too. One does not have to embrace Eastern philosophy to recognize that there is a state of preverbal being which exerts a powerful influence over life. The nature of this state is most difficult to characterize, and it is beyond our present scope to do more than suggest it. We may regard the pre- or nonverbal state as an undifferentiated form of being in which the subjective and objective worlds are not experienced as sharply distinguished from each other. It derives from early infantile experience, and persists through life as our grounding in nature, a root that thrives though covered by all the soil of civilization. We shall have more to say of this in a later chapter; here it may be claimed that the preverbal state can never be fully grasped with words, and yet enters into every form of therapy. In analytic treatment it makes itself felt in the silent interstices between verbalization. The words by which truth is brought to consciousness are, figuratively speaking, formations of new psychic stuff out of this inner preverbal core. Under good analytic conditions the new structures will be genuinely less neurotic than the old. But they do not replace the nonverbal substratum of being, only develop an improved structure around it.

By the same token, other forms of therapy can, by eschewing the analytic goal, take greater advantage of the preverbal state by encouraging modes of expression that are more fully representative of nonverbal being than is the verbalization of the analytic approach. One thinks here of the basically nonverbal treatments that utilize bodily movement, or emotive expressiveness. No doubt the experiences so induced are closer to the preverbal state and can have genuine therapeutic impact. Yet they, too, suffer their own brand of limitation, namely that of not being able to clearly and objectively understand one's full situation.

The dichotomy is not between the ignorance of nonverbal therapy as against the truth-telling of analysis; nor is it between the sterile verbal intellectualization of analysis and the vitality of a nonverbal therapy—though in the heat of propaganda it is sometimes presented this way. Rather is the dilemma intrinsic to all therapy. Intellectualization is the hallmark of bad analysis, just as obscurantism is the hallmark of bad nonverbal therapy. Each is a problem in its own right, but neither is basic. The fundamental problem has to do with the inherent limits of human truth itself and the grounding of our lives in contradiction.

Thus, there is no such thing as a utopian therapy, and any therapy that sets itself up as such is perforce bad therapy. Not bad in being ineffective, but bad in the sense that it promotes unworthy goals, goals that people might have been expected to outgrow in this late age of consciousness, but from which we will never completely escape, for they stem from our earliest narcissistic wishes for perfection via the union with an all-powerful parent.

It should be made clear that though I am asserting that no therapy can be absolute, or millennial, it by no means follows that all therapies that modestly admit their limitations are of equal merit. They all, I suppose, have their place, and each may have an area of special application with respect to which they have worth equivalent to all the others. But beyond this rather obvious level of equality they have major differences: in intellectual substructure, in susceptibility to corruption or trivialization and, most importantly, in their different implications for the organization of the human community. Here is where the question of values takes on its most serious form. To state the limits of therapy is also to recognize that the human situation has no closed end, but is rather in a state of continuous historical evolution. Whatever therapies are to the individual in neurotic distress, they are also significant institutional trends within society; and our position with respect to the organization of society is deeply interlocked with attitudes toward therapy. Before we can explore this further, we need to sort out the varieties of therapeutic experience; and in order to do this we had best shift gears and consider the main forms of therapy we shall be exploring in brief historical perspective.

HISTORICAL SYNOPSIS

It is commonly agreed that what we call "therapy" corresponds to an institution that has existed in every known differentiated society. Therapists today are the heirs to the priest class, shamans dressed up in a new professional garb (though at times reverting to the original costume). Indeed, the set of therapies we know today in the Western world have grown out of the crack in our culture created by the decline of the traditional priestly function. Since emotional unhappiness is continually generated by civilized life, alternates to the shaman have appeared according to other cultural types more suitable to contemporary life, with all its complexity and rationalization.

The most successful candidate for this role in the modern world has been the physician-psychiatrist, standard-bearer of a triumphant science. Modern science did not merely create today's psychiatrist; it also defined for him the object of his attention, "mental illness" itself. The past two centuries have witnessed the differentiation of the insane and emotionally troubled from the general class of misfits, paupers and criminals into which they had been previously thrown.[4] Through the nineteenth and well into the twentieth century, these twin concepts—the madman *cum* psychotic and the doctor *cum* alienist *cum* psychiatrist—developed jointly.[5]

The difficulties in arriving at clear ideas of phenomena such as madness and neurosis spring, as we have seen, from a number of sources. Of these, the problem of defining the irrational—which is what madness is about—using rational forms of thought has been from the beginning one of the most formidable. Here, more than in other areas of science, the field has been preempted from time to time by charismatic individuals who have been able to establish contact with irrational forms of experience ruled out of bounds by dominant social interests—including the mainstream of science itself. The history of the therapies in the modern world has by and large been a fitful wrestling between the recognition of madness and the demonic on the one hand, and scientific objective, "civilized" control of the irrational on the other. And where organized society would not be able to assimilate the demon, there would arise cults, sects and "schools" of therapy that would stay for a while, then pass away. They were usually dominated by some eccentric, stubborn, forceful individual who stood against official institutions, and so became the nucleus of a little "countersociety."

Anton Mesmer (1734–1815), the Austrian discoverer of hypnosis, was the first major example of such a type. Mesmer essentially found a technique—suggestion—for altering the play of mental forces in his subjects and so produced remarkable, if short-lived, changes in behavior, including the "cure" of neurotic phenomena of the hysterical kind. Mesmer also became the focus of a cult which lasted a number of years, then folded. However, hypnosis was rejuvenated toward the close of the nineteenth century, principally in France where it reappeared under the respectable aegis of Jean-Martin Charcot (1825–93) and his powerful rival, Hippolyte Bernheim (1840–1919).

The details of this development are of no present concern to us. However, some of its features are characteristic of schools of therapy. Note the impact of a new technique (here, suggestion) which upsets a previously held pattern of relating and thinking, hence changes behavior and introduces new knowledge. Note, too, that such a method has to have a "disease" on which to work—in this case hysteria of the conversion type (simulation of fainting spells, seizures, blindness, or other organic conditions), a disorder that was widespread in the nineteenth century and considerably less so now. Note therefore that the "disease" must express something that is specific to the period—i.e., that it, along with the technique used to address it, are each historical in some measure. Note further that the discoverer of the technique can set himself up as a hero or god, especially a rebellious one, and can develop his cult and receive his punishment from the established system whose regulations (embodied in the historical disease) he is defying. And note finally the reemergence of the technique, modified, more respectable, yet subject to increasing factionalism.

Squabbles between various advocates, each of whom claims to have exclusive purchase on the truth—especially when that truth was the work of a past master—may signal nothing so much as the inadequacy and obsolescence of all of them. In short, they may herald the coming of a new discoverer-hero. In the history of therapies, one man, Sigmund Freud (1856–1939), stands out as the embodiment of that role, which he picked up from the confused amalgam of late-nineteenth-century neuropsychiatry.[6]

Freud studied with Charcot, and joined the late-nineteenth-century debate on hypnosis. His achievement lay, however, in vastly extending our grasp of something hypnosis had afforded but a glimpse of—the unconscious. Freud provided the first, and still the definitive, calculus for conceptualizing the irrational in rational terms. His work was much more than a therapy based on this calculus; it was rather a new outpost of the scientific approach, and at the same time the most relentless critique yet seen of the optimistic and positivistic world view that science was supposed to exemplify.

Freud was a transformer of Western culture, hence his influence is incalculable. It certainly far exceeds whatever particular impact the therapy founded in his name may have. Whatever the fate of Freudian psychoanalysis as an institution—and it has already sunk to a relatively minor role so far as actual therapeutic practice goes—Freud with his methods and central insight remains the progenitor of modern therapy. It is striking to see work after work, new method after new method, define itself by reference to Freud, usually as an alleged breakthrough past his limits. Through the years, a thousand commentators, mostly long forgotten, have labeled Freud passé. Buried countless times, just as perpetually resurrected, the spirit of Freud continues to brood over contemporary therapy. All of the analytic schools of psychotherapy derive directly from Freud, while many of the non-analytic therapies owe much of their impetus to ideas introduced by him. Adler, Jung, Rank, Horney, Reich, Fromm, Perls, Berne—names that have come to be identified as the bearers of immensely divergent therapeutic systems—all share a common inheritance of Freudian psychoanalysis (and in most cases an intense and ambivalent tie to the master himself). It is, of course, not just one idea but an organized complex of belief and practice that defines a therapy. Thus Freud's therapy remains distinct for having been borrowed from, though other therapies have managed to achieve their own identities for all their borrowing. Nonetheless it is helpful up to a point to relate therapies to Freud's psychoanalysis, since this reflects something of their historical development.

For all its complexity, Freudian therapy is defined by a rather limited set of criteria: theoretically, by an emphasis on infantile sexuality and dynamically repressed unconscious mental processes; and in practice, by what is called the Basic Rule—i.e., the imperative to say whatever comes to mind, as well as by attention to *resistance*—i.e., blocks in the path of revealing unconscious mental life, and *transference*—i.e, the reliving of the past in the therapeutic setting.

In this Freudian unity a number of schisms occurred, developing different facets of Freud's theory, and downplaying others.[7] Thus, C. G. Jung (1875–1961) minimized the importance of infantile sexuality and introduced a drastically different, expanded idea of the unconscious; while Alfred Adler (1870–1937) downplayed sexuality and the unconscious altogether and focused instead on social factors and what might be called "egoistic" elements—assertiveness, strivings for power, self-esteem, etc.

Jung and Adler defined two main types of alternate approaches, the transcendent and the social, and most subsequent analytic schisms have occurred along these lines, especially the Adlerian. Included among such approaches—which are usually termed (with little justification or usefulness to anyone) Neo-Freudian— are the schools associated with figures such as Otto Rank (1884–1939), Karen Horney (1885–1952), Harry Stack Sullivan (1892–1949) and Eric Fromm (b.1900). These schools have had wide influence in the United States, especially in the fields of education and social work.

Two other schools of therapy that originated in close connection with Freudian analysis should be noted also, although they are widely divergent from each other, and from psychoanalysis as well. One is the central-European school of existential analysis,[8] founded mainly on the philosophical principles of Kierkegaard, Husserl and Heidegger and developed by psychiatrists such as Ludwig Binswanger (1881–1966) and Medard Boss (b.1903). Existential analysis has a highly limited role as a school of therapy in the United States, but as a point of view it has become quite influential through the work of Rollo May and, especially, that of R. D. Laing and his group.

The second was the Reichian school. Wilhelm Reich (1897–1957), another powerful figure who defined his early efforts in relation to Freud, was originally a leading psychoanalyst (and Marxist) but became increasingly preoccupied with the biological sources of neurosis.[9] Thus from psychoanalysis came orgone therapy (after the form of life energy Reich claimed to have discovered) and, from that, bioenergetic therapy, which is, roughly speaking, Reichian therapy stripped of the orgone hypothesis. As with existential analysis, this approach has had less impact on its own than as the source of a point of view which has influenced therapeutic practice at many levels.

For example, the important contemporary approach of *gestalt therapy*, though developed mainly by F. S. Perls (1893–1970), was influenced by Reich (through Paul Goodman), Jung and Freud, as well as by the school of academic psychology to which it owes its name.[10] As so often happens, the approach took on its own form under the charismatic influence of Perls and has continued to evolve with the changing American scene.

The American climate has produced several influential schools of therapy which, though influenced by older developments, have yet achieved a specifically American identity. Of these perhaps the most important is the approach (or, rather, evolving set of approaches) developed by the psychologist Carl Rogers (b.1902).[11] More than anyone else, Rogers has brought the psychological profession into the business of therapy, thus breaking the monopoly that medicine and its psychiatric specialty long held. Rogers' ideas, compounded of a little Freud, somewhat more Otto Rank— i.e., Neo-Freudianism—but mainly of a highly individual yet typically American blend of pragmatism and optimistic faith in the individual, have had a major impact on the conduct of therapy in the United States.

The optimistic melioristic streak in American culture has also borne fruit in other prominent contemporary approaches to therapy. Usually these rely on *group* experience, at times conducted along psychoanalytic lines, at times of a brief and intense nature. One thinks here of the whole *encounter* movement (in which Rogerian and gestalt therapy have played important roles); or of another approach, the *transactional analysis* founded by Eric Berne; or of Werner Erhard's more recent *est*. Many of these methods give some recognition to earlier work, but they really constitute a distinct form, which shall be discussed in more detail below, but may be called for now the *human potential* approach.[12]

The main point about therapies such as these is that, rather than give the patient a traditional and asymmetric relationship with a helping doctor, therapist or some other expert, they attempt to produce an altered life experience with peers—and a leader-guide—who are to directly affect the person and somehow "open" him or her up. All such therapies are greatly indebted also to the *psychodrama* of J. L. Moreno (who also introduced the concept of group therapy itself back in 1932).

A similar notion—that direct alteration of the living unit of personal life would change neurotic behavior for the better—also underlies the major recent development of *family therapy*. Again, one should perhaps use the plural, therapies, since there are several approaches. Some are relatively psychoanalytic in basic framework, while others use a radically different approach derived from the study of communication theory and ethology—i.e., the naturalistic study of animal behavior.[13]

Another group of therapies has recently arisen exploring the possibility of reaching directly and rapidly what might be considered deep and preverbal layers of the mind. Some of these draw upon Eastern transcendental approaches, while others attempt to use consciousness-altering drugs (i.e., the work of Claudio Naranjo) or neurological means to the same end. A fast-growing newcomer to the field is the *primal therapy* of Arthur Janov, who uses psychological methods to break through to the traumatic roots of neurosis.[14]

Finally, we should include discussion of an important therapeutic approach that has been around for the past thirty years and is perhaps, of all the schools, the furthest removed from Freudian concepts. This is the *behavioral therapy* associated with the names of H. J. Eysenck in England and Joseph Wolpe in America.[15] Therapies of this type, which are based upon the learning theory of academic psychology, are growing rapidly in influence.

THE AXIOMS OF THERAPY

From this brief synopsis it appears that therapy in the modern world is precisely in that stage of confusion and heterogeneity as would await the coming of a new, unifying system.

As observed above, this is not likely to occur in advanced industrial society. Given the state of our culture, searching for a therapeutic synthesis is like hunting a unicorn. Instead, let us try to analyze the existing therapies according to their basic assumptions—much as one would search for the axioms out of which different geometries are built. In this way we will be able to grasp more clearly essential differences between the various schools.

Surveying the field, it would seem that each therapy addresses itself to the basic dialectic between the mind, biology and society by emphasizing one or another as the main causal factor in neurosis and consequently as the main area to be influenced. Thus we have *psychotherapy, biotherapy* and *sociotherapy.* Of course all therapy is ultimately *psycho*therapeutic in that it affects the psychology of the neurotic person. But so is all therapy ultimately *bio*therapeutic and *socio*therapeutic in that this person has a body and lives with other people. We need to focus not on the therapy's areas of ultimate influence but on its main area of concern.

The type of therapy tells us the direction in which neurotic contradictions will be pursued—and what holes are likely to be left behind. Freud's psychoanalysis—to choose the most distinctive psychotherapy—zeroes in on thought and fantasy and suspends action and real social consequences. Bioenergetic therapy explores contradictions as they are immediately manifest in breathing, muscular tension and so forth, and shelves much attention to fantasy or social relations (at least the attention given is minuscule in proportion to psychotherapy or sociotherapy). Finally, family therapy, a fairly clear-cut sociotherapy, deals with current social interactions within the family, and seeks to influence these, rather than fantasy or bodily attitudes.

Obviously these are matters of emphasis, not exclusion. It has always to be borne in mind that the writings and official teachings of the leading schools of therapy usually turn out to be a lot purer than what is practiced. In addition, most practitioners develop an individual style that mixes a number of levels of approach. This is less a synthesis than a compromise dictated by practical necessity.

However even at the level of pure doctrine things are never too neat. The people who developed these therapies were not blind men groping about an elephant and confusing the appendage they were grasping with the whole beast (there are exceptions who have done just this, but they needn't concern us now). Most of them recognized the many layers of the human situation and paid some respect to all aspects. But whether the developer of a therapy was an ignoramus or not, his conceptual money went to one place and not the other, and this determined the broad direction of his treatment.

Some words of definition here. To me, "nature" means whatever arises outside of history and is indifferent to our striving, our will and our morality. Death and the stars are alike forms of nature, as is the basic plan of our body and, it may be, the deep preverbal core of being. Therefore I would regard any therapy that tries to heal by putting us in touch with a transcendent dimension of experience, or some form of universal principle, as more a biotherapy than a psychotherapy. Similarly, behavioral therapy comes under this heading, since it radically downplays the role of subjective fantasy as well as social relations, and uses instead a conditioning model of behavior that is generalized from animal psychology. And of course these approaches have to be set alongside the more traditional biotherapies, which rely directly on the medical approach, with an emphasis on drugs, shock treatment, etc.; as well as the rather more radical biotherapy of Wilhelm Reich, who sought the key in the functioning of the total organism in relation to the cosmos.

Thus each dimension has to be subject to further analysis, and the really essential distinctions between therapies emerge only after close inspection. Within the social therapies there arises, for example, an important distinction between (to choose extremes) those who think that immediate family relations are crucial and those—the so-called radical therapists—who would go beyond the direct personal relation entirely and take society as the essential level of intervention.

Even more elaborate distinctions crop up within psychotherapeutic schools. Roughly put, we may distinguish between biopsychological and social-psychological factions. The former is more likely, for example, to emphasize instincts and drives—which are basically biological notions—as main determinants of the psyche; while the latter focuses more on the mental aspects of interpersonal relations—feelings of security, self-esteem, etc. The Kleinian group of Freudian psychoanalysts would be an example of the former type,[16] while the work of Harry Stack Sullivan epitomizes the latter.[17] Or, a psychotherapy may take the path of existentialism and stake its claim on the ground of a pure phenomenology, seeing drives or social explanations as only the mask over naked, unmediated experience. And so it goes.

Another axiom that all therapies of whatever type have to include is some position about the source of woe and the hopes for doing something about it. There has to be, in other words, some optimistic attitude toward the demonic, whether the latter is called "radical irrationality," "destructiveness," "evil" or the "id." No therapy can be grossly pessimistic and stay in business long, but there is room for a wide range of optimism.

Usually this has a distinctly cultural flair. The closest thing to a pessimistic therapy was European existentialism, with Freud's stoicism next in line. The Americanized versions of each became much more optimistic, which was in accord with cultural expectations. Americans have generally been unable to recognize the ample streak of diabolism in their national experience, and thus American culture has always played down any sense of radical evil and merely continued to do so when it embraced therapy. Indeed, the fact that therapy has become so ineradicable a part of American life can only be due to our undying faith in technique and meliorism. Consequently much therapy practiced in the United States is highly optimistic and by the same token has a rather attenuated perspective on evil—i.e., any radical sense of wrong. The individual is granted an ample repertoire of active purposiveness; illness is often regarded as held-back bad feeling, which can be expressed without much harm; or disturbances are seen to be rooted in the body, where they can be managed as though they were medical conditions; and/or the source of the problem is seen restricted to an immediate environment of other people, each of whom can presumably be reasoned with and educated in a positive direction no less than the patient himself. Thus the most prevalent model of therapy in America is one in which an individual either strives alone or in a limited association with others to better himself through technical means, hard work and optimism. We can recognize here yet another version of the basic bourgeois myth. It may be that therapy, at least of this kind, succeeds by putting the person in touch with an elemental part of his heritage. This of course still begs many questions of detail, and fails to provide any kind of guide for rational choice— all the more so as the heritage on which it is based is fraying quite a bit around the edges.

With this reminder we may turn to the therapies themselves.

The account that is to follow is necessarily a compromised one. Were it comprehensive enough to fully describe even the major schools extant in America, it would be unwieldy for the purpose of a general critique and tedious to boot. Therefore it must include only the salient points from a general standpoint, yet without wounding the essence of any particular school. Our work is further complicated by the fact that, while the approaches are organized into distinct schools, with official training programs and institutional trappings, they are also diffused outward as points of view with widespread, uneven and intermixed influence. Happily there are several compendia of therapies to which the reader may turn if further knowledge is sought.[18]

New schools may spring up between the writing of this manuscript and its publication; and even some schools we do take up here will doubtless feel slighted by what follows, while others may consider themselves misrepresented. I hope these reactions will be minimal. Should they occur, I have only human failings to plead in defense.

Part TWO

The Varieties Of Therapeutic Experience

Section A
Analytic
Therapies

INTRODUCTION

Our survey commences with the group of analytic therapies. No longer the sole form of psychotherapy, as they had virtually been for many years, the analytic schools still play an important role and are usually what comes first to mind when one thinks of therapy. As we shall see, there are many varieties of analytic approach. Despite their serious differences, however, all generally rely on verbal means to place a person in greater contact with split-off elements of his or her mental life. Hence the therapy "analyses," leaving the patient to resynthesize. We begin with the oldest and most influential variety, the Freudian.

3

Freudian Psychoanalysis And Psychoanalytic Psychotherapy

PSYCHOANALYSIS

There are actually two systems to be considered in Freudian psychoanalysis—psychoanalysis proper and psychotherapy based on psychoanalytic principles. The former is what has generated the theory, the point of view and the great influence, while the latter is what is more widely practiced. This is because of the particular nature of psychoanalysis proper, which pretty much disqualifies it as a general approach.

For one thing, classical Freudian treatment requires a sizeable investment in time and money—four to five days a week for three or more years—which few people can make. A more fundamental obstacle to popularity lies however in the nature of the changes that this intense procedure is designed to bring about.[1]

The intense, regular and prolonged contact, along with the traditional analytic use of the couch, so that the patient, or analysand, is both supine and faced away from the analyst, sets going a psychological current in which unconscious, psychologically less mature forms of thought press for realization and discharge. This current is mobilized and brought into play with more mature, verbal aspects of thought through the imperative of the analytic Basic Rule. That amazingly simple dictum which generates the data for the structure of Freudian thought, and which is found in no other variant of therapy, is the directive to *say whatever comes to mind.*

Or, rather, *try* to say whatever comes to mind, since the analysand soon finds out that the imperative cannot be satisfied, for the simple reason that a vast territory of his experience is actively repressed though intensely active. The analyst sits there behind him, having established the principle of fidelity to the Basic Rule and then, so to speak, moved out of ken. The analysand is now left in the silence of his inner discourse, with the rueful realization that he must verbalize publicly that which wants to be thought but has never been allowed clear access even to private awareness. Thus at the edge of "what comes to mind" is the muffled cry of the repressed, drawing conscious attention to it, yet forbidding expression.

The analysand can deal with this dilemma in countless ways, which we need not go into here, but all of which have the common property of keeping unconscious experience out of awareness. The analyst's business, meanwhile, is strictly defined: It is to labor patiently, nonjudgmently, tirelessly insistent at the edge of awareness, to dissolve those countless ways the analysand *resists* the emergence of his psychic interior. The analyst does this by simply commenting on, without either gratifying or suppressing, the clotted tangle of thought at the edge of awareness. In doing this, he uses three techniques:

1. *Confrontation*—a mirroring technique in which the analyst tells the analysand what the analysand is revealing at the moment. For example: "You are denying your anger to me."

2. *Interpretation*—also an empirical statement, but this time explaining the analysand's behavior in a way that is new to him and thus reflecting some of the unconscious. For example: "You are angry because I remind you of your colleague and rival, John; and you deny this because you have always sought to get ahead by being a nice guy."

3. *Reconstruction*—the providing of hypothetical historical statements of hitherto buried fragments of the analysand's infantile past. For example: "Your anger and defense against it must be a repetition of how you felt when you were little, John and I standing for your brother."

Through these three maneuvers, the analyst both draws the unconscious into the range of awareness and encourages its further elaboration. For in the unconscious lie those memory traces of living and impossible desire, which never give up their demand.

Analysis lures them out of hiding, then bids the patient wrestle, Jacob-like, with them—which is to say, with himself. Through the process of wrestling, the patient increasingly invests the dispassionate, out-of-ken analyst with hitherto split-off, unconscious feeling—which the analyst simply accepts and comments on to the extent that the analysand is blocked in his own self-revelation. Eventually this dialectic reproduces the analysand's original childhood neurotic conflict in terms of the analytic situation. And from this comes the so-called *transference neurosis,* which is the *sine qua non* of Freudian analysis, not because it has any curative power—far from it—but because its attainment signals maximum engagement with the unconscious world. When the transference neurosis is fully accepted and integrated—i.e., when its many wishes are worked through by repeated analysis—the analytic work may be said to be finished.

The healing power of psychoanalysis lies then in the hoary dictum "Know thyself." Again, not because such knowledge need be beneficial—it is often enough quite noxious—but because the self which has succeeded to such knowledge is a self transformed, tempered, made supple, truer, a self that is master—insofar as one can be—of its internal forms.

Why this should be a less then tumultuously popular therapy is not hard to see. For the attainment of knowledge of this sort requires tempering of the self—and tempering entails a fire, not merely the fire of repressed wishes, but the fire of such wishes played out in an actual, if highly unusual, relationship with another person—the fire, in short, of human enthrallment. Enthrallment, moreover, with someone who is pledged not to gratify the wishes set free—not on moral grounds, but because such gratification favors repression. Since it is not the current wish so much as the memory, or trace, to which it is attached that forms the substance of unconscious thought, a partial gratification by the analyst, rather than by the past object of desire, would bleed just enough tension off from the unconscious impulse to secure its further repression.

Freud observed early in the development of his method that the good is the enemy of the best. He recognized that people were only too willing to accept some intermediate boon rather than look fully at themselves. As soon as their distress waned they became eager to avoid further exploration; indeed, people would go to virtually any lengths, including the most extravagant kind of self-destruction, to avoid awareness of their unconscious minds.

This fact in itself would be enough to ensure the unpopularity of any therapy based primarily on making the unconscious conscious. But the full explanation is by no means so simple. The fact is, people suffer by and large from specific problems in living, problems in which neurotic tendencies intermesh with a host of environmental forces. And they have every reason to reach for a solution to those problems within the terms of everyday discourse, and only special or particular grounds for seeking that fuller self-knowledge which psychoanalysis offers, grounds that are ultimately a matter of personal values. Further, since Freudian treatment specifically rules out rapid resolution of distress as one of its goals—indeed, since it can safely promise to make the analysand temporarily feel worse in the interests of its long-range objectives—alternate forms of treatment may make sense in many instances.

PSYCHOANALYTIC PSYCHOTHERAPY

Psychoanalytic psychotherapy is just such a modification in psychoanalytic method to take into account some of these realities.[2] The basic variation in technique concerns the role of the analyst—now, therapist—who, instead of sitting out of view and encouraging the unfolding of the unconscious, confronts the patient directly and focuses attention on specific problems in living. The patient meets with the therapist less often than with the analyst, so that the therapy becomes less of an end in itself and is rather more preoccupied with the events of everyday life. Moreover, the patient is sitting up, engaging in a dialogue with the therapist, rather than reclining with his own phantoms. And within this dialogue, current problems in living—work, family life, human relations—receive the major share of attention.

To the extent that the understanding of what is going on is based on Freudian principles, and some of the goals of psychoanalytic treatment itself are retained, this treatment may be called psychoanalytic psychotherapy. However, we are in no-man's-land here, or, rather, any-man's-land, since the infinite variety of situations and the lack of any systematically defined structure of treatment admit of numberless varieties of approach, generally heavily influenced by the personality of the therapist, and varying widely in quality. Further, since the innovation of therapy points away from the unconscious, and places a greater emphasis on external reality and the relationship with the therapist, such therapies inevitably come to resemble the so-called Neo-Freudian analyses, to be discussed in the next chapter.

We may summarize the Freudian position with respect to the axioms of therapy.

First of all, it is unequivocally a psychological—as against a biological or social—therapy. That is, the decisive events are inner experience and fantasy rather than what one *is* with respect to the world of nature, or *does* in the world of other people.

Secondly, it is based on a view of the psyche according to which behavior is *critically* regulated by radically repressed unconscious thought, which in turn is based upon infantile, bodily desire— Freud's essential concept of infantile sexuality as the basis of what is repressed. Now there is an important point here, indicated above by the word "critically," about which there is rampant confusion. Freud never uttered the nonsense that behavior was simply determined by the unconscious. He held rather that it emerged out of the impact of unconscious wishes on given reality. Behavior is formed, so to speak, at the boundary between unconscious and conscious thought (which latter registers the objective world)—a radical boundary, given the nature of repression which sees to it that the unconscious never rejoins its conscious correlate. So Freud's thought can be called "dialectical," in that it is the interplay between forms of experience rather than any one of them that determines behavior. The unconscious is in need of special attention because under everyday circumstances it gets no attention. Psychoanalysis is therefore but a form of compensatory attention.

Given the dialectic between conscious and unconscious, the strict determinism that has been ascribed to Freudianism ("Everything we do is determined by unconscious ideas") melts away. True, thoughts are determined, but not in a linear way. Psychoanalysis teaches a person that his behavior is far more complex than had been imagined. And he will learn, as Freud pointed out, that he is both more moral and more wicked than he seems. But the upshot of his knowledge can only be to increase the number of choices before him. Thus the practical consequence of psychoanalytic determinism is to establish the necessity of freedom.

Thus, too, moral standards continue to apply to a fully analyzed person (whose unconscious is quite present, indeed who mainly differs from his preanalyzed state in the subtlety and range of his conscious judgment). By the same token, moral judgments are suspended in the analytic hours, increasing the power of unconscious impulses in a way that would be legitimately unacceptable in everyday life.

Thus the demonic is amply recognized in Freudian thought. Owing to the dispassionate role of the analyst and the prohibition on his activity within the session, the demonic, which, needless to add, is only the old word for Freud's unconscious, is let out of its cage—or, at any rate, the doors of the cage are opened.

Although psychoanalysis is rigorously psychological as a theory, it is, as noted above, a dialectical psychology, and the dialectic may be resolved into an interplay between biological and social factors as they impinge on the psyche. Biology is represented in the drives, sexual and aggressive, which have a somatic source, and in the infantile situation of dependency, which leads to our intractable narcissism; while society is mediated by the family, which is internalized in the Oedipal complex, but which itself looks outward on society. Thus according to Freud the innards of the self are formed from the outside—real people, real social roles—and folded inward, but the folding has to take into account the laws of the biological drives. Hence what is "inside" our psyche, and plays a role in all neurotic phenomena, never simply reflects the everyday laws of social relations or biology; it is different from each, yet derived from both.

The special status of psychic reality should not be confused, however, with any kind of transcendent or supernatural explanation. Freud was firmly in the camp of science, and his achievement was to discover, using scientific principles of explanation, uncharted forms of mental territory. If acquaintance with this territory has a certain therapeutic effect, it is by no means a simple or obvious one; indeed it can be profoundly unsettling, calling into question the very foundation of the social order. Thus Freud's remark upon arriving in America that, though his ideas might be embraced there, little did people know that "I am bringing them the plague."

PRACTICAL SYNOPSIS

The days when psychoanalysis was recommended for any and all emotional disturbances are gone, never to return. And the same has to be said for all the other treatment modalities. What follows is a schematic and personal guide by which the reader can begin to orient himself vis-à-vis psychoanalysis.

How Widely Is Psychoanalysis Employed?

This is difficult to answer, as there are few terms more loosely used. Classical, full-scale analysis remains widely practiced, probably to the same or even a slightly greater extent than a decade ago. However, as a percentage of the total amount of therapy given, it has diminished notably. The greatest share of the total is now perhaps taken by some form of Freudian or Neo-Freudian analytic psychotherapy. Most training programs, whether of psychiatrists, clinical psychologists or social workers, produce therapists versed in a modified Freudianism; and when one talks in general about visiting a therapist, psychiatrist, analyst or "shrink," this is what is usually meant. As should be clear by now, it is a statement that leaves a great deal unsaid.

What Sort Of Problem Is Full-Scale Psychoanalysis Most Fitted For?

There has been a major effort to widen the scope of psychoanalysis, but by and large the treatment remains most clearly suited for neurotic problems, in contrast to psychoses or other kinds of severe impairments, such as alcoholism, where the person's life is, practically speaking, out of control. It is also not designed for situations where an acute problem is closely associated with a sudden environmental change. It is most indicated when the neurotic problems—which may include sexual difficulties, disturbances in mood and general impairment of personal relations, as well as the more classical symptoms—are diffuse and relatively chronic, and when they are felt subjectively. In other words, the neurosis should be experienced mainly as something within oneself, not simply between oneself and the rest of the world.

What Kind Of Person Is Most Likely To Benefit From It?

Generally speaking, one with some verbal capacity, the ability to form relationships and to conduct something of a settled life. More essential perhaps is a genuine curiosity about oneself and the ability to tolerate frustration, especially the painful nongratification of transference feelings. If unambiguous and rapid answers are demanded of life, this is not a recommended form of treatment.

What Goals Does Psychoanalysis Set?

The goals are twofold. From the clinical standpoint, analysis aims to remove the underlying basis of neurotic behavior. This means that it is less concerned with symptomatic or conscious change than are other therapies. More generally, the goal is to promote a self-reflective process and to take it to the point where the individual can continue on his or her own. The ultimate aim is to master neurotic desires by bringing them into the dialectic of reflection.

How Realizable Are The Goals, And What Minimum Benefit May Be Reasonably Expected?

The former question is most difficult to answer, as the outcome cannot be measured except on individual, subjective grounds. Much hinges on whether one forms a good working relationship with the analyst. At a minimum, psychoanalysis and analytic therapy can provide a degree of clarification and the relief that comes from being seriously listened to.

Can There Be Any Undesirable Outcomes?

Yes. The two most common are, first, a neglect of needed changes in the external world in the interest of exploring the subjective realm; and, second, an interminable stalemate in which dependent transference needs are gratified by the treatment process itself. Often the sign of this is excessive intellectualization; language, which is the medium of analytic work, becomes corrupted by the defensive process and used for the gratification of hidden passive wishes toward the analyst.

Wouldn't It Be Better If The Analyst (Or Therapist) Were More Real?

People often raise this question, forgetting that what is "real" in human relations is never simply defined. In fact there are multiple human realities, only a limited number of which can be established in any relationship. Usually, "real" in the question above is taken to mean friendly, warm, self-revelatory, etc.; in short, a desirable feature of everyday social conduct.

This is indeed a valuable type of human reality and it can have beneficial therapeutic effects—in some instances. But there are other valuable types of "real" relatedness, such as a quiet receptivity, which will have different kinds of beneficial effects—in other instances, namely where a psychoanalytic goal is sought. The effect of the analytic receptivity is to tilt the relationship toward subjective reflection on the part of the analysand, this constituting the goal of analysis. At the same time an extremely deep relationship is growing—and being analyzed—between the quiet pair. Needless to add, the analyst's reserve should not be a cover for actually being unfeeling, withholding or cruel, and there are rigorous training standards set up to ensure that such does not occur—though it still rarely may. But even where the analyst is not in reality sadistically withholding, the analysand can be expected at times to feel that he is, such being the nature of the transference, which in turn is but the neurosis played outwardly. And this tension is exactly what the analysand has to bear and work out if the treatment is to be of benefit. In analytic psychotherapy, on the other hand, the therapist tends to remain more real in the first, social, sense, although his behavior needn't be as reciprocal, as, say, friendship would have it. This follows from the fact that his function is realistically not that of a friend.

What About Time And Money?

No one should enter analysis unless he is willing to make an open-ended commitment. The unfolding of the unconscious has to be given time, and a successful analysis can take years—usually three to five. Since one should go four or five times a week for the duration, analysis will obviously be an expensive proposition, even though most analysts charge no more per session than other therapists. In recognition of this problem, a number are willing to see people for lower fees per session in analysis. Further, in many large cities (psychoanalysis tends to be concentrated in large urban regions) there are training institutes with clinics where one can be analyzed (usually by an analyst in training) for whatever fee can be afforded.

How Sharp A Distinction Is There Between Analysis And Analytic Psychotherapy?

It is by no means absolute. In some instances a treatment that is conducted sitting up twice a week can approximate a full-scale analysis; while in others a five-times-a-week treatment on the couch turns out to be mainly psychotherapeutic.

Is There A Difference In Value Between The Two Types?

More prestige is usually given to the more intensive procedure, but this is not a legitimate indicator of real value. Legitimate, though different, goals can be served by both forms; and value depends on how well those goals can be met.

4

Neo-Freudian
Analysis

As noted earlier, "Neo-Freudian analysis" is not a happy name since it tends to distract from the specific identity of what the Neo-Freudians have accomplished and keeps them too much in the master's shadow. Nonetheless, it has stuck, and I shall use it. I fear, however, that the exposition to follow may further perpetuate the injustice since I propose to group together all of the "Neo-Freudian" schools—the best-known being Adler, Rank, Horney, Sullivan and Fromm. My reason for grouping these schools together stems in part from their very abundance. They represent the differentiated effort of powerful figures each of whom stamped his or her work with individuality, wrote extensively and coined many notable and variegated concepts. To summarize it all would lose the reader in enormous detail[1] and would miss the key point—that for all the variety, these schools make certain common axiomatic assumptions and represent an identifiable type of therapy from which individual practitioners and theoreticians may differ in lesser or greater degree, but which deserves nonetheless its characterization. It should be observed, though, that Adler came first, and in some measure originated the basic thrust of Neo-Freudian thought. However, although his influence has been enormous, it also has been indirect, owing to his inability to systematically formulate his ideas or to found a "school."[2]

One ground for the name "Neo-Freudian" is clear: These approaches all stemmed from dissatisfaction with Freud and the official Freudian establishment.[3] The reasons for the rebellion should not be considered a straightforward matter of objective theory or practice; nor can they be written off as peevishness owing to exclusion from the Freudian fold. The clash between personalities and ideas in a movement that was transforming twentieth-century thought is too rich and complex a story to be simplified in the interests of ideology. Justice cannot be done here to the wars that have beset psychoanalysis, in part because that would divert us from our aim, in part because an adequate—much less a definitive—history of the psychoanalytic movement has not yet been written. Perhaps the events in question are still too close for historical perspective. For example, many key archives pertaining to Freud are ensconced in the Library of Congress and elsewhere, not to be examined for years. Though this reflects consideration of the fact that many of those involved in the struggle are still alive, it also hints at a reality of the psychoanalytic movement that has been itself implicated in much of the factionalism—namely, the aura of arcane mystery and grandeur that has come to be associated with the figure of Freud (and in turn with other Founding Fathers), made especially intense by the very madness dredged up in the course of analytic work and training.

Whatever has become of it since in the way of rationalization, psychoanalysis in its earlier days was not a line of work to attract the timid or banal. On the contrary, many of its pioneers were storm-tossed individuals with more than a touch of megalomania. As for Freud himself, everything we know tells us he was a heroic genius but no angel, and that his character, no less than his work, was well suited to stir up extremes of loyalty and rebellion in those who followed.[4] Indeed, the personal and conceptual issues are bound to run together in a field such as psychoanalysis, where the instrument of knowledge is the self of the analyst.

In any event, the key distinctions from Freud that crystallized out of all the personal, intellectual and political turmoil to form the nucleus of Neo-Freudian thought may be summarized as follows:

1. Rejection of Freud's theory of instinctual drive, also known as the libido theory.

2. A complementary emphasis on "culture" or "interpersonal relations"—i.e., on the influence from the world of other people.

3. Coordinated with the above, an emphasis on those areas of mental life that reflect the interpersonal world: self-

assertiveness, feelings of self-evaluation, security and so forth.

4. Modifications in practice that reflected this theoretical shift.

There are, of course, many areas of continuity with Freudian thought, in particular the idea of intrapsychic conflict and an emphasis on development and childhood experience. Neuroses are still seen as unassimilated particles of infantile life, and analysis—i.e., resolving current experience into its neurotic elements through verbal exploration—is still the major means of intervention. Nonetheless, there is a shift of focus and of emphasis within the axiom, out of which emerges a human image distinctly different from Freud's version.

Neo-Freudian man is clearly a less driven creature, more directly in touch with his environment, less demonic and much more hopeful. Hence the theoretical necessity to downplay Freud's libido theory in favor of an equally powerful force that may be roughly described, in the terms of Karen Horney, as the "healthy striving toward self-realization." There is, in short, a "real self," constituted of one's "particular human potentialities," with "unique alive forces" and "that central inner force, common to all human beings and yet unique in each, which is the deep source of growth."[5]

With prime position given to the self system, it follows that the infantile sexual forces, for which Freud claimed so much, fade out of their privileged role in psychological causation. Harry Stack Sullivan (whose theory is the most systematic of the Neo-Freudians) eschews the concept of libido entirely, and discusses sexuality under the rubric of "lust dynamism." By this he means that lust is one of a number of "patterns of energy transformation" which develop in the growing organism, are extensively modifiable by experience and interact with each other. For example, what is most important about the lust dynamism is its collision with other dynamisms that center about the need for intimacy and security. And in these conflicts the sexual force, lust, is given no special status, as Freud accorded it when he held that infantile sexuality was radically repressed. Instead, direct social influence in general, and "interpersonal relations" in particular, are the main forces for Neo-Freudians. Therefore, security needs (Sullivan) the pride system (Horney) and their felt aspect, *self-esteem,* are the prime movers of the person, subordinating sex to their social interests.

Closer inspection reveals however that Neo-Freudians and Freudians are not really talking about the same things in the realm of sexuality. As Sullivan wrote, "lust, in my sense, is not some great diffuse striving, 'libido' or what not. By lust I mean simply the felt aspect of the genital drive."[6] The differences here are indeed striking, for we see that what Sullivan has in mind are mainly the *conscious* ("felt") aspects of sex. Moreover, these are referred to the genitals—naturally enough, since feelings arise so strongly there. But what Freud postulated was drastically different: an unconscious, radically split-off, *repressed* system of sexuality, not of libido as such (which is an abstract theoretical concept, not the concrete focus of Freud's interest), but of *fantasies* which involved every sexual facet of the body, and, so to speak, chronicled the individual's lost past as it was bodily played out.

So what critically differentiates Freud from the Neo-Freudians is not so much sex as the concepts of repression and unconscious thought. These are considerably weaker in the Neo-Freudian view, their strength having been ceded to the direct relationship with the interpersonal environment, We have here a view that lends itself to an optimistic interpretation of the human situation, since improved infantile experience—i.e., more love, acceptance, constancy and so forth from the parent—will have a more beneficial effect on a creature who accepts experience directly than on one who screens it through a mediating system of unconscious fantasy.

This is especially true in that Freud held that repressed fantasies were formed in a state of terror and impossible yearning, hence were turned away from the start from any beneficial ministrations of the external world. Freud saw the person as being somewhat like Dostoevski's "underground man," who has seen too much and walled it off, unable to forgive, because he has forgotten, yet who must live with the source of his rage and spite. Thus in Freud we have a quite radical conception of human evil, a concept foreign to Neo-Freudians. Sullivan, for example, is readily able to dispense with evil on the basis of his direct reading of experience: "My interest in understanding why there is so much deviltry in human living culminated in the observation that if the child had certain kinds of very early experience, this malevolent attitude toward his fellows seemed to be conspicuous. And when the child did not have these particular types of experience, then this malevolent attitude was not a major component." And so, malevolent development, which is Sullivan's terms for the evil, or demonic, in man, "is obviously a failure of the parents to discharge their social responsibility to produce a well-behaved, well-socialized person."[7]

I have dwelt upon these themes because the basic view of the human order which underlies them extends well beyond the theories of the Neo-Freudians to inform most of the therapeutic approaches now extant in America.[8] In fact, given this basic view, the nature of therapy itself follows logically: If what is wrong with people follows directly from bad experience, then therapy can be in its basics nothing but good experience as a corrective.

Neo-Freudian analysts recognize this in their technique, which bears down heavily then upon the actual relationship with the analyst as a reliving of outside and past relationships. By the same token, the relationship is less structured toward exploration of the unconscious mind. Missing from the technique is that strict emphasis on the Basic Rule—to say what comes to mind—which characterizes the Freudian approach. The Neo-Freudian analyst actively intervenes to a much greater extent. Although past development has its role in theory, therapeutic practice is inevitably drawn toward the here and now, and, as Adler emphasized, beyond, to the *goals,* the active strivings of the patient. As a consequence the regressive fantasy tie to the hidden, impersonal analyst is considerably attenuated; treatment tends to be briefer and more immediately productive of discernible change; and the techniques and strategies of living—what might be called our adaptation to the world and the feelings of self-evaluation connected with adaptation—become the centerpiece of what is altered.

As noted, the Neo-Freudian concept of analysis tends to converge with the psychotherapy which has developed out of classical Freudian technique. In general, however, the Neo-Freudian approach is more eclectic and less theoretically stringent than the Freudian, concerned as the latter is to develop the transference neurosis and explore the unconscious mind. Neo-Freudians, lacking this goal, can quite readily extend their method to include, for example, group treatment as well as individual treatment. This certainly amplifies the interpersonal dimension—in a way however that can best be discussed below when we consider the group approach as a whole.

In conclusion, Neo-Freudianism comprises an important school with wide influence throughout the world of therapy, social work and education. Its basic thrust is to deemphasize the repressed and to focus on interpersonal factors. Thus it remains a psychotherapy, yet one weighted in a straightforward, positive way (as against the dialectic of Freud) with the psychosocial dimension.

PRACTICAL SYNOPSIS

What Are The Significant Differences Between Neo-Freudian Schools?

Neo-Freudian treatment varies widely. It includes people (often within the Sullivanian camp) whose work is nearly indistinguishable from classical Freudian psychoanalysis—and for whom the practical advice at the end of the previous chapter holds. And at the opposite pole it also includes those widely engaged in all kinds of theoretical variations and florid experimentation, including quasi-communal living arrangements between therapist and patients. Furthermore, all of the schools are undergoing a fluctuating development. Thus it would be difficult for anyone to predict in advance just what one might encounter in Neo-Freudian analysis. Some particular knowledge of how one's local practitioners see things is advisable.

As an outline, however, it can be said that the followers of *Adler,* being uninterested in working analytically with the unconscious life, practice an active, focused, goal-setting kind of therapy; that *Rank* has more or less faded out as a distinguishable approach to therapy; that *Fromm,* though influential for his social point of view, is not identified with any particular variant of therapy;[9] that followers of *Horney* have split into several factions, including one that is responsive to the mysticotranscendent tradition (see Chapter 11); and that the *Sullivanian* groups are the most institutionally organized and currently influential amongst the Neo-Freudians, especially in the treatment of psychosis. Needless to add, these are not meant as definite or final judgments. However, as a rough guide it may be anticipated that the analytic schools range along the following spectrum: Freud–Sullivan–Horney–Adler; the former end more concerned with analyzing split-off fragments of early experience, and the latter more interested in the holistic current functioning of the total person.

Does This Shift Mean That Different Kinds Of Problems Are Better Treated By Different Schools?

This is very difficult to judge, since at best each school has a rather hazily outlined area of application. The issue may turn less on the kind of presenting problem than on the ability of the patient to put up with the regression and frustration of the classical Freudian setup. The more intolerant a person is of this, whatever his or her problem, the more likely he is to be helped by approaches that emphasize current interactions of the whole personality rather than analysis of what is deeply buried.

What Are The Main Practical Differences Reflected In This Shift?

With all due allowances for the tremendous variations that exist, these can be summarized as: less use of the couch; fewer sessions per week; less emphasis on free association, with more active, focused intervention on the part of the analyst; greater attention paid to unrealistic attitudes, which in turn diminishes the range of free-floating fantasy (which is, by its very nature, unrealistic); and greater attention to self-assertion, self-regard and the everyday coping with felt needs.

Are These Not Shortcuts To The Same Goal?

I think this is an unhappy way to state the problem, one that too readily lends itself to the hurling of brickbats—for it establishes the original Freudian analysis as a waste of time, money and effort, and/or sets up the Neo-Freudian alternatives as trivial. It is better to consider these variations as embodying different goals, which entail different practices. Since all analytic schools regard neuroses as complex, multilayered structures, the question before each individual is whether they want to pursue their neurosis into the deep unconscious or along the path of social relations. Each of the schools offers its own direction, and each direction has an area within which it makes sense and will satisfy some value positions. Although my personal opinion is that the Freudian approach offers the more definitive encounter, there is no positive proof that this is so, nor, considering the nature of the problem, can such a proof be developed.

But Doesn't Each School Claim To Offer Insight And To Work With Transference?

Yes, but the insight offered is into that which the therapeutic technique succeeds in bringing into focus. Similarly, the transference attitudes explored and/or used will vary with the kind of relationship established. At one end—the classical Freudian—the patient will be projecting a host of archaic images stirred up by the perceptually absent analyst; at the other end—the Adlerian—the patient will be engaged in a relatively more mature, yet still childlike, relation with an active, highly present analyst. Just as we have a multiplicity of relationships with each figure of the past, so can there be many transferences.

Is Freudian Analytic Psychotherapy The Same, Then, As Some Types Of Neo-Freudian Analysis?

To some extent, simply because it is briefer and more directed than classical Freudian analysis. However, differences in emphasis would still emerge because of the Freudian interest in repressed infantile sexuality and the Neo-Freudian concern with security and the needs of the self.

It has perhaps been overstated by now, but a good practitioner of any school begins with the actual person before him, not with a theory. The theory may help him select various things for emphasis, but these always have to be communicated in recognizable terms to the patient if they are to have any bearing on his life.

What Are The Main Potential Advantages And Disadvantages Of Neo-Freudian Treatment?

Its main advantage is that it has been more open to innovation and more accessible to social intervention, thus it allows for a more flexible repertoire of therapeutic strategies and is more readily attuned to problems where the external situation plays a heavy role.

A disadvantage is that it is more likely than the Freudian treatment to settle for a shallower self-understanding in instances where a person might otherwise go on to a deeper reflectivity. There is also the question whether making social influence the main force leads to the imposition of conformity. Possibly so, because of the greater weight placed on confrontation with unrealistic attitudes. Such judgments always involve the benchmark of what is "realistic," and this is likely to touch upon social mores. We shall have more to say of this below as it affects other therapies.

5

Jung And
Analytical Psychology

We enter here a dramatically different territory, though one which manifestly remains in touch with other varieties of psychoanalysis. Although Jungian analysis in its strict form comprises only a minuscule fraction of the therapeutic effort now underway, the work of Jung himself has a scope, range and general influence second only to that of Freud among all the individuals who have entered the therapeutic movement. Certain of his fundamental assumptions have had an influence that extends well beyond the bounds of his own terminology and school (which, lest it be overlooked, remains a significant effort in England and the European continent, as well as keeping its toehold in several American cities, notably San Francisco). It is these ideas that I shall briefly present rather than the prodigious exploration into mythology and symbolism which gives Jung's thought its fascination.[1]

Although the vast corpus of Jung's work resists summarization, there is one basic organizing assumption that runs through it. This is the concept that the mind consists of far more than can be given by experience; and that this additional part, which goes under several names but is best called the "collective unconscious," is the most important of all the mental systems and has causal priority. Jung thus moves in an opposite direction from Adler and the Neo-Freudians, who tended to collapse the unconscious into consciousness. But he moves well beyond Freud's version of the unconscious, too. Indeed, it is hard to conceive of two major thinkers who shared so much and yet diverged so widely in basic aims as Freud and Jung. Thus it would be a disservice to both of them to call Jung's work a variant of psychoanalysis instead of by his own term, "analytic psychology." The difference is not merely semantic. To Jung, the unconscious only became interesting beyond the point where Freud's method left off.

Freud's work remained rooted in empirical reality. His technique of free association and the intense neutrality of the analytic setting yielded the repressed contents of the unconscious—the chronicle of the actual life of the patient as it had become enmeshed in conflict between natural wish and social control. Thus for Freud our unconscious was created out of experience; then, in its repressed state, affected further experience. True, his thought strayed from this perspective at certain points,[2] but on the whole it remained true to this principle.

For Jung, however, there is a deeper, *transpersonal* unconscious, something that reflects the history of the human species and indeed the cosmic order, and which arises prior to an individual's experience. Within this collective unconscious are the so-called *archetypes,* which may be roughly defined as nuclear mythic themes (the Hero, the Great Mother, etc.). The manifestations of the archetypes occur in a profusion of *symbols* that appear in dreams, disturbed states of mind, certain cultural products, or through the process of what Jung terms "active imagination."

Jung claimed to have objective evidence of the archetypes in the form of spontaneous production of symbolism that could not have been known to the subject by ordinary means (e.g., an ignorant schizophrenic has a vision of the sun as a wheel, which matches a similar vision reported in an ancient and forgotten text). And his deep rejection of the primacy of ordinary experience and causality led Jung to seek manifestations of the collective unconscious in realms that are by and large today regarded as occult and mystical —alchemy, oriental religions, flying saucers and so forth. Given the omnipresence of so powerful and transpersonal a force, Jung was able to use it as a principle of explanation, something that caused other things to happen, something, indeed, that contained the germ of the future.

Thus for Jung the Freudian "personal unconscious" and its complexes were "banal and uninteresting." "All those personal things like incestuous tendencies and other childish tunes are mere surface; what the unconscious really contains are the great collective events of the time. In the collective unconscious of the individual, history prepares itself."[3]

With this *primum mobile* it is quite logical then that Jungians should be little interested in infantile development or in the intra-psychic conflict between wishes and counterforces that Freud (and, allowing for the difference in the nature of the forces, the Neo-Freudians) so attended to. Rather was the problem of neurosis or health more one of integration between different parts of the person and that which is transpersonal, transcendent. The goal of therapy was to mend those splits and lead a person into philosophic ripeness. Thus Jung focused, in a way that no other school has been able to do, on problems of the middle and later years of life. The prime objective was to allow a person to experience the split-off parts of himself, especially the archetypal emissaries of the collective unconscious and certain other psychological forma-tions which were, so to speak, contiguous with it, such as the *anima,* or split-off female quality in the male (*animus* for the woman), and the *shadow,* a negated or inferior self-image. The goal of the Jungian voyage may thus be defined as the rapprochement of the self with that which is ineffable, that which is beyond the person yet expressive *through* him. Jung called this goal *individuation*— roughly translated into everyday terms, the attainment of wisdom.

I do not mean to imply that Jung was without resource for deal-ing with the more readily observable aspects of life. Far from it. As is well known, his work included a vast amount of effort applied to concrete problems of personality (especially to char-acter typology). As these are less critical for purposes of therapy, they will not be discussed here. But even if they were, the reader would be able to observe a constant effort on Jung's part to bring these elements into line with what he regarded as crucial, the deep unconscious.

Jungian analysis itself developed into a method designed to bring about rapprochement with the deep unconscious. Within its scheme, prime place was given to dream analysis. For Jung, Freud's characterization of the dream as a distorted representation of a hidden wish bordered on anathema. The dream, remember, was the most notable way the archetypes had of making themselves known. Therefore, to explicate it by following the patient's spon-taneous associations to its details was to muddy the water. No, the dream itself, the manifest dream, was sacrosanct. It should be regarded as one regards a hieroglyph, as needing translation, not interpretation.

Thus Jung deliberately prohibited free association, which he called "Freud's reductive method." Instead he used the technique of *amplification*, which amounted to expanding the dream content in dramatic terms within the dreamer's life (as by asking the patient to imagine his way further into the dream scenario), and then situating the forms of the dream within the world tradition of myth and symbol. In this way the dream itself was revealed to be a higher form of cognition, guiding the patient to a superordinate knowledge rather than leading to what he had to hide.

Jung regarded this technique as the way to bring a person into greater and greater contact with the deep unconscious; and this contact itself, without any external practice or mediation with the personal unconscious, was considered the main healing principle. Thus, Jung's approach to dreams sometimes resembled the work of the biblical Joseph or Daniel rather than the modern analytic dissector—nor was this an image he would have shunned, as he never tired of pointing out the high value, indeed the superiority, of the ancient ways of thought.

In light of the above, it should not be surprising that Jungian treatment takes a drastically different course than Freudian. Paradoxically, in many respects it is closer to the Neo-Freudian, due to the fact that both forms really downplay Freud's unconscious— the Neo-Freudians by minimizing the whole idea, Jung by maximizing an alternate form of unconscious. It would obviously be disadvantageous, therefore, for a patient in Jungian analysis to develop a transference neurosis: For one thing, he might not dream, out of spite; for another, his dreams would be "contaminated" by interference from the personal unconscious; and finally, he would not be in a position to engage in the active exploration of symbolism which is the heart of Jungian treatment.

Thus in much of its aspect Jungian treatment resembles what can be called "supportive psychotherapy": The patient and analyst sit face-to-face, practical advice is dispensed, a sort of folk wisdom (of which the paradoxical Dr. Jung had much) reigns, and neurotic behavior is handled on a matter-of-fact, conscious level. Further, a warm and positive relation with the analyst is maintained through active intervention on the latter's part. The general attitude conveyed is that one's neurosis is part of a much larger whole. By attaining philosophic calm and detachment, the patient prepares the way for that encounter with the transcendent toward which the Jungian aims.

Detachment from neurotic turmoil can itself have obvious therapeutic advantage. Whether this factor or the professed one of contact with the deep unconscious is the agent of whatever benefit emerges from Jungian treatment is an interesting question. However, whatever the actual active principle, it is the *idea* of the transcendent force of the impersonal collective unconscious that constitutes the germ and soul of Jung's influence.

For what Jung did was to keep the door open to the ineffable and mysterious. It is open in Freud, too, but on condition that the passerby submit the mystery to a new form of dialectic within which it is translated into the language of the lost infantile body. Jung, however, keeps the mystery intact. While remaining an advocate of the scientific approach, he refuses to reduce the spirit into the scientific canon. The spirit still reigns supreme in Jung. It lets us see a little of its power; and what we see can be encompassed by science. But the unseen remains infinitely greater than our paltry effort at comprehension. Jung thus keeps the idea of faith alive within the purlieus of therapy.[4] Indeed, he does more than rescue it from Freud's baleful eye; he grants it intellectual respectability.

Jung, therefore, provides the most systematic and serious grounding for the *transcendent* approach to therapy. With the prestige of science more or less in shambles in the eyes of many, especially youth, Jungian thought has come to exert an influence, albeit indirect, far greater than the actual practice of his therapy.

In summary, C. G. Jung's analytic psychology affords a psychotherapy radically tilted toward the transcendent, which is to say nature. "The unconscious is nature, and nature never lies," said Jung, and by that he meant that a princple in the world existed beyond individual experience or material history, and determined both. Although Jung's work is heavily influenced by biological thinking, he differs greatly, of course, from the more biological approach to nature as this approach is manifested in therapy (such as drug approaches, behavior therapy, bioenergetic therapy), but he shares with it a major indifference to what society has to say about behavior. In other words, he generally takes social factors for granted in their given state.

It should be added that for all its spiritual bent, Jung's thought is rather worldly and tolerant. He refused to pigeonhole mental illness or to regard it pejoratively; indeed, he was much given to proclaiming neurosis to be an attempt at self-cure, and madness to be the striving for superior insight. This was because of the fact that though he retained a keen sense of the demonic, he referred it to a much wider stage than the individual. Hence there was no need to segregate the mad from the sane in an effort to cleanse the latter; all of us, mad and sane alike, being equal in the impersonal eyes of Jung's godhead, the collective unconscious.

PRACTICAL SYNOPSIS

Does Analytical Psychology Deal With Different Kinds Of Problems Than The Other Analytic Schools?

This is a difficult question, to be sure, and made more so by the widespread confusion of tongues between all schools. Jungians claim that their method works well with every type of emotional disturbance, but that it is especially designed for the normal individual in middle life or beyond who seeks wisdom and enlightenment. In other words, Jungians make an explicit leap into positive therapy, therapy designed to add something along with relieving neurotic distress. Whether this therapy works at all depends to a greater degree on the patient's willingness to believe its terms than is the case with other forms of treatment, which by and large stay with the empirical data of life. If this belief is there, then a wide range of emotional problems—including psychosis—would be accessible. Jungians also claim to be specially qualified to deal with problems of creativity. It is hard to see how this claim could be substantiated, but many patients of Jungians through the years have been artists.

What Are The Chief Practical Consequences Of Jung's Change In Direction?

The couch is generally not used, and sessions usually are only once or twice a week for a year or more. Two phases of treatment exist (and overlap): One is a supportive psychotherapy, which is down-to-earth and not very far-reaching—in contrast to the second, which is the exploration of the archetypal world through dreams, etc. In both cases a direct, personally involved attitude by the therapist is cultivated. Linked with this, transference is regarded as an interference and downplayed.

What Are The Potential Advantages And
Disadvantages Of This Approach?

The gains are self-evident so long as one accepts Jung's view of a transcendent mind. Even without this belief, the treatment can provide an opportunity for gaining a broad, synthesizing perspective on one's life. For many people, this, plus the positive relationship with the analyst, will be of definite help.

On the other side, it can be argued that a positive indifference to the actual details of life is a dangerous way to approach emotional conflicts. Further, those to whom Jung's view of the universe does not represent truth would have to regard it as mystifying, since it replaces mundane and material explanations with transcendent ones. Of greater significance is the potential that such an outlook holds for being identified with politically backward trends. Reactionaries have always found those who seek causes in the stars useful for their ends.

6

The Existential Approach

I use the term "approach" in introducing a discussion of this form of analysis because the trends in question defy (deliberately) systematization into any coherent school. It would perhaps be more accurate to refer to it as the existential "dimension" in therapy. If this is borne in mind we shall be in a position to understand how this approach significantly enters into a wide range of therapeutic arrangements without being in itself a therapy.

Existential analysis is more of an institution in Central Europe, where people take philosophy seriously and where a substantial tradition of practice and exegesis has grown up. Attempts to graft this tradition onto the American scene seemed about to flourish some fifteen years ago with the publication of the anthology *Existence,* edited by Rollo May;[1] but—for reasons that are of some interest—the organism rejected the transplant. Rejected it, that is, in the form in which it was offered; choosing instead to transform existentialism into terms with which American culture is more congenial and mix it with native strains of therapy. So arose the hybrid *humanist psychology* movement of the Sixties, which shall concern us further in other sections. This existential attitude remains, however, a notable trend within therapy and so deserves brief description.

It would be going too far afield to explore the European roots in any depth, especially in light of the fact that they themselves are in much of a tangle. Many of the main figures of modern Western thought stalk about in the history of existential analysis, and cross paths with one another, often against the wishes of their exegetes. Thus we have the antirational philosophies of Kierkegaard and Nietzsche running together with that of Edmund Husserl, the founder of the new metascience, phenomenology; or the cloud-capped right-wing thought of Martin Heidegger with that of the passionate atheistic rebel Sartre and the Neo-Lutheran Tillich; and we have distinguished practitioners Minkowski, Boss, Straus and, above all, Binswanger going their various ways under these sundry banners while placing themselves in varying degrees of opposition or accordance with Freud or Jung. Add to this pastiche the deliberate flaunting of rules of evidence or explanation and we can see why the existential approach resists summarization—and why, perhaps, it has been doomed to remain a trend only.

And yet a powerful one. For what existential analysis does is tap directly into the chaos of modern experience, the runaway world, godless, without any inherent moral authority or belief system, a world that so many take for granted. Here is an approach that meets the fact of chaos squarely and says, in effect, that something good, a new order perhaps, can be built from the encounter. The existential appoach begins then not with conflict or disease but with the general spirit of alienation. Sharing with Jung an assault upon our alienating scientific tradition, but eschewing Jung's flight into an alternate, mystical order of the universe, existential analysis stays on the ground of disconsolateness, working from within despair, not beyond it.

Staying within the level of experienced despair leads to a concept of anxiety radically different from the one Freud advanced—albeit one which remains central to its own system. Freud held that the anxiety which entered into neurosis was a signal of impending danger—i.e., danger which would arise were an unconscious wish to be realized. But existential anxiety is not anticipatory; it involves neither past nor future, but is the immediate awareness of incompleteness, meaninglessness, contingency—of "being-in-the-world." And it is this threat, say the existentialists, from which we flee in neurotic disorder—which is manifest as a false order, rigidity, including the false order of scientism.

In more concrete terms this means an emphasis upon the given, spontaneous moment of experience and a reluctance to pin down this moment into any explanatory scheme. The most subtle explanation is both a plot and a fixed order, something to tie down the spontaneous and human heart of experience. Opening this heart, facing it, confronting it, even though it appears an abyss—this is the nucleus of the existential approach.

Still more concretely, the existential approach has to be carried out in the here and now of the therapeutic relationship. Once again then, though from different grounds, we have a therapeutic approach criticizing the reserve and impersonality of the Freudian relationship, with its emphasis on the Basic Rule of free association, in favor of an approach in which there is an active dialogue between therapist and patient. The Neo-Freudians justify the dialogue on the basis that it brings the patient and therapist closer to the interpersonal ground from which both neurosis and health spring; while Jungians claim that it facilitates a working rapport necessary for the arduous voyage through the sea of the unconscious. The existentialist proclaims it as the fundamental structure of being-in-the-world. As Binswanger put it, the existential analyst

> will always stand on the same level with his patients, namely on the level of their common reality [*Dasein*]. Consequently he will not turn the patient into an object in contrast to himself as a subject but will regard him as a partner in human reality [*Dasein*]. [He will regard the relationship] as a *meeting* on what Martin Buber has called the 'abyss of human reality' . . . and will denote it not only as self but also as 'Being with' in personal intercourse and as 'Being together' or love. And in an existential sense the condition which Freud has taught us to call *transference* is also a mode of the meeting [italics Binswanger's].[2]

The mode of dialogue here is more radical than that of the Neo-Freudian, where the relationship is *inter*personal and consequently open to explanation. A Neo-Freudian still keeps within Freud's developmental and dynamic framework in which present events can be referred to past events, and manifest factors (the dream contact) to latent ones (the hidden wish). In other words, he believes in the power of explanation. The Neo-Freudian analyst mainly differs from the Freudian in how he selects the key events and forces. The existentialist refuses from the start, however, to take that step away from the given phenomenon, which would be tantamount to avoiding the anxiety of being-in-the-world. He is guided here by Husserl's cardinal phenomenological method of "bracketing," by which the investigator, through strict intention of his subjectivity, strips the object of all secondary, acquired and referred qualities; strips it down, insofar as humanly possible, to the "thing-in-itself." Thus he refuses to *ex*-plain, which is to take away from the moment; he only indicates, and shares.

Practically speaking, this allows the existential therapist to be much more open in his response to the patient. Where the Freudian listens, and draws out of the patient his immersed thoughts, the existentialist works to push the patient toward immediacy and away from false generalization or categories. Associated with this is a kind of therapeutic nihilism. Freud had counseled against the furor to cure; yet he claimed to have developed a technique that would get to the heart of neurotic darkness and illuminate it, hence bring help to the afflicted ego. But if the anxiety arises, not from the danger of realizing repressed and invisible wishes, but simply from being unable to face what is there already, then there may be no help at all except to face the horror directly. The extreme example is Binswanger's well-known case of Ellen West,[3] in which it is claimed that the patient had been helped existentially even though the choice she was able to make—by virtue of finding her being-in-the-world—was suicide. While it should not be felt that Binswanger would want to do no more for a patient, an indifference to commonly held views of health is intrinsic to the existential approach.

As noted, this approach persists mainly as a dimension of other therapeutic efforts[4]—in part, no doubt, because few can stand to practice therapy without some explanatory guidelines.[5] Indeed, an absolute existential attitude is pretty much inconceivable. Rollo May, for example, who was instrumental in introducing the ideas to America, continues to touch upon this tradition, but he has also moved from it toward an idiosyncratic blend of existentialism, psychoanalysis and a native American brand of pragmatism. As with Jung, the existentialists have found a home with many current therapists unhappy with the alienating scientific tradition.[6] Existentialism's concern for shared experience, what we may call *intersubjectivity,* brings it into line with many of the transcendent approaches, particularly those which draw on the Oriental tradition. Also, as noted above, we may see its influence in the humanist psychology movement, and in the Gestalt approach, with its premium on immediacy.

One of the most influential figures of the last decade, R. D. Laing, may also be considered an existential analyst—although, like all good existentialists, he resists classification. Laing has proven true to existentialism by refusing to define a system or to allow himself to get pinned down to any particular concept. However, a series of themes that have appeared in his works are in line with basic existential ideas, in particular those of Sartre.

Although Laing has been much more sluggish than Sartre in trying to relate the radical implications of his thought to a concrete political reality, nonetheless the basic existential terms are there. "No one can begin to think, feel or act now except from the starting point of his or her own alienation." So begins *The Politics of Experience*,[7] Laing's most celebrated book. And he goes on to claim that "Psychotherapy must remain *an obstinate attempt of two people to recover the wholeness of being human through the relationship between them*" (italics Laing's). Further, "Existence is a flame which constantly melts and recasts our theories. Existential thinking offers no security, no home for the homeless. It addresses no one except you and me."

Laing, however, goes decisively beyond earlier existential analysts to actively implicate the environment—especially the family —as the alienating agent. Consequently, Laing is not content to merely tolerate madness as a valid form of experience; it becomes rather an act of heroism, a positive virtue, the negation of negative experience in alienated culture. The real madness is of those in power, from parent to president; the lunatic, socially defined, is potentially freed by his exclusion from society's power and bureaucracy; like Lear's Fool, like the maddened king himself, his craziness becomes the way out to a higher light.

This is an ancient notion, which extends well back before the psychiatric tradition and was picked up by psychiatrists before Laing. But only Laing championed it with charisma at a moment —the mid-Sixties—when the legitimation of authority was crumbling. The resulting furor polarized the world of psychiatry into a medical establishment that stood for repression and segregation of the deviant-insane and an antipsychiatry faction standing for rebellious madness.[8]

As is history now, Laing grounded his antipsychiatric critique in practice, especially in the celebrated Kingsley Hall, in London. Here the existential approach was pursued to conclusion: a community of helped and helper, without professional trappings, a place where one could "go down," go through the voyage of madness and emerge at the other side, not back in society's alienation, but into a new freedom.

Kingsley Hall is no more, and its makings need not concern us further here.[9] It is hard to see much of the new freedom it promised. However, the Laingian experiment was an important trend. In the history of therapy, the existential approach has been a pathway of development leading from Freud's original breakthrough to forms rather markedly different from psychoanalysis, through its emphasis on lived, shared experience as the critical agent. It is not the only path of development, as we shall see in subsequent sections, but it deserves emphasis as a major root of contemporary practice.

To sum up, the existential approach is perhaps the most radically psychological of all the therapeutic strategies. In its essential form it posits pure consciousness as the object of therapeutic attention. That is to say, consciousness is held to be unmediated: The source of psychic content is referred neither to an unconscious, nor to bodily events, transcendent influence or social factors. Since, for whatever reason, contemporary experience is felt as blunted, the existential approach, which so to speak hurls us into our being and removes explanatory support ("It's only your nerves"), cannot be but a radical method if seriously applied. By removing explanatory props, the existentialist puts us face-to-face with the pain of inner suffering—that is to say, with the demonic; moreover he bids us take full responsibility for it, such being the condition of freedom.

As noted, the purity of this attitude is rarely sustained. Many take refuge in religious consolation; some, like Laing, keep paths open to the world of society and the family;[10] while others—we shall touch on them soon—refer experience to the body. Some even refer experience back to deeper mental layers—the unconscious of Freud or Jung—but to this extent, of course, they are either psychoanalysts or analytical psychologists. It might be noted in passing that for Freud, both social and biological forces were mediated through the unconscious layers of the mind. Consciousness, pure experience, could be both accepted as the empirical base of psychological knowledge and analyzed as to its unconscious aspects, which would implicate biology and society together.

Thus the pure existential approach, in eschewing explanation, forfeits also a grasp of Freud's breakthrough into the unconscious. And this feature continues on in the application of existentialism to other varieties of therapeutic experience.

PRACTICAL SYNOPSIS

For What Sorts Of Problem Is The Existential Approach Most Suited?

As elaborated above, the existential attitude mainly defines a line of approach to emotional disorder, and is not in itself a complete therapy. Thus its usefulness can be fully ascertained only in light of the complete pattern of therapy with which it is articulated— and this will of course vary considerably. Nonetheless, the approach itself may be a useful way of angling in on neurotic distress wherever the neurosis is combined with a more or less acute sense of estrangement from the world. Generally speaking, such a condition is felt by people of rather heightened self-awareness who have lost faith in traditional reassurances, whether these be of reason or of faith.

In my own opinion, the existential attitude itself is not an adequate recourse against the feeling of estrangement, since its essentially individualistic structure only further cuts a person off from the dimension of real social causes and remedies that apply to alienation in all its forms. Those who do not share this view, however, may find that an existential attitude corresponds to their view of the world.

Is The Existential Approach Helpful In Dealing With Psychotic Feelings Of Estrangement?

There has been considerable confusion about this issue, to some extent perpetrated by Laing. Most of Laing's research was about the Dark Continent of psychopathology, schizophrenia; and much of it—including the part that led to therapeutics—was about the family dynamics and the family therapy (see Chapter 13) of schizophrenia.[11] In this area the existential concern, though there, was marginal. Laing also called attention to the pernicious labeling and social objectification of the psychotic. Although this was not the first time anyone had done that, Laing's critique was a valuable one, pursued with skill and vigor—but it, too, was only marginally existential.

The existential attitude itself applies not so much to actual neurotic or psychotic processes as to the general and increasing spirit of alienation that afflicts contemporary society. But this spirit, which in fact exists on a spectrum with neurosis or psychosis in great numbers of people, can be made to seemingly merge with these disorders, and be confused with them. Laingians have tended to consider neurosis or psychosis as wholly a matter of social alienation—instead of a *self*-alienation which may begin in a setting of social alienation but thereafter takes on a course of its own for which the individual is quite responsible, albeit not in a moralistic sense.

Laing thus did a major disservice to the treatment of schizophrenia, which became almost as much of a caricature of a complex reality in his system as it had been in the rigid medical orthodoxy he attacked. To do justice to schizophrenia, the problem has to be approached as a real disorder within the individual—one that can have a biological basis—as well as between the individual and the world. This is more so the case in that Laingian ideas are virtually inapplicable to the great majority of actual psychotics, whose desperate social and personal position would never permit even the beginning of existential treatment.

Is Existential Treatment Simply A Waste Of Time Then, Without Any Actual Base Of Application?

As an unadulterated, total treatment, this would probably be the case, since its extreme subjectivism rules out any realistic attitude. However, as an ancilla to other methods it may, as stated above, have value where consciousness is dominated by feelings of alienation, whatever the full picture of emotional trouble. And there can be no doubt that this is a growing concern. Neurosis is always a function of historical development. It takes on a different face in our time from that of Freud's—or Sullivan's, Jung's and so forth. Consequently the face of therapy becomes different, too.

What Kinds Of Practical Modifications Are Implied And By What Methods?

These would have to vary greatly, and are virtually impossible to characterize in view of the lack of definition provided by existential writers. Actually, "practical" modification is against the spirit of existentialism, which disdains technique. What is sought is mainly intense awareness and feeling, and the technique chosen should be one that does not intrude too much on this. Thus classical Freudian technique has been appropriated by some existential workers—e.g., Medard Boss, and Laing himself—while others will use techniques of greater activity, including having the analyst share with the patient his own emotional state. The important point is to select themes of the immediate moment and to downplay explanations in terms of the past.

What Are The Advantages And Disadvantages Of This Innovation?

The advantage is that the intensification of awareness leads the individual to question all ready-made explanations, and makes possible a new leap. Existentialism throws people back on their creativity. And by minimizing explanation, it minimizes the chance for rationalization (e.g., "I'm sick because my parents made me so"), and thus promotes acceptance of responsibility for one's life.

The disadvantage would seem to follow from the other side of this advantage: By cultivating the moment and bracketing out interpretative explanations, the individual is left wallowing in his or her immediate subjectivity. With explanation comes an appreciation of the past, and hence a sense of history and of continuity with the human community in its *present* form, since current relationships cannot really be grasped except as continuations of old ones.

If untempered, then, the existential approach can lead to yet another version of the shortsightedness from which it bids to free us, since a world seen as without history is a world of no depth or form.

Section B
The Postanalytic Therapies—
The Human Potential Movement

INTRODUCTION

We come now upon a distinctly American and contemporary trend in therapy—the postanalytic, or humanistic, therapies. An overview is in order, since each of these therapies has a distinct approach, yet all flow together, as a glance at an Esalen catalogue will convince you. In this group may be found types of therapy as diverse as Rogerian psychotherapy and bioenergetics, encounter groups and mystical therapy. With roots everywhere—in Neo-Freudian and Jungian analysis, as well as existentialism and revival meetings—the product is yet a distinct type. The human-potential movement, or humanist psychology, is not a system but an overarching mood that tends to affect all of these variegated therapies—even if some of the approaches have outgrowths that do not consider themselves part of the movement itself.

The lack of system is no happenstance but an essential ingredient of the humanist approach. Even though a certain inevitable institutionalization has set in, the manifest intent of the human-potential movement has been to break down boundaries, to keep moving, to be, above all, open.

The human-potential idea consists of an amalgamation of the existential attitude—direct experience as the touchstone—with that most basic of American ideologies, the perfectibility of man. The latter notion is what we mean by the *humanistic* orientation—a hallowed, hard-to-define tradition basic to the notion of progress in the Western world, and the fundamental principle of which is that "man is the measure of all things." The word "man" here denotes a distinct entity, a whole greater than the sum of the parts into which he may be analyzed. It is this whole man who is celebrated by the humanists, whether they approach him from the psychoanalytic side (Eric Fromm is the best-known exponent of this attitude, though all of Neo-Freudian analysis shares it, indeed is virtually defined by it), or from the standpoint of the existential attitude, where man's wholeness is to be sought through direct experience rather than analytic reflection.

Existential humanism constitutes nothing less than a determined effort to salvage faith in a godless world. God has left the world, the humanists claim, so that man can elevate himself to the level of God. There is, or should be, no limit; our current state is only a fragment of what can be attained. "We will work to increase our capacity, to take in and assimilate energy, to allow *more* to flow through us, holding onto nothing," so reads a course description of Esalen. "You don't have to suffer to feel good," "Creating Positive Struggle," "How do you want to be alive in this world?" are the titles of others that convey the message. In short, we are in touch with the infinite, only we don't know it— yet. Consciousness is blurred, but it can be raised and cleansed, directly, through new forms of experience. Gone is the *angst* of European existential analysis. Gone too is the doubt and ambiguity, the skepticism of Freudian psychoanalysis. In other words, the demons have faded away. In their place is energy, flow, acceptance, nurture, tenderness: joy.

Along with this, another decisive shift of emphasis occurs. The concern is less with the pathological—the classic neurosis and psychosis—and more with ordinary unhappiness and alienation. As we have seen, when feelings of alienation are concerned, the distinction between normal and sick melts away; and while neurotic features exist, they are more or less articulated with the patterns of everyday life. While some elements of the human-potential movement—one thinks of Rogerian therapy in particular—are focused on the alleviation of neurotic suffering (though they define neurosis and treatment differently from, say, psychoanalysis), much of the movement sees itself mainly as an educational venture, primed to spread good tidings to the citizens of the New Age. In some humanist exercises, seriously disturbed people are urged not to take part, owing to the potential of some of these techniques for stirring up feelings beyond the control of an already troubled individual.

The humanist centers started in California and have since

spread to many urban and suburban areas. Although it is impossible to usefully describe the individual variations, their sum amounts to a new element in the American cultural scene. Esalen and its cohorts have succeeded in taking the original impulse of Freud's therapy—that there are forces hidden within one's self, consciousness of which will have a liberating effect—and giving it a genuine cultural base. This was done by extending the technique of therapy beyond the range of neurosis and into ordinary alienated unhappiness. The existential approach, with its therapeutic nihilism, mainly brought the alienated end of the spectrum of unhappiness into view alongside the neurotic. And taken wholly as a therapy it tends to confuse the two, as we observed in the preceding chapter. However, the humanist movement succeeded in fleshing out the existential impulse with new therapeutic techniques, thus making social alienation directly accessible to therapy.

The techniques employed by humanistic psychology to achieve its goals are several: group work, direct influence by leadership, attention to the body, consciousness alteration, and so forth. All of these techniques are buttressed by an ethos of spontaneity, self-expression and emotional honesty, and an ideal of personal happiness in the here and now. We shall explore some of these options in chapters to come, but here it should be noted that, while pure existentialism remains preoccupied with subjectivity, humanist therapy adds an appropriation of the external, objective world, whether it be the world of one's own body or the world of other people. This explains how the humanist approach has managed to become institutionalized while pure existentialism remained on the fringes. It also should be noted that, like so much of therapy, the human-potential movement has mainly been a province of those who could satisfy material needs and indeed could afford an extra share of the world, for it is to the middle and upper classes, unfulfilled by their wealth, placing their hopes for fulfillment in the acquisition of the ultimate luxury, Joy, that the human-potential movement addresses its positive message.

7

Rogerian Therapy

Carl Rogers is a complete representative of the humanist approach. Perhaps it would be better to call the approach representative of him, for none of its exponents have been around so long, spread their influence so widely nor been so imbued with native American influence as he. Scion of the midwestern farm tradition, a man whose first calling was Christian evangelism through the YMCA, Rogers was well into ministerial training at the Union Theological Seminary, when he discovered his true bent for psychological counseling.[1]

Through his lengthy and distinguished career, Rogers has continued to develop his approaches to therapy; indeed he has moved beyond the essentially individual psychotherapy we are about to describe, into group and encounter methods. Nonetheless, all of his work bears a distinct stamp, and the psychotherapy he worked out remains a coherent and viable system, widely practiced, especially in the psychological profession, and widely studied.

Rogers stands out in two ways from most of the progenitors of therapy. First, he comes from an academic background, and is correspondingly much more concerned with the scientific standards common to academic settings, such as experimental testing. Second, being more thoroughly native American, he is substantially less influenced by Freud and psychoanalysis than virtually any other major figure aside from the behaviorists.

What Rogers developed is strongly *psycho*therapeutic, in that verbal exchange is the means of influence, and just as strongly non*analytic,* in that this influence is not brought to bear in order to ferret out split-off, unacceptable, radically repressed infantile fantasies. Quite the contrary: Rogers is positively existential and humanistic; he has a very definite idea of the wholeness of the self (the humanist's "man"), and he finds it good. He holds that our culture has been dominated by the puritanical idea of original sin—and he sees Freud's psychology as the main representative of this doleful perspective in the world of therapy. By contrast, Rogers claims to have discovered a truer, better man at the deepest level: "One of the most revolutionary concepts to grow out of our clinical experience is the growing recognition that the innermost core of man's nature, the deepest layers of his personality, the base of his 'animal nature' is positive in nature—is basically socialized, forward-moving, rational and realistic."[2]

This is the heart of humanism—that there is a *whole* person, distinctly organized, slumbering beneath the rubble of such fragmentary impulses and fears as Freud discerned with his analytic wrecking equipment. And being whole, he can be approached directly, roused up and led out into the light. It is thus on the individual's holistic self-perception that Rogers focuses, with the firm conviction that this underlying core of good self-feeling can be brought out in therapy, and that the process of its emergence will counteract neurotic distortions.

Rogers goes further than the Neo-Freudians in postulating interpersonal relations as the ground of neurosis and health alike, a ground on which the consciously felt therapeutic relationship itself becomes more important than anything particular learned from it. It would be more accurate to say, perhaps, that the Neo-Freudians and Rogers worked with the same basic concept (see page 85 above, Karen Horney's idea of the "real self," which is very akin to Rogers's concept), but that the former attempted to synthesize it with the analytic model, while Rogers went straight in a positive direction.

The word "positive" is key to understanding Rogers in particular and the human-potential movement in general. Objectively speaking, to be positive means to rely mainly on what is immediately available to consciousness as a way to the truth. By contrast, the negative attitude—such as Freud's—relies more on contradiction and that which is split off from the surface. Rogers's positivism is not so far-reaching as that of Skinner and the behaviorists, in that he works with inner subjective states of mind instead of objectified descriptions of behavior from the standpoint of the observer. However, for Rogers, consciousness is basically transparent; it provides a reliable guide to knowledge, a direct read-out of reality. In this sense he may be said to offer a subjectivist positivism as his basic philosophy of knowledge.

Thus, Rogers feels that therapy can be experimentally validated. And he critically relies on felt experience as a guide to the truth. *"Experience is, for me, the highest authority"* (italics Rogers's) is part of his credo; "This is Me" is the first chapter of his major work, *On Becoming a Person*, elsewhere in which he adds that "when an activity *feels* as though it is valuable or worth doing, it *is* worth doing. Put another way, I have learned that my total organismic sensing of a situation is more trustworthy than my intellect."[3] Here Rogers situates himself and his therapy squarely in the midst of the pragmatic American tradition, in contrast to Freud, for example, who, for all his reliance on the facts of what the patient said, remained very much part of a more speculative European mode.

But the word "positive" has its value side, too. In Rogers we see it as an intense belief in the goodness of man. Though his conviction is grounded in trust, it is certified—as one would expect Rogers to find—by experience. *"The facts are friendly,"* he states in his manifesto, and goes on to assert, on the basis of a life's work, *"It has been my experience that persons have a basically positive direction"*—that is, "constructive, moving toward self-actualization, growing toward maturity, growing toward socialization." (Italics Rogers's.)

Clearly such an attitude is going to have therapeutic effect whether or not it corresponds to the whole truth about the human situation. However, positive concern has to be actively conveyed to the patient; and it will only make a dent, given the alienation of neurotic experience, if applied wholeheartedly. Rogers insists, quite consistently, on the positive value of sincerity in the therapist. The therapist must be "what he is"; there must be (in one of the few technical terms to which Rogers ever resorted) a *congruence* in him, a matchup between what he is experiencing, what he is aware of, and what he conveys to the patient, or—to use Rogers's preferred term—client. Rogers seems to assume that in such a state the therapist, being human, will feel warm and positive toward the client. The therapist must do more than just accept the client; he must experience what the client is experiencing (have what is called "empathy" for him), and at the same time evince what Rogers calls "unconditional positive regard" for him. This attitude may not be that easy to attain. In any event, therapists who cannot muster it are advised to look elsewhere for a therapy to practice.

Thus, rather than a screen on which the client projects his

fantasies, the Rogerian therapist is an active transmitter of regard to him. He does this in the simplest way possible, not by probing beneath the surface but by reflecting that surface back to the client, rephrasing the client's words so that the statement he has just made is relayed back to him, charged this time not with the masochistic self-hatred of neurosis but with the positive esteem of the therapist.

Thus Rogerian therapy—and to some extent all the humanist-existential approaches—bears down on creating a setting in which a person can become intensely aware of how he is evaluating himself. The therapist tries neither to actively change this nor to interpretatively explain it. Again, he merely reflects it back to the client filtered through his own subjectively benign state of unconditional regard—regard not for what a person does or says, but for what he *is*, for that wholeness within. Rogers's experience has shown him that if this is done consistently, beneficial results will be observed, the stasis of neurotic experience will begin to break up, and the freedom of the "true self" will take over.

Rogers sees therapy as akin to good education and, more fundamentally, to the basic socialization process. And since the problem can be approached positively, Rogers is able to propose a relatively brief corrective. Immediacy is the key, "to be" the main operative verb—"It is a richly rewarding experience to be what one deeply is"—therefore a briefer course of treatment—say, once a week for a year or less—is commonly the case, in contrast to the long, drawn-out period of psychoanalysis. This abbreviation has obvious advantages, and not simply from the standpoint of savings in time and money. One advantage is that it tends to thwart the development of complicating feelings such as the transference, and thereby fosters the positive climate Rogers so esteems. The positive climate is promoted both by the therapist's regard and by a certain degree of suggestion which, so to speak, nudges the client's thinking into a more humanistic direction.

For example, consider the case of "Mrs. Oak" in *On Becoming a Person,* an important instance in which Rogers attempts to demonstrate that "the inner core of man's personality is the organism itself, which is essentially both self-preserving and social," by providing verbatim excerpts of the therapeutic exchange. The critical moment occurs in the eighth interview when the client talks bitterly of having felt cheated all her life and first becomes aware, as she comes in touch with this attitude, of a feeling which she describes as "murderous." At this instant Rogers intervenes, emphasizes the *bitter* feeling—i.e., the one implying that she has been the victim of a bad environment—and ignores the murderous one with its more ominous implication. *Implication* is all one can make of these feelings; they point somewhere unknown, at least in advance. But Rogers actively seizes on the feeling of bitterness, of being hurt and mistreated; and not surprisingly, Mrs. Oak follows right along with this approach, which is obviously more in line with the demands of conscious morality and with the view of human nature Rogers is propounding.

It is a simple matter to see how Mrs. Oak would quickly feel better under such ministration. It is rather more problematic to regard the results, gleaned over thirty-nine sessions (equivalent to two months of psychoanalysis), as providing proof of an "inner core of man's personality." Of course, the matter is not closed here. All therapies, psychoanalysis included, have their measure of suggestion, and all tend to reproduce the world outlook of the therapist's system. But we can best consider this later on.

To summarize, Carl Rogers has provided a workable, clearly defined psychotherapeutic approach based on humanist-existential principles. The therapy is popular, and its underlying approach has had wide influence in counseling, social work and education. Rogers derives from Adler; more exactly, Rogers was able to introduce a parallel stream of development to the Adlerian in American clinical psychology. In terms of our axioms we have a psychological system, with a considerable emphasis on subjective awareness, yet extensively articulated with social, interpersonal factors along with being strongly rooted in a naturalistic base of an essential, good human core. This base does not extend very far into biology or transcendence; the social dimension remains tied to the immediate human surroundings—i.e., not to society as a whole. Further, there is little theory of infantile development and no emphasis on the kind of instinctual explanations favored by Freud; in fact, almost a repulsion. Another way of putting this—and one that perhaps most sharply distinguishes the Rogerian approach—is that there is a drastic minimization of the demonic and of repressed unconscious factors in general. Where the deepest layer is the "whole man," from that realm has the devil been expelled.

PRACTICAL SYNOPSIS

For What Types Of Problems Is The
Rogerian Approach Suited?

Rogerian therapy is designed for a wide spectrum of emotional states. People from the relatively normal end have worked with it, as have hospitalized schizophrenics. This range probably derives from its preoccupation with problems of self-regard. Since these are universal, almost anyone can find some point of personal reference in Rogers's approach. The therapy would seem to be especially well suited for counseling people in times of stress when the environmental situation is not in itself overwhelming but where it brings out self-defeating feelings of inferiority or insecurity—e.g., students adjusting to school. Others who could be helped by this approach are the relatively nonneurotic people of the middle classes who are experiencing loneliness and isolation as a result of alienation. Whether this is the best they can do to combat such feelings is another matter; but there is no doubt that Rogerian treatment applies to them.

What Are Its Limits?

As with therapies in general, its limits stem from its strong points. Rogerian treatment is unabashedly inspirational: Its fundamental concern is to get people to feel better about themselves by setting the therapist's positive regard against bad self-images that have become internalized. To do this, the therapist has to engage in a good deal of positive reinforcement, which is fine—except for people who don't like such an approach and, more importantly (since the former can be expected to stay away of their own accord), people who might be attracted to it by virtue of their despair, but who would be better served by a more intensive evaluation of their total problem. And this would include people who had severe environmental problems—with their families or society—as well as those with more involved psychological states that could be remedied. Rogerian treatment, like its existential relative, gains its grasp of consciousness by forfeiting some appreciation of both the real environment and the dark side of the self.

Thus Rogerian treatment works best where the person doesn't have to go very far or deep—as with the student needing to steady down—or where, practically speaking, he can't—as with chronic schizophrenics in a hospital.

What Are The Pros And Cons Of "Unconditional Positive Regard" By The Therapist?

As we observed earlier, there is no single "reality" in human relations. The reality of the Rogerian relationship (and this point extends across the humanist spectrum) is one in which the awareness of the client is enhanced through direct exposure to a therapist who is, so to speak, undergoing the same process and sharing it with him. This can certainly make people feel better about themselves so long as they are disposed to accept the basic terms of the treatment. But there are limits: A therapist focused on conveying his positive regard for the client cannot at the same time regard the situation with the eye of a circling hawk looking for a disturbance in the underbrush. No doubt this metaphor expresses an undesirable extreme; yet it is equally certain that it reflects a critical attitude that, in proper proportion, is essential for good therapeutic work. And it is an attitude that the Rogerian philosophy makes difficult for a therapist to sustain. In other terms, he pays for his subjectivity with objectivity; and the client pays too. It all hinges on whether the price is right for the goals that have been set.

8

Gestalt Therapy

So far all of the therapies we have discussed have shared one feature despite profound differences in theory and values: They have all relied on verbal communication between therapist and patient to achieve their aims. However, there is no reason why words should be sacrosanct; and where the value is placed more on feeling and less on thinking, as has been the case with the existential approaches, then verbalization as the tool, and the whole idea of *psycho*therapy itself, are potentially subject to the scrap heap.

Such a development underlies Gestalt therapy, which, while not eschewing language completely (indeed, can be presented in the form of *Gestalt Therapy Verbatim*),[1] still makes the decisive break into nonverbal experience. By denying the special status of *mind*—in fact, by regarding any special concern with the psyche as a kind of neurosis—Gestalt therapy also undercuts language, the tool of thought, and clears the way for an approach that is explicitly *organismic*. This type of therapy places the body, with its movement and sensations, on entirely the same level as the mind and its abstract thoughts and verbal symbols. And this in turn opens another window on the transcendent.

These attitudes being rather popular nowadays, especially on the West Coast, it may be forgotten that Gestalt therapy has a rather elaborate theoretical base that is firmly grounded in the traditions of modern psychology and psychotherapy.[2] Its name and fundamental point of view derive, of course, from Gestalt psychology; but where the psychology was mainly about perception and cognition, the therapy, properly enough, attends to the emotional life of the whole person. In this respect Gestalt is tied fairly closely in its origins to the Freudian psychoanalysis it seeks to supersede.

Frederick (Fritz) Perls, the principal founder and undisputed sage of Gestalt therapy, was at one point a Freudian training analyst. And to judge by his writings, he remained the true apostate, whose love turns to hate, not indifference, and so keeps a tie to the parent-authority.

Significantly enough, the contributions of another great Freudian apostate, Wilhelm Reich, also loom over Gestalt therapy. As we shall see in the next chapter, Reich made the decisive psychoanalytic breakthrough into the body by his character analysis and later biofunctional therapy. Perls himself does not seem to have been too directly influenced by Reich, but another founder of Gestalt therapy, the anarchist critic and poet Paul Goodman, was.

In any event, Reich's organismic-functional approach and his obliteration of the mind-body gap are heavily represented in Gestalt thinking, and certain of its key terms, such as the "contact" between an organism and its environment, seem directly taken from Reichian thought.

Aside from Reich and Freud, Perls also borrowed something of C. G. Jung's approach to dreams, according to which all elements of the manifest dream stand for parts of the dreamer's self. For all these debts, Gestalt managed to become its own unique synthesis by mixing the idea of the psychology from which it takes its name with psychoanalytic characterology and existential humanism. The key idea is a simple one—indeed Perls kept trying to make it simpler and simpler—but it's hard to pin down. It is that the structure of *awareness* was overlooked by Freud to the detriment of therapy; and that awareness, properly understood, is an active process that moves toward the construction of meaningful organized wholes (the *Gestalten*, or *gestalts*) between an organism and its environment. Gestalten are patterns involving all the layers of organismic function—thought, feeling and activity—and their formation is seen to be part of the lawfulness of nature. Consequently neurosis is nothing but an unnatural splitting in the formation of gestalten, and anxiety (as against Freud's idea of the anticipation of an inner danger) is basically the organism's sensing of the struggle toward its creative unification.

Like Freud then, the Gestaltist believes that a person's neurosis is the result of warping incurred in the warding off of forbidden trends. Unlike Freud though, these trends are seen as needs of the total organism rather than as repressed fantasies—i.e., the whole mental side is downplayed. Further, the organism is endowed with a drive to put itself together; and conscious awareness, rather than being the inert registration Freud made of it, is the active sign of this process. Therefore, reasoned Perls, cure lay, as Freud himself had held, in expanding consciousness.

This, however, was to be done by placing the person in touch not with repressed memories but with current, immediate organismic needs. Freud's program for expanding consciousness involved a person's holding himself still. The bodily inactivity on the couch and the impersonality of the analyst, combined with the Basic Rule (to verbalize whatever one was experiencing), all forced hidden thoughts to the surface of consciousness. In this way what was past and repressed could be eventually recaptured and integrated with the present. But Perls felt that this very stillness and skewing toward the verbal only perpetuated the neurotic split between thought and feeling. The therapist's job is to forestall any excursion into the past, or indeed outside the immediate therapeutic situation. Instead, it is to catalyze greater awareness into the here and now—i.e., therapy works toward allowing the organism to fulfill the potential inherent in the current situation, to let the natural process of gestalt formation take place. Active awareness of the present is what promotes healing, not the reflective and synoptic picture of one's entire life that is the goal of psychoanalysis. Interpretation, the principal technique of analysis, thus becomes an antitherapeutic interruption of the healing process.

Gestalt therapy is an avowedly existential approach, though with none of the gloom of "being-in-the-world" that characterizes European existential analysis. Rather is it thoroughly, positively American—positive in its assumption (with Rogers) that the obvious, most consciously held fact is the guide to truth, positive in its assertion that excitement and growth are the key processes of the human organism, and positive in giving active permission for the patient to express, openly and in public, all felt needs and resentments.

To summarize some of this, in Perls's own words:

> anyone who has a little bit of good will will benefit from the gestalt approach because the simplicity of the gestalt approach is that we pay attention to the obvious, to the utmost surface. We don't delve into a region which we don't know anything about, into the so-called "unconscious." I don't believe in repressions [sic]. The whole

theory of repression is a fallacy. We can't repress a need.
We have only repressed certain expressions of these
needs. We have blocked one side, and then the self-
expression comes out somewhere else, in our movements,
in our posture, and most of all in our voice. A good
therapist doesn't listen to the content of the bullshit the
patient produces, but to the sound, to the music, to the
hesitations. Verbal communication is usually a lie. The
real communication is beyond words.[3]

In practice, a person who undertakes Gestalt therapy will be
doing a good bit of talking, but it will be more for purposes of
expression than explanation or the attainment of comprehensive
self-knowledge. The treatment is usually conducted in groups, although *group process* as such (see below) is not much taken into
account. Neither is the relationship with the therapist drawn upon
for reflective insight into the patient's pattern of human relationships.

Further, instead of meeting regularly over a long period of time,
the Gestalt approach favors a concentrated "workshop" setting
where therapeutic sessions are part of a total living experience for
brief periods of time. Such workshops now dot the landscape of
therapy. Usually a weekend is set aside, though any concentrated
span of time, either singly or in series, may be chosen. Workshops
constitute a notable alternative to the regular one-hour (or less)
session. In the evolution of several therapies—Gestalt included—
the workshop idea has been developed to the extent of new forms
of communal living where life and therapy become virtually indistinguishable. Of such trends and their general social significance,
more below. To return to the therapeutic experience per se, the
workshop is no trivial innovation. Besides shortening the treatment (Perls estimated that three months of concentrated effort
might be enough, though other Gestalt therapists are more
cautious), such a format certainly tends to intensify the experience
and thus leads to more dramatic results.

Dramatization is a key to the Gestalt approach. Instead of relating a conflict in words, and following their track to deeper
levels, the Gestalt subject enacts it, alternately playing out its different parts. Usually several chairs are used and the patient shifts
back and forth between them as different parts of the conflict are
enacted. He may first play his overbearing conscience, or "over-
dog," and yell at an imaginary self in the other chair to do better,

shape up and so forth; then, switching chairs, he will be the submissive, whining, yet obstinate and tricky, "underdog" who limps through life spitefully defying his conscience. The point, of course, is that both parts are really himself, though each is trapped in struggle against the other. By getting the patient to give each part its say, he is led to realize vividly and immediately that, for all of its splits, there is only his one organism.

The therapist's job is mainly to catalyze awareness of this kind. Though he is generally quite active, he keeps himself offstage, in the prompter's box. All is referred to the patient. For example, if the patient feels criticized by the therapist, he is urged to play the therapist and utter aloud the criticism he has been imagining. Similarly figures from the past, and images from dreams and fantasies, are brought into the ambit of the patient's expression. No comment *about*, no reference *to*, is tolerated; everything must be dealt with here, now, and with as much full being as the patient can muster. Perls called his approach to dreams the "identification" technique, but the term applies as well to the therapy as a whole. To bring split-off projections back to the self—"You are you and I am I," goes Perls's "Gestalt Prayer"—and to let the self identify with, accept, all its urgings and sensations—this is the core of the Gestalt method.

Of course the patient resists this: He interrupts his organismic self-expression in countless ways, and at times he simply refuses to go along. But the therapist works to make the patient aware of these obstacles, using as a main trump card a call to the patient's responsibility for his neurosis. There is no "can't" in Gestalt therapy, only "won't." This judgment is made in the interest of putting the patient in touch with his human potential and not to make him feel guilty through implying that he wishes to be ill.

In fact the very existence of guilt feeling is minimized in Gestalt —as it is whenever a therapy adopts the positive approach. Perls said (quite correctly) that "in the Freudian system, the guilt is very complicated. In Gestalt Therapy, the guilt thing is much simpler. We see guilt as projected *resentment* [italics Perls's]. Whenever you feel guilty, find out what you resent, and the guilt will vanish and you will try to make the other person feel guilty." And later: "The expression of resentment is one of the most important ways to help you to make your life a little bit more easy."[4]

This is a far cry from Freud's "Whether one has killed one's father or has abstained from doing so is not really the decisive thing. One is bound to feel guilty in either case. . . ." and it reflects a world of difference in philosophic outlook and general view of the human condition. For resentment is an organismic *need* that can be expressed and hence satisfied; while Freud's guilt is grounded in an unconscious murderous *wish* that is denied access to consciousness because it is buried in a thought that refuses to collapse itself into total organismic functioning. In other words, it is a specific wishful idea, a *fantasy*—"kill father"—based upon lost infantile experience, a precise piece of history that will not be forgotten and can be neither gratified nor completed. Perls and Gestaltists (and almost every other school of therapy in one way or another) hold that Freud was unduly pessimistic and that current organismic expression of resentment will, if it is "wholehearted" enough, put together what history has put asunder. To do this they have to (quite consistently) minimize the demonic, minimize the past, minimize any special quality of verbalization (for only language can differentiate sharply enough between the specific forms of past and present experience) and minimize the distinction between thought and action. In sum, the Gestalt goal is to diminish the gap between the objective and subjective modes, and to restore to a person the wholeness of nonverbal experience, conceived as a kind of *élan vital*.

We may therefore characterize Gestalt therapy as a mode which, while remaining psychological, grounds itself equally in the biological—not, certainly, in any kind of mechanistic way (Gestalt is a long way from being accepted by the official world of medicine and psychiatry), but rather in the sense of a nature philosophy. The wisdom of the body, the unity of all experience—these are Gestalt tenets, and, combined with a basic view of the goodness of man, they lead readily to a positive, American form of Eastern religion. The transcendent quality emerges in a certain seer-like strain in Perl's personality, in the "Gestalt Prayer" and in the emanation of a general air of salvation from Gestalt literature.

By the same token, verbal explanation of the actual content of a person's life is downplayed. And though it may seem incongruous for a therapy that is run in groups, calls for *communitas* and has an explicit social critique, social factors are scarcely included in any systematic way. There is no theory of transference to speak of, nor of group process, interpersonal relations or social psychology. The de-emphasis of verbal knowledge plays into the social myopia of Gestalt therapy, which mainly stems, however, from Perl's near-exclusive attention to *projection* as the major form of disturbed communication between the self and other people. When we project, we attribute to an outside force something that is subjectively within ourselves. If everything I see in you is only a projection of my inner resentment, longing or whatnot, then the You I see has nothing to say that is your own, no genuinely social bond, hardly any interdependent reality. And while societal criticism is liberally spread through the Gestalt literature, it rarely goes beyond the well-known indictment that our society, or at least normal life in it, is neurotic—dull, lifeless, hyperabstract and alienated.

In other words, the basic judgment of Gestalt therapy, a verdict that derives mainly from biopsychological thinking, is simply extended to society; the therapy does not employ insight into the actual structure of society itself. This may have something to do with its appeal—but that is a matter that cannot be decided at present.

PRACTICAL SYNOPSIS

For What Problems Is Gestalt Therapy Best Suited?

Gestalt is part of the humanist movement and shares its range of application from moderately severe neuroses to middle-class alienation and anomie. It is more emotionally demanding than Rogerian therapy, however, and since it concentrates heavily on dealing with resistances instead of offering affirmation, it is less suited for counseling or for support of the chronically psychotic. I should think it would be most helpful to excessively intellectualized neurotic people whose personal relations have become stultified, or who feel pent-up. Gestalt mainly heals through fostering intense emotional experiences in a group setting. It works best, then, for people whose lives are deficient in emotional intensity and group relations, and who are not too frightened of either. It is limited, as is the existential-humanist sphere in general, by being unable to deal with problems for which comprehensive knowledge of either the individual or the environment is required. Perls never clearly distinguished between the creative use of the intellect and the abuse of our rational power by the defense of intellectualization. As his therapy was expressly designed to attack the latter, it cannot make good use of the former.

What Is The Role Of The Therapist?

Because Gestalt therapy is so emotionally demanding, it can induce a state of near hysteria. Its conditions thus require that the therapist be of exceptional caliber. If he is too wooden, he gets nowhere at all; but on the other hand, it is easy to go too fast and to stir up more than can be assimilated.

The problem goes deeper. Every therapist—no matter what the therapy—has an opportunity to exploit the infantile attitudes of the transference by setting himself up as a seer or shaman. And frequently this unscrupulous attitude—so termed because it does violence to an individual's capacity for autonomy—is combined with a substantial intuition and sensitivity, hence is compatible with a considerable degree of success.

As stated, all therapies may include among their practitioners some of this type. However in Gestalt we come for the first time upon a therapy whose basic terms offer a particularly tempting target for individuals of this kind. We shall find other therapies with a similar predisposition—biofunctionalism, primal therapy and encounter groups being only the most obvious. All share a pronounced emphasis on emotional as against intellectual experience; and this is what creates the opening for mystification and hysterical possession. Clearly this is an unwanted extreme—just as the cold, detached analyst is an unwanted extreme—it needn't occur, and many, probably the great majority, practitioners of these therapies do not succumb to the vice of seerdom. Nonetheless, anyone considering a course of one of these therapies is well advised to consider the possibility carefully and in advance, since under the intense emotional impact (especially with group experience) of the therapy itself, it may be much less possible to determine just what is going on.

Can Gestalt Offer The Same Benefits As Other Group Therapies?

As we will see, group therapies themselves vary widely; furthermore, many Gestaltists are willing to experiment and hybridize their treatment with other group modalities. Thus it is difficult to generalize. However, in pure form Gestalt, though carried out in groups, is quite different from group therapy proper in that the interactions between the members of the group, and the development of the group as a whole, are not attended to. The group continues to exert influence, however, mainly by establishing a climate of approval for emotional expression.

9

Biofunctional Therapies: Wilhelm Reich And Bioenergetics

The biofunctional therapies all rely on the assumption that we live fundamentally through the body. Hence neurosis and healing alike are to be thought of as conditions affecting our bodily organism, and verbalization and social intervention are correspondingly minimized. While biofunctional forms of therapy mix readily with the human-potential values of existential humanism and play an important role in centers such as Esalen, they also stand as individual schools, such as Alexander Lowen's bioenergetics. And they originate in the work of one of the major figures in the history of psychoanalysis and therapy, Wilhelm Reich.

We observed in the preceding chapter that Gestalt therapy could be viewed as a decisive rupture with the psychological approaches, the Gestaltists turning instead in the direction of organismic functioning, the realm of the body. This is so if we trace the line of therapy through the existential approach and the human-potential movement. However, such a line bypasses Wilhelm Reich, who, from within Freudian psychoanalysis, and via a detour through Marxism, made the definitive breakthrough into the body.

Reich stands in the tradition of fallen angels. One of the early-twentieth-century generation that was attracted to psychoanalysis by its radical lure (as against those who came later, after it had become an institutionalized "ego psychology"), Reich fell early into the "special son" role that had once been Jung's and which it was ever Freud's penchant to cultivate. And like others—Jung,

Adler, Rank, Horney, even the loyal Ferenczi—Reich found it necessary to stake out territory of his own rather than stay faithfully in the master's shadow. Unlike these others, though, he took the protest to its extreme. Reich was never one for the middle of the road. The stormiest petrel, the most uncompromisingly—even compulsively—original of men, he would not rest, indeed it seemed he could not work creatively, unless he was in opposition to—even expelled from—the main body of society.

Thus, it was when, in the mid-Thirties, he had been read out of the psychoanalytic movement (for being too political) and the Communist party (for being too psychological) and Germany itself (for being a menace to fascism), that Reich began his definitive shift to the biological—and eventually the cosmic—base of human functioning.

These developments are all chronicled and need not concern us in detail here.[1] However, it should be noted that, as with all major original figures, the works which appear so at variance with tradition on the surface are seen to have considerable continuity with it when examined in depth. What looks like a quantum leap or a bolt from the blue will generally turn out to be a synthesis of elements that had been there all along, both in the originator's past and in his intellectual milieu. Hence, Reich's seemingly astounding biological break with psychotherapeutics was fundamentally the logical development of an idea Freud had developed at the beginning of his psychoanalytic investigation, then superseded but never finally discarded—the concept of the *Actual-neurosis* and a theory of anxiety based upon the idea of dammed-up libido (sexual energy).

As Freud first saw it, what had *really* happened to a person (the "actual") determined the neurotic disposition. This applied both to the infantile situation—where seductions and other concrete traumata were sought as the causes of later neuroses—and to the onset of neurotic difficulty in the adult. In the latter case the prime offender was thought to be incomplete sexual release. Indeed, through the 1890s and to a diminishing extent thereafter, Freud was seriously interested in social reform that would permit full sexual discharge. Coitus interruptus (which was especially common, in part because of inadequate contraception) was the main target, but his concern was for the whole range of sexuality. As late as 1908, in his essay on "'Civilized' Sexual Morality and Modern Nervous Illness," Freud held that the intellectual backwardness of women had to do with the degree of sexual supression forced upon them by a patriarchal society.[2]

Linked with these attitudes was the view that anxiety was the direct outcome of somatic changes brought about by incomplete sexual release. Freud went so far as to speculate that a direct chemical transformation, unknown to the science of the time, occurred in sexual hormones as a result of their incomplete discharge and turned them into anxiety-stimulating substances. Since all neurotic manifestations were held to be the outcome of defenses against anxiety, it followed then that *actual* sexual traumas and *actual* failure of discharge were the root causes of neurosis. Strongly implied was the projected obsolescence of the psychotherapies and the future ascendance of sexual hygiene and sexual therapy for the prevention and cure of neurosis.

Of course, this view never prevailed with Freud; if it had, he would have never bothered to develop psychoanalysis. From the start there were also the *psychoneuroses*—i.e., disorders mediated not by unfulfilled needs or acts but by unacceptable thoughts. As Freud developed his theory, these psychoneuroses, which at first were considered secondary elaborations of biological states, became more and more the true representatives of the whole class of neurotic phenomena. And as this later view slowly took hold (it did not achieve primacy in Freud's thought until 1926, when he was seventy years old), the view of mind became more and more a *psychoanalytic* one. The *wish* became the unit of psychological interest, replacing the biological *need*. The prime explanatory concept of instinctual drive came to be regarded as a mental state—the mind's looking at bodily demand—rather than the somatic play of hormones and innervation; and anxiety became the *signal*—i.e., a communication—of impending danger to the ego, a danger that could be equally a matter of an immoral thought or a life-threatening illness. With the passage of time and the development of ego psychology, the second, signal, anxiety theory became virtually the only concept of anxiety and hence of neurosis formation and therapy.

But not for Reich. From his earliest days in psychoanalysis he felt that actual experience, and notably sexual experience, remained the touchstone. While he continued to do important psychological work for a number of years, one senses that for Reich, mind—the whole congerie of fantasy and thought, wish and desire—was always epiphenomenal to the reality of the functioning body. By the mid-Twenties he had already taken Freud's original ideas about sexual release to the point of specifying the orgasm as the criteria of healthy function.[3] At the same time, he was developing his ideas about character into a form that would later take shape, first as "muscular armor," and eventually as a transducer of universal biological energy, the *orgone*.

During his psychoanalytic days, Reich made important contributions to the theory of technique by emphasizing that analysis had to proceed from a person's chronic, automatic character attitudes down to repressed fantasies.[4] Since character is, among other things, a defense against stress, this means that analysis could not wait for the fantasies to bubble up to consciousness but would have to actively approach the patient's resistance as they manifested themselves in the treatment setting.

In this way Reich developed an active confrontation style which challenged a patient's character resistances. It occurred to him that these attitudes seemed especially prominent as manifested in the patient's bodily carriage and expression—in the fixed smile, the stiff neck, the fortress chest or the passive slouch. Confronting these postures and vigorously interpreting their meaning would frequently result in a rush of contrary emotion (spiteful rage behind the smile, passive yearning behind the military bearing, and so forth) that would in turn open up new therapeutic ground.

One thing led to another, and Reich focused more and more on characterological blocks, which he came to call "muscular armor." After his break with psychoanalysis, he began combining verbal techniques with nonverbal, direct bodily intervention. Through attention to breathing, muscular tension and movement pattern, either by encouraging emotional expression or by direct bodily manipulation, frozen emotional attitudes were released. With the actual outpouring of feeling, Reich held, came the bottled-up residue of infantile damage. And with a functioning, real organism in mind, the therapeutic goal became more specific: no longer self-knowledge, but flow and motility; no longer consciousness of forbidden wishes with repudiation of same, but full expression and gratification of sexual needs.

Thus we can call this whole approach to therapy the "biofunctional." As Reich became convinced that a real physical energy-flow lay beneath these changes, he named his treatment after it: "orgone therapy." Those who came later and essentially dropped the orgone hypothesis prefer to call the treatment "bio-energetic therapy." All versions are based, however, upon the nuclear idea that emotional health depends upon organismic function, the wisdom of the body and instinct.

Reich went further than Freud in one direction of instinct theory by giving sexuality greater sway than Freud had ever intended. At the same time, he refused to follow the master into the reaches of duality. Where Freud later engrained his skeptical view of human nature in a theory that built ambivalence into us by its postulation of life-and-death drives locked in eternal combat, Reich continued to hold to a monistic theory. Eros alone drove life; and only the repressing environment would stop it. This accorded with the original idea of the Actualneurosis, where trouble was caused by blockage, and it was explicitly opposed to Freud's view of the individual who could repress himself, and had to do so because of the awful ideas he was generating out of innate ambivalence.

Reich's theory was compatible with an active approach to therapy that sought to recapture concrete traumatic memories; and it was compatible, too, with his uncompromising insistence on the need for complete orgasm as the *sine qua non* of health—an imperative that led him to remorselessly criticize all existing moral restrictions on sexuality. He did not, however, advocate sexual promiscuity, although rumors to this effect were spread by those who found him too threatening. What Reich's biological imperative did lead him to advocate was serial monogamy, and it also led him to prohibit any kind of deviation for its own sake, including homosexuality. The point was that the body needed genital orgasm in order to stay healthy; anything less was not sexuality. Promiscuity implied a restless search, hence a lack of orgastic fulfillment; while perversion denied to the body its natural path of sexual discharge. Hence both were wrong—i.e., unhealthy—and neither more nor less so than abstinence or compulsive faithfulness to an unsatisfying partner.

Reich's single-instinct theory and relentless biologism was also compatible with—even mandated by, if a thinker were to be consistent and audacious enough—a concretization of libido. No longer a theoretical metaphor for displaceable, transformable sexual interest, libido became physically grounded in the body, and in nature at large, as orgone energy.

A thinker of Reich's stamp had to have some tangible postulate on which to moor his hopes for humanity. Through the Twenties and early Thirties it was Marxism. During this period Reich made many notable contributions toward the amalgamation of psycho-analysis and Marxism, seeing in the former the radical psychology necessary to carry out a revolutionary strategy; and in the latter a form of social organization necessary for the carrying forward of the sexual liberation which in turn would free the human spirit. When his hopes in each field were dashed, he turned to biology itself and found the same liberating principle in the energy field known as the orgone.

From this point forward, Reich's development becomes both too problematic and too far afield from the question of therapy for adequate and relevant discussion here. The facile assumption that his later work was simply madness (as though that could be, for a person so productive and organized right up to the end) has been pretty well discredited. But this only begins to frame the question of how far Reich's late work strayed into vitalist fantasy and how much of it was inspired insight into biological theory—a question that cannot be answered by the customary *ad hoc* arguments but only by a more systematic reexamination of Reich's work than has yet been attempted.

Whatever its scientific value, the late phase continued the early trajectory—accelerated it in fact to outer space and specula-tion about galaxies in collision. What had begun as a fission within psychoanalysis became not just biopsychological but reached beyond the personal as well, extending the same form of functional analysis from neurosis to carcinogenesis and cloud formation. Consequently the later modes of therapy became more nonpsychological as well as nonverbal.

Although the use of the notorious orgone accumulator—in the defense of which Reich was to be subjected to his fatal last per-secution at the hands of the U.S. government—has slackened off (for reasons that have never been clearly articulated),[5] Reichian therapy in its final stage was a long way from its psychoanalytic origin. The couch was still used, to foster relaxation; and at times Reich, adhering to his basic functional point of view in which all behavior could express the organism, would resort to verbal character-analytic work. But the therapy pointed toward something markedly different, a state in which word-symbols would be eventually dropped as superfluous mediators. At that point the patient would be mostly or entirely unclothed, and the therapist no longer an impersonal screen but an active prodder, kneading blocked muscles, pressing on frozen chests, sticking rubber tubes into static throats to induce gagging. Then he would sit back to observe respirations or emotional flow, sometimes directly provoking strong feeling, such as rage; sometimes comforting a sob; sometimes just waiting.

Reich conceived the therapeutic progress segmentally (based upon the phylogenetic insight that we all are descended from earthworms). Thus, blockages would be opened up from the forehead down—through the eyes, mouth, throat, neck, shoulders, thorax, diaphragm, belly, perineum and genitals, with the diaphragm the key midstage, and the genitals, of course, the end point, for when orgastic potency had been securely achieved, then therapy could end.

Reich realized that progress could not be linear in a biofunctional system, that it was resisted as tenaciously in the body as Freud had found it to be in the mind. But he realized also that the resistances had their function, since too rapid a breakthrough of blocked feeling could prove devastating. Thus his therapy, for all its activity and audacity, had its cautious, painstaking side. Yet, for all this, one complication that Freudian thought had increasingly taken into account was eliminated by Reich and the orgonomists, bioenergeticists and Gestaltists who came after him— namely, the transference relationship with the therapist.

The less the therapist does in response to the patient's behavior—i.e., the more "Freudian" he becomes—the more floridly will transference fantasy develop as the patient struggles with the enigma of the therapist's response. Hence, the elaboration of transference fantasy is played down by the active role of the therapist in all the biofunctional therapies. In these therapies the therapist stands for one definite, active pattern of relationship. Moreover, he is continually translating away from symbol and fantasy toward bodily experience. What in other modes of treatment is considered to have a communicational value between therapist and patient is now mainly localized—physically—in the patient himself.

Thus fantasy, transference and the entire interpersonal and social dimension is played down. The Reichian therapist in effect says to his patient: The fact that my standing over you kneading your unclothed flesh suggests a rape at the hands of your father is in no way a drawback to this therapy. Quite the contrary, for it mobilizes your doubtlessly powerful feelings about such an eventuality and then lets you "get them out."

In other words, it gets the energy moving, and that is what really counts. And by and large, people who have already made the commitment to biofunctional therapy accept formulations such as these. At any rate, though they may have an emotional storm, they quiet down and resume cordial or at least reasonably neutral relations with their therapist. Indeed, if one does not take into account the unconscious mind, the evidence would appear to support Reich's contention that his biofunctional approach successfully bypasses the problem of transference in therapy. Of course that is no mean caveat, but we shall have to let the matter rest for now. It should be apparent, however, that the claims made by biofunctional therapists that they also do "analysis" are spurious on the face of it, since they are eliminating the very conditions necessary to illuminate the psychological depths. What passes for analysis then in such approaches is generally a rather directive psychotherapy based upon the agreeable truism that one's parents were stifling and repressive. Reich may have been able to do more than this—but he was nothing if not extraordinary.

In fact Reich was an impossible act to follow—too gigantic and uncompromising a figure, and notwithstanding his Marxist phase, too ultimately indifferent to social reality, to ever successfully found a "school." After his untimely death in 1957, his followers, many of whom had congregated at his Orgone Institute in Rangeley, Maine, tended to go their own ways. The closest thing to a Reichian organization, run by Dr. Elsworth Baker in New York City, is still a long way from the original. Meanwhile, Reich's biofunctional concept has been gaining in popularity, owing no doubt to its compatibility with the human-potential movement. Most programs for self-expansion these days are liberally sprinkled with Reichian phrases, and his ideas have entered—though without the systematic elaboration which was his hallmark—into innumerable massage and movement therapies, where they either stand alone, as a monument to his genius, or become amalgamated with other approaches such as dance, psychodrama, Gestalt and so forth.

An erstwhile pupil of Reich's, Dr. Alexander Lowen, has gone ahead and recoined the same therapy *sans* the orgone hypothesis, under the name of "bioenergetics therapy."[6] Since his therapy is both biological and energetic, Dr. Lowen has succeeded in promoting it as the current major manifestation of the biofunctional approach. Lowen claims to have improved upon Reich by being less one-sided—i.e., by paying substantial attention to the psychotherapeutic as well as the biofunctional. He considers his bodily tactic more flexible and sophisticated in that he relies on exercises, group work and often has the patient standing on the floor rather than lying on the couch as Reich emphasized. In short, if one forgets the question of intellectual stature, he stands in roughly the same relation to Reich as Non-Freudian revisionists do to Freud. Whether this constitutes a watering-down—as Freud put it, an amalgamation of the pure gold of the original with some baser metal—or whether it represents a progressive adaptation to the realities of the therapeutic task is difficult to decide. In any event, it is another example of the "Americanization" of therapy.

PRACTICAL SYNOPSIS

For What Problems Is Biofunctional Therapy Suited?
Is It Limited To Neuroses That Have Bodily Manifestations?

The second question is best answered with the observation that all neuroses have bodily manifestations, if one looks closely enough. That is what Reich did; and that is what has to be done if one is to gain anything from the treatment. In other words, the somatic face of the neurosis is there in everyone: Biofunctionalism is for those who are able and willing to show that face—and correspondingly less inclined to present their neuroses in other ways. With this in mind, it can be said that biofunctional treatment, like the other humanist psychologies, applies to the general range of neuroses with feelings of inhibition and deadness. And like these other psychologies, it finds easy extension to the syndromes of anomie. Here the biofunctional therapist says in effect: If society has taken from you real power over your lives, at least I can restore a sense of it to your body.

Of all the manifestations of neurosis, however, one group is especially open to biofunctional treatment—the sexual. For a Reichian, the standard of health is unequivocally orgastic potency; hence disturbances in this area of function will be specially attended to in Reichian therapy. But it should not be thought that sexual problems will be treated as isolated or symptomatically. Many tend to forget that Reich never considered performance in itself—what he called erective potency—a reliable standard of functioning.

What Are Its Limits?

Reich, needless to say, saw few or none. He applied orgonomy to everything from schizophrenia (where the energy block was thought to be behind the eyes) to cancer (where it was felt to be a total body depletion). In the absence of any proof that such an approach makes a real impact on the disease, we would have to regard biofunctionalism as without value in these disorders except as a kind of invigorating physical therapy. Again, because it does not take a person's environment or detailed psychological makeup seriously, biofunctionalism, like other humanist psychologies, is not recommended where extensive interpersonal factors are present or where deep self-knowledge is either needed or wanted.

What Is Its Relationship To The Sex Therapies?

There is a certain overlapping in goal, needless to say, and in technique as well (see the discussion of the sex therapies in Chapter 14), since biofunctionalists will not hesitate to give advice and counseling, while sex therapists focus directly on bodily performance. Also, the conceptual bases of the two therapies, while quite different in their origins—Reich coming out of psychoanalytic dialectics, and the sex therapists out of behaviorism—tend to converge in mutual positivism where the only meaningful events are physical observables. Still, biofunctionalism remains a broad approach that regards sex as a cornerstone, while sex therapy makes sexual performance much more of an explicit goal in itself. Sex therapy also works in a counseling and learning model, and is closely allied to family approaches (see Chapter 13) while biofunctionalism remains essentially an individual therapy.

What Are Its Main Advantages
And Disadvantages?

Its main advantage is that it provides contact with an undeniable part of reality—the body. And this is also its major disadvantage, since it makes the body an end in itself, thereby slighting other aspects of life. The same criticism can—and should—be made of other therapies, of course, but the omission here, as with Gestalt, is perhaps more severe: In cutting out the psychosocial dimension, the way is made that much easier for excesses on the part of the therapist, who can justify any nonsense and mischief in the name of providing contact with the body.

10

Primal
Therapy

Lately another claimant for the title of therapeutic paladin has emerged, this time from Southern California. And while Dr. Arthur Janov and his "primal therapy" have yet to become part of the therapeutic Establishment, nor even a media success on the order of transactional analysis, there is little question that his work has been a notable addition to the field. It is doubtful that Janov would be pleased to know he has merely added to the field without eliminating the rest of it, since he is of the opinion that "if one theory is valid, and I believe the Primal notions are valid, then other approaches are invalid." This quote places him in the ranks of the "saviors" who congregate in the history of therapy, an impression confirmed by a study of *The Primal Scream*.[1]

Dr. Janov's work bristles with certitude and is laced with rapturous expressions of gratitude by ex-patients. The dustjacket is emblazoned with the most extravagant praise: "Sigmund Freud presented *The Interpretation of Dreams* in 1900. Dr. Janov's work may be quite as important," writes the *Chattanooga Times*. The *Berkeley Gazette,* making the same comparison with Freud, adds that Janov's endeavor will "probably work to a much better end."

Arthur Janov must be on to something. Whatever its ultimate merit, primal therapy taps a bedrock of great emotional power. Janov sees the force as the truth of deeply buried painful childhood experience that sits like a lump in the breast through all later days. And he asserts that only he—not Freud, who got lost in psychologizing; not Reich, who swung too far to the bodily extreme; neither the existentialists nor the Gestaltists who remain trapped in the present—only Janov himself goes deep enough into the past and puts it all together in terms of the organism to offer a genuinely curative treatment for neurosis.

Janov had practiced what sounds like fairly straightforward Freudian/Neo-Freudian individual and group therapy for a number of years until awakened from his dogmatic slumbers by the scream of a patient. On a hunch, Janov had urged him to call out, "Mommy! Daddy!" and as the patient did so he seemed to become possessed and passed into an infantile crying state that culminated in a "piercing, deathlike scream that rattled the walls of my office." Following this the patient reported a kind of breakthrough into more genuine feeling, which set Janov to thinking, and thus primal therapy was born.

One fundamental point underlies primal therapy: It is that neurosis consists of a warded-off, actual Pain (Janov often resorts to capitalization to underscore the monumentality of his concepts) that contains all of an individual's infantile hurts and wrongs. The neurosis is composed of, first, all the symbolic attempts a person makes to shun his Pain—the defenses—and second, the chronic state of tension set going as a result of this state of affairs.

So far this sounds like plain psychoanalytic theory, especially in its emphasis on early childhood experience. For Janov as for Freud, the neurotic is a man haunted by unfinished business. Unlike Perls, Janov places no faith in the integrative power of current awareness; and unlike Reich, he feels that therapy cannot simply dissolve body armor but must recapture specific, psychological memories. Yet the differences from Freud, though not as obvious, are even more profound. For, along with Perls and Reich (and virtually everybody else in therapy), Janov holds that the child's own wishes and longings are only *secondarily* involved in the neurotic process. In other words, neurosis starts as something done to the child by the parent.

Thus, we are back again to the theory of the Actualneurosis, only in an extreme version emphasizing the unbearable pain of infantile emotional trauma. The pain of this hurt is not admitted to himself by the child; and because he cannot believe in the *reality* of what happened, he builds neurotic defenses. In Janov's theory the hurt lies very deep, and neither verbal insight nor superficial tinkering with love, support, drugs, group pressure, existential awareness or what-have-you will suffice to dredge it up. But *it*— something specific and focal—is there to be dredged up, and once the defenses are down and *it* is really felt and screamed out for the first time, health will ensue. Hence Janov's proof-positive attitude, his belief in cure for neurosis, and his amazing certitude: "I believe that there is one reality, a single, precise set of truths about each of us that is not open to interpretation."[2]

Now, unidimensionality was exactly what Freud abandoned in 1897 when he decided that not all of his high-bourgeois Viennese ladies could have been seduced by their fathers, as they claimed, but that they all had fantasies of the event because they all wished for it to be so. "Our patients suffer from reminiscences," Freud had written earlier in *Studies in Hysteria*. He was to decide soon after that what they were afraid to remember included their own desire. With this insight the new science became *psycho*analysis, and from it Freud was led inexorably to infantile sexuality as the matrix of desire. Of course, his patients hadn't just desired; something real had to happen too. The fine ladies must have seen and experienced more as little girls than they were prepared to acknowledge. As we observed earlier, Freud never wholly dropped the idea of Actual-neurosis. But his point became that there could never be a "single, precise set of truths about each of us," because the mind would meet reality with its own fantasy and form experience at the boundary between desire and actuality.

Janov, on the other hand, is very explicit in denying that this could be so, that mind could have its own laws, or that these would matter much in the scheme of things. Therefore he does not have a dynamic psychology as such, but a nature psychology in the manner of Perls and Reich in which *need* is primary and *wish* not only derivative but dispensable once need is met. For all the surface similarity to Freud's theory, Janov's point of view lacks that theory's two most indispensable components: repression (i.e., a strictly psychological account of the unconscious) and a theory of infantile sexuality.

Freud postulated a hierarchy of danger situations, corresponding to the developmental progression of the child and marked at each stage by a new and potentially traumatic source of anxiety. Thus the infant had first to contend with loss of the needed object (mother herself, or her breast); then with fear of loss of the parent's love; then with fear of bodily danger (here the castration complex intervenes—i.e., infantile sexuality is at its height); and lastly, grown post-Oedipal, fear of superego or conscience, whose signal is the sense of guilt. In each instance, Freud held, the child has to contend with some wish of its own implicated in the danger. In other words, if mother goes out, might that not be experienced by the child as a consequence of its own greedy feeling for her; or if father forbids, as a result of the child's hostility?

Janov, however, in every case so far as I could see, discovers only one really troubling event, the Primal Trauma—awareness that the parents do not love the child. Thus even guilt is regarded as "at its base . . . no more than *fear* of loss of parental love" (italics Janov's).[3] Somehow every patient ends up screaming out that mommy or daddy didn't love him. Needless to add, the child becomes no more than a blank slate here, someone who would grow free were he loved. No intrinsic complications in the structure of mind are admitted, no inherent, unattainable desire or fantasy—only the failure of parental love. The question is whether this is the true ultimate Primal Trauma, or whether it is the most accessible to consciousness under the specific therapeutic situations Janov sets up.

To some extent the latter case must hold. Even Janov's terminology sets a one-dimensional stage. For example, readers of Freud are accustomed to the use of the phrase "Primal Scene" in reference to the intensely charged spectacle of parental intercourse. For Janov, however, the "Primal Scene" becomes the "time in the young child's life when all the past humiliations, negations and deprivations accumulate into an inchoate realization: 'There is no hope of being loved for what I am,'" following which the child "slips quietly into neurosis."[4]

Of course, there is no reason why Janov can't recoin the phrase, so long as he is consistent. And by and large he is so consistent that any individual who comes to him will find himself overwhelmingly likely to have an experience in accordance with Janov's definition of "Primal Trauma." So relentless is Janov's consistency that it enables him to say that all defenses can be broken down, that absolute cure is possible, and that Freud's idea that we are inevitably neurotic is so much Old World despair.

The therapeutic approach that sets out to capture Primal Pain is similarly striking in its intensity and unambiguity.[5] The patient is given a written set of instructions in advance which defines the terms of the therapy. Included is the directive "Do exactly as the therapist says. In no case will any harm be allowed to come to you. . . ." The patient is told to check into a hotel and remove himself from regular pursuits for three weeks, to abstain from all drugs and tension-reducing diversions, and to give himself entirely over to the treatment for this period. During this intense phase of the therapy the patient has one open-ended session each day and is the only patient of the therapist for the whole period. Sessions generally last from two to three hours each and are stopped when the therapist decides the patient can't take any more (in contrast to the vast majority of therapeutic compacts, which allocate a fixed block of time on a regular basis over an indefinite period).

In each session the therapist works actively toward a specific goal (in contrast to having the patient free-associate): to get the patient to express his deepest feelings toward his parents. And this he eventually does, with gut-wrenching, baby-talking calls and screams of inchoate pain. Everything else is interdicted—dealing with current life situations, explanations of behavior, exploration of fantasy for its own sake, bodily attitude as such and, most significantly, feelings toward the therapist. Janov is at his most positive on this point, saying:

> Primal Therapy shuts off any transference and does not permit neurotic behavior of any kind because that means the patient isn't feeling; he is acting out. We force the patient to be direct. Instead of allowing him to be obsequious or intellectual, we tell him to fall on the floor, screaming, "Love me, love me!" directly to his *parents*. This usually makes all discussion of how the patient might feel toward his therapist superfluous. It seems such a simple notion that if the patient is carrying forward feelings about his parents and projecting them onto the doctor, the projected and displaced feelings are really unimportant. What is crucial are those early feelings toward the parents. Feeling them will eliminate neurosis and transference.[6]

The truth of this "simple notion" would only be as obvious to me as it is to Dr. Janov if I were prepared to believe with him that forcibly prohibiting a patient from having feelings about the therapist actually succeeds in eliminating such feeling. Given the ultimate privacy of thought, it would seem rather more likely to have two linked effects—one, of driving expression of transference feeling underground; and two, of intensifying it along certain narrow channels, channels as deep as the archaic law-giving, absolute parent-god is high.

The fact is that the patient has to be quite aware that he is talking to Janov while fantasizing about his parents. The two streams of thought run together, and the object in each—parents and Janov—comes to represent the other. That the therapist would set going so dramatic an occurrence, then decree that what is in fact happening is really not happening, can only have the effect of recapitulating the image of the omnipotent, reality-defining parent. Further, it skews the communication between the two of them in a way that has powerful emotional consequences.

The situation is more than casually reminiscent of a model of disturbed communication worked out by Gregory Bateson and associates in the 1950s—the "double-bind."[7] (The terms of the bind are drawn from Bateson et al. and given in italics below):

1. *A primary negative injunction:* "Do not have or act out feelings about me, the real person in the room in whose hands you have placed your destiny";

2. *A secondary injunction conflicting with the first on a more abstract* (less immediate) *level.* The secondary injunction is delivered in multiple ways—by orders; by deprivation of ordinary stimuli; by directives to express readily accessible memories of parental rejection—in short, by doing everything possible to stir up the most extreme transference feeling;

3. *A tertiary injunction prohibiting the subject* (Bateson et al. used the term "victim" here) *from leaving the field.* Here, too, the impact is multiple, consisting of the therapeutic compact, the fee that has been paid, the expectation of help, the gratification at being the object of so much attention, the deep gratification of the transference wish itself, etc.

The double-bind hypothesis was originally developed to explain how families drove their children mad. That situation does not precisely obtain here. Yet the model is also useful in accounting for a wide range of human entrapment. We can go further, and call it *enthrallment,* a word that is very pertinent in considering therapies, since one can feel very good while being enthralled, good enough to quite forget about the unfree nature of the relationship.

In any event it seems that the initial phase of primal therapy is fertile soil for enthrallment, whether or not it actually occurs. It could well be that any sufficiently intense emotional experience carries a risk of this sort. Certainly no religious conversion would be without such a hazard, and indeed the thread of enthrallment runs through the whole history of human social organization. What is notable about primal therapy, however, is that it so determinedly legislates the social factor out of its hypotheses while in fact employing it in the most profound way.

After completing the three-week intensive phase, the patient returns to normal life while continuing his treatment for another six months ar so with a Primal Group. This is a group as unlike those that have formed the traditional fabric of group therapy as can be imagined. There is virtually no group activity as such, none of the struggles about communication, interaction, intimacy and power. The people in the group have as little overtly to do with each other as possible. Each instead seeks his "Primal" in relative isolation, tied to the others only by their facilitating example. The group thus becomes a backdrop rather than a direct instrument of change.

Remarkable results have been claimed for primal therapy; and whether these are due to the expulsion of poisonous feelings, as Janov claims, or to a rather more subtle process akin to religious conversion, there is no doubt of its power. That fact that very few people can be treated at a time, and only those who can make a prior commitment to devote three weeks exclusively to treatment, as well as afford a substantial financial outlay, amounts to something of a drawback. But this has to be set against the brevity of the treatment process, compared to the considerably greater long-term investment in time and expense involved in traditional analysis.

Other costs may be greater if less obvious. By its very nature, primal therapy is radical at the cost of any attention to the superstructure of life. Janov's goal is to transform a person's state of feeling; those concerns that form the matrix of everyday life—interpersonal relations, the family, moral dilemmas, specific issues of work, etc.—are assumed to fall into place automatically once the postprimal person gets back to his/her "real self." But as described in *The Primal Scream*, this is a self rather devoid of social interest, one able to live so immediately in the here and now that it becomes indifferent to the whole dimension of striving, struggle and aspirations. And while Janov dismisses these as "symbolic substitutes," mere neurosis, others will recognize them as the rich, ambiguous bed of being human itself.

One cannot be sure that the "real selves" who emerge from the primal cocoon are as zombielike as Janov's description makes them sound. However, there is an ominous fit here—seen no doubt down through the ages and not just in therapies—between the possibilities of enthrallment, conversion, "peak" experiences and the like, and a dangerous attenuation of a person's contact with the maze of life. Thus it has to be said of primal therapy that, for all its wondrous promise, it may ultimately succeed in doing no more than renewing the question of whether its version of "health" is to be preferred to ordinary neurosis.

PRACTICAL SYNOPSIS

For What Kinds Of Problems Is Primal Therapy Suited?

This question has to be approached on two levels. First, insofar as it works with the basic model of psychodynamic treatment— that of putting a person in emotional touch with split-off, lost feelings—primal therapy may be considered applicable to the whole gamut of neurotic problems. And second, since it deals with so much emotion, it can be considered a relative of the human-potential movement in its attack on feelings of alienation. However, since it goes so much further than earlier forms of therapy in the direction of religious conversion, it should only be considered by those who want to undergo extremes of experience and to drastically experiment with their lives. In this respect it is somewhat analogous to classical psychoanalysis, but while the older treatment pursues an unhurried course of self-reflection, primal therapy bores down immediately to emotional bedrock.

Is This Not Just A Faster, Because More Intense, Route To The Same Goal?

No. Here, as elsewhere, the goal is foreshadowed in the method. And in primal therapy emotional upheaval takes prime place as means and end. Though emotional catharsis may—indeed should—affect neurotic functioning, a person should not enter this treatment thinking it is simply an instrument to "cure" neurosis.

Are There Any Particular Types of People Who Are Likely To Be Harmed By Such An Approach?

As a general rule, the more emotionally extreme and anti-intellectual a therapy, the less likely it is to be of benefit to people who have problems that require complex judgments about the real world for their solution. Further, people who are particularly suggestible, or those who are emotionally fragile for whatever reason, are placing themselves in positions of risk in therapies of this sort.

What About Abuses By The Therapist?

For the reasons given above, there are few therapies so susceptible to charlatanism as primal therapy—indeed it seems a throwback to Mesmerism in this respect—although, generally speaking, primal therapists are concerned not to abuse their power. Unfortunately, as primal therapy has been spreading widely, and undoubtedly has undergone many developments from the original model, it is impossible to give any firm guidelines as to where the reader can stay clear of potential abuses, especially by unqualified people who set themselves up as therapists with only a smattering of knowledge and experience. Therefore a special measure of caution is recommended in checking out the credentials of the primal therapist.

11

The Mysticotranscendent Approach

A fundamental theme of many therapies is to get down to "basics," to strip outer layers of experience away and return us to its ultimate inner unity. Neurosis in this light is a distraction standing in the way of the unified core of life. Reich, Perls and now Janov all share this attitude despite their divergences; hence their positive conviction and messianism, and the religious aura which surrounds their therapies.

Some variety of religious feeling has existed from time without end in all the cultures of the world. The yearning for ultimates has been a defining quality of our species, so fundamental that the scientific attitude itself may be only a momentary distraction. Gravest, perhaps, of Freud's affronts to tradition was his insistence that religious belief was merely an illusion, both masking and expressing unconscious concerns that were not only more repellent than spiritual aspiration but more immediately fascinating as well. This claim has stuck in many a throat and inspired a ceaseless counterattack on Freudian skepticism. And no wonder, for Freud undermined the cherished belief that behind the veil of ordinary experiences lies a more valid and precious form of experience— untapped universes of transcendent light.

The mystical tradition at all times has stood for the primacy of the transcendent, and documented it with innumerable examples of other-worldly bliss and doctrines of spiritual attainment. And while this tradition vastly antecedes therapy, indeed quite swallows it up, and will in any event go its own way no matter what relationship is established between itself and therapy, many leading exponents of therapeutic schools have touched upon the transcendent tradition, while others have embraced it openly. Jung's approach is only the most prominent example of a trend that includes Fromm's collaboration with Zen Buddhism,[1] Karen Horney's exploration of Eastern religion toward the end of her life, and Laing's voyage to India. Even a relatively orthodox Freudianism is turned by Herbert Fingarette, in his penetrating study, *The Self in Transformation*,[2] toward an unexpected congruence with Eastern thought. We have touched upon some of these matters in preceding chapters. It remains now to raise a few general themes—bearing in mind the caveat that I am no guide who is retracing his own steps when describing the mystical dimension. This may put me in the category of those who read the seed catalogue instead of planting their own garden, but that risk will have to be taken.

The mysticotranscendent dimension is perhaps even more difficult to pin down than the existential attitude, as it encompasses a vastly broader cultural sweep and has been less specifically defined as a part of therapy. Like existentialism, however, it has become just that—a dimension of numerous therapeutic approaches; and again like existentialism, it has at times been formulated as a therapeutic possibility all by itself.[3] And if the transcendent approaches, taken as a class, differ from existentialism in being more closely tied to traditional religious practice rather than in rebellion from it, they share with existentialism an antiestablishment attitude and a willingness to break into esoteric grounds of experience. In fact at times the distinction may be blurred between the two, each committed to the cultivation of special forms of consciousness. And if we consider that the most ancient and other-worldly approach to the dilemmas of life has in recent years been joined by hard technical and quite new-fangled scientific inquiry into the nature of consciousness and brain function,[4] the situation becomes puzzling indeed.

Of course these puzzles need not concern the neurotically hobbled and socially alienated individual limping through life. For many, the transcendent approach—whether offered by any of the Eastern meditative practices, including Yoga, Zen, Sufism and Tibetan Buddhism, or by variants of the Judeo-Christian mystical tradition—has offered the solace of belief and a coherent approach to the world, while promising relief from neurotic tension. Others, less needful of a framework of belief and ritual, have adopted the artificial aids of alpha-wave conditioning (the elec-

trical waves associated with brain activity during the state of meditation can be monitored on an EEG machine, thus allowing a
person to program his own meditation progress), and (in much
greater numbers of course) some type of "mind-expanding" drug
to achieve the desired calm. And while there may be a world of
difference between the ends of this spectrum, ranging as it does
from the most promiscuous kind of faddism to devotions of indescribable discipline and commitment, there is also a common
thread within all of it that intersects with the domain of therapy.

There is a difference of opinion here. Many devotees of transcendent practice claim that it begins where therapy leaves off.
First clear up the neurotic blocks, by whatever means necessary,
then find the path to the beyond—so goes this line of reasoning.
Others, however, hold that mystical practice achieves the same
kind of goal as therapy, but by a different route, one that simply
takes a person further along the path of enlightenment. Still
others argue that mystical practice circumvents the actual work
of therapy and, by ignoring the real therapeutic task, shortchanges
the patient. Again, as with much in therapy, it comes down to a
mixture of knowable fact and personal value. But what are the
facts here? Does the transcendent approach consist of anything
that can have an effect termed "therapeutic"?

The basis of the transcendent approach, no matter what the
particular pathway, is the attainment of a different state of consciousness, or, more exactly, a set of states of consciousness all
of which go together by virtue of being felt as different from
ordinary waking consciousness in an emotionally compelling way.
The transcendent approach becomes a religious one insofar as
its altered state of consciousness is made meaningful, especially
in the extent to which it may be said to correspond to some general truth about reality as against mere subjectivity.

Obviously a religious elaboration will go a long way toward
structuring the transcendent state of mind, and it will introduce
powerful social effects related to the institutionalization of the
religion. These factors cannot fail to have important emotional
consequences whether or not the objective superstructure of the
religion has any validity on its own terms. It was William James
who observed that more alcoholics have been cured by religious
conversion than by all the medicine in the world. For all the
immense apparatus of modern psychiatry, I suspect the same observation would hold true today.

Although the effects of the powerful social superstructure of religion cannot be ultimately (or in practice) separated from the alteration in consciousness that lies at its heart, it remains important to define this alteration in its own terms. But of course this cannot be done: To define something, one needs words, but the mystical experience is inherently ineffable; words can only suggest it, for in itself it consists of a state of purified awareness, where things have no name. In the mystical state the self, all that we attach to "me," the subject and center of experience, ceases to exist in its ordinary condition of separateness. Instead the person feels himself as extended in a unified field with the rest of the world. Words are tags we put to elements of our experience after the self has become differentiated from that experience; they are, so to speak, attempts to recapture the world from a distance. But what if we feel ourselves as already one with that world? What is the point of words then? Thus the mystical state is nonverbal.

All who have experienced the sense of identity between the knower and the known have not failed to be deeply impressed by it. Many have reported, after their return to the ordinary state of consciousness where verbal representation once again makes sense, that the reality of the transcendent mode is "more real" than the everyday reality in which we find ourselves split into a knowing subject and a known object. Indeed, for the true Buddha, the term "transcendent" itself becomes superfluous. There is no transcendence except for the uninitiate who looks over the wall at something special and not yet his. For, being an uninitiate, he does not know that the wall is only an illusion, and that the whole need for transcendence is created out of the yearning to vault the illusion, and hence is an illusion itself. Once the illusory barrier is dissolved by means of the appropriate devotions, then one is just there—here, everywhere, timeless: one.

Freud the skeptic termed this state of mind the "oceanic experience" and he traced it back to a very primitive stage all of us have gone through in early infancy when the self was just in the process of formation.[5] Freud held that in this stage the baby—especially in periods of satiation when hunger has been assuaged—is prone to experience the sense that he and the breast are one. This experience has all of the essential elements of the later mystical one—ecstasy, the feeling of unity, denial of separation, and, it may be speculated, a heightened sense of reality—and it may be regarded as a genuine precursor of the transcendent state, memories of which could be activated in later mystical modes. Thus the nonverbal state is also *preverbal*.

But (as Freud was careful to point out) it should not be argued from this that the mysticotranscendent state of consciousness has no validity of its own, that it is only an infantile aberration come back to turn the adult away from reality. The most that can be absolutely said is that the infantile experience is the first *occasion* of a kind of subjective enrichment that is potentially available throughout life. In other words, it may be the first of a series of doors onto unified experience, doors that we are free to open at any time to reassert unity. In this light, the transcendent experience itself is not necessarily any less valid than any other form.

On the other hand, it should be said that just because a thing *feels* more real it need not *be* more real. In truth, the whole question of what is ultimately real we may leave to philosophers. All one can be certain of is that down through the ages people have had varying interpretations of reality. Moreover, it seems there have always been two broad classes of states of consciousness—one buttressed by everyday life and divided into a knowing subject and known object; and the other, much more varied, consisting of sexual passion, dreams, trances, moments of artistic creativity, meditative conditions, drug-induced states and so forth, in which the boundary between subject and object becomes to some extent breached. And these latter states are always called "altered," since in all but a few idiosyncratic societies the conditions of everyday life militate against them, or, as in the case of sex, strive to regulate them closely. Of all major societies, India seems to have been the most traditionally tolerant toward altered states of mind, but even there it must be recognized that the *sadhu*, or holy man, is given a special, albeit widely accepted, status.

Further, the meditation rituals have to be continually retaught; they do not come naturally. To put the matter more precisely, they may perhaps come naturally in the biological sense, but in virtually every instance the order of society stands in the way of their automatic realization. And Man, as we know, is a political animal. Society is our "natural" surround. If societies are traditionally more skewed to the transcendent way, as the cultures of the East are said to be, then this consists essentially in having a cultural orientation that gives more weight to the subjective than the objective dimension (in contrast to Western culture, which accentuates the objective). In other words, no culture obliterates the gap between subject and object.

But it is not simply "Society" in the abstract aggregate that rules against obliterating the gap; the everyday fine structure of human relations sees to it that some distinction remains. For each person only becomes a self by separating him- or herself from an infantile condition in which there is no differentiation between the self and the other. Thus we become individuals, hes or shes subject to the endless differentiated roles of social and family life. Only in the grave does this differentiation stop.

Yet, while we are never fully happy with our separateness, we are usually even less willing to give it up on another's terms, since that would mean becoming absorbed into the other, losing one's identity utterly. And this is the great snag in all efforts to impose a subjective unity on the field of reality: they involve *de*differentiating all the objects in that field, making them give up their identity and, in a sense, swallowing them up in the self like ingested food. This is fine until you become one of the objects, which is why societies invariably, and to everyone's relief, put institutional checks on the process of achieving unified experience.

Thus when advocates of the Eastern way criticize the "dualism" of the West, they are proposing as better two kinds of things. One is an ideal, the state of mystic selflessness, or the unity of subject and object, an ideal that can be approached and valued but is simply not given within the terms of human discourse. The other is a realistic goal—namely, taking more seriously the subjective dimension, along with a set of practices that will further subjectivity. Viewed in this light, much Eastern doctrine is equivalent to a Western psychology as seen by a mind that gives greater weight—hence "reality"—to its subjective forms. From another angle, this amounts to asserting the greater interrelatedness of all things—man-nature, male-female, knower-known, nation-nation—as against their separateness and opposition.

What does this have to do with therapy? The answer is complex, as the transcendent state potentially permits a spectrum of experiential states to emerge. At one end is the attainment of the blissful state of reunion and unity; while the other faces the terror of repressed demonic fantasies. The situation is very much the same as having a good or bad drug trip. The agent of change, be it the drug or meditative ritual, succeeds in disengaging the person from everyday expectations and perceptions.

At the same time the focus is different from that of psychoanalysis, where free association of subjective ideas is encouraged but combined with *verbalization*—i.e., made part of an objective communication with the analyst. In meditation, naming thoughts is discouraged. Instead, a purified, special subjectivity is sought through control of one's attention. The exceptional degree of concentration attained by the Yoga is associated then with a two-fold narrowing: first, an attention to the subjective as such; and second, an exclusion from subjectivity of the free play of verbaliz-able fantasy that would result if the situation in all its real diversity were attended to. Turning attention away from the common flow of ideas and images, and placing it instead on the mantra, or simply (if this can be done) on a void, shifts the ordinary balance of our experience.[6] And, as when people are put in an experimental setting where the normal input of sensory data is minimized (as by being floated in a pitch-black pool, temperature 98.6 degrees, with ears plugged, etc.) they begin to undergo hallucinatory changes as the subjective input fills in the objective blanks, so too does the subjective world take over in the meditative ritual.

What becomes of the shift to subjectivity depends on how far it is pursued and with what ideology. Most meditative rituals are well suited to keeping defenses against unpleasant feelings intact, while others run the gauntlet of demonic states of possession. It all depends on the attitude one brings to it, the setting and the intensity with which the ritual is carried out. In the case of blissful quiescence, the individual is in effect summoning up a new, harmonious subjective state to be layered over his old one. If that old one was one of neurotic tension—i.e., one in which repressed destructive forces were breaking through, yielding anxiety, symptoms and inhibitions—then the new state of mind may, so to speak, seal things off again. The transcendent attitude provides a fantasy of reunion to be set against the fear, more or less present in some form in every neurotic situation, that needed objects will be destroyed. Here all is one, so naught can be lost. At the same time the meditator, by turning his attention away from bodily striving, is able to still aggressive and sexual impulses. In this frame of mind he can become convinced that what had appeared to be life's intractable dilemmas are really no problem at all. And the relief afforded by this maneuver can have a reinforcing effect, encouraging further centering of consciousness.

The experiences so induced are powerful enough to bypass the neurotic labyrinth entirely. However, to really work they have to be backed up with a major reorientation in life, else they will accomplish no more palliation than a few ounces of alcohol. Here many might decide that the game is not worth the candle, especially when they realize that to make these changes stick requires substantially more discipline than they had bargained for. As R. C. Zaehner says of the "alleged spontaneity" of Zen Buddhism in his excellent study *Zen, Drugs and Mysticism*, "nothing could be farther from the truth. For the achievement of Zen enlightenment an apprenticeship of gruelling toil is the indispensable prerequisite."[7]

No doubt some minor alteration can be accomplished with proportionately less effort, and to this extent meditation may have some broad usefulness as a quasi therapy. For the frantic executive it may be just the thing to relax him, may even help him cut down on his smoking. But the real changes do not come so readily. And this statement is not so much due to elitist bias as to the actual nature of things. There is simply too much inertia in the world to be wished away by acts of contemplation, even if one found this a worthwhile goal. And on closer examination, what appears inert will reveal a dynamic core, the outcome of active forces, clashing and frozen in combat—forces coming from diverse sources: from the body, from the unconscious mind and from the real, material objective and social world. To break through all this requires more than meditation; it demands a coherent system of belief, discipline to tame the unruly self, and a social fabric to support the whole enterprise. Simple appeals to transcendence, or what Zaehner terms "nature mysticism," ignore the fact that nature is indifferent to good and evil, while the human nature that is summoned up whenever ordinary consciousness is interrupted is just as likely to contain demons as angels.

Thus, if it goes no further than simple changes in consciousness, therapeutic results obtained by the transcendent approach are bound to be either shallow and/or fortuitous, with the worsening that attends the nightmare or bad drug trip always a possibility in the background. And if it does go further, then the social dimension must be introduced—some system of practice, some doctrine, some politic has to be invoked. However, any system that builds on subjectivity is bound to be compromised by the fact that the altered state of consciousness it is designed to secure can only be evoked through a narrowing of attention. For this reason, all mysticotranscendent practices, whether they be religious or therapeutic, depend for their very nature on the subject's not looking too closely at what is going on. The mystic is expected to look *through* things, to see their ultimate unity; not *at* them, to see their particular differentiation and all the meanings that everyday social life attaches.

But if the institutions by which the self is surrounded are to be regarded as a game, or illusion, what about the institutions that make possible this kind of vision?

Such sects are inevitably torn two ways. From one side they propose a dramatic alteration in all forms of human relationship; from the other they depend upon stability and quiescence. The result, in contradiction to the ideology that all is one, is to split their program between a spiritual endeavor that is intensely cultivated and a mundane one that is allowed to pretty much conform to the established order. As an example, consider Tantric Yoga, one variety of Eastern practice often singled out as especially suitable for synthesis with the ways of the West by virtue of remaining in touch with the body and sensuous enjoyment. Of this sect, the great indologist Heinrich Zimmer wrote that it must not be supposed that tantrism "implies any kind of revolution within the social sphere, as distinguished from the sphere of spiritual progress. The initiate returns to his post in society; for there too is the manifestation of Sakti. The world is affirmed, just as it is—neither renounced, as by an ascetic, nor corrected, as by a social reformer."[8]

Now this is obviously a problematic point and cannot be lightly settled, as the career of a Gandhi indicates. To take it up any further with respect to religion in general would be too far afield. But with respect to transcendent forms of therapy, even if—one could almost say, because—they do not take it up explicitly, we must ask: To what extent do the results of the transcendent approach (taken beyond isolated meditation, which is, as we have noted, not likely to suffice) depend upon the alteration in consciousness *per se,* and to what extent upon the influence of the social setting in which that alteration is carried out?

For example, recently the Chilean psychiatrist Claudio Naranjo has attempted to use certain drugs along with psychotherapy.[9] The drugs are "mind-manifesting," in that they facilitate special types of consciousness, without being as disorganizing as LSD or mescaline. Naranjo's aim is to gain the best of both worlds—the deeper access of the transcendent experience and the coming to terms with the objective side of life of psychotherapy. The psychological technique is something like a mixture of Gestalt therapy and psychoanalysis, without the latter's laborious, resistive path of free association and transference analysis—and without the vast output of time and money as well. The goal, as revealed in the title *The Healing Journey*, is the Dantean vision that Freud, too, may be said to have drawn upon. The person voyages through his unconscious, touches upon his personal hell and emerges transformed.

Naranjo's work is highly interesting, albeit risky. Each drug produces its own type of effect, the patients are obviously deeply affected, and one gets the impression of a field that is just beginning to reveal its potentialities. But it is also significant to note that Naranjo leaves out of his account the interpersonal dimension, here in particular the question of transference, but more generally the entire social factor. As with primal therapy, we have prolonged contact between a patient who is undergoing a markedly regressed, infantile form of experience and a therapist (or guru or shaman) who is guiding him, Virgil-like, on his journey. And while Naranjo is not grandiose like Janov, he is even more taciturn on the question of suggestion and enthrallment by transference—indeed, he leaves the issue a virtual blank.

The questions go beyond the direct influence of the therapist. What of the drug itself? Aside from pharmacological dangers (which are not trivial, at least in one instance), can the patient claim that these are his own truths which have been achieved? Is this his genuine inner subjective nature, or is it an illusion that he can usefully embrace? Has the individual actually worked through the resistance to self-revelation, or has he simply blitzed it aside, snatched at what he could and beat a hasty retreat to everyday alienation?

I doubt whether these questions can be adequately answered within the scope of what we now know. In any event, they can never be answered outside the framework of personal and political values. And this dimension is especially pertinent for a choice that involves the devaluation of the entire objective world in all its differentiated misery and splendor.

PRACTICAL SYNOPSIS

Should The Adjective "Practical" Be Applied At All To The Mysticotranscendent Approaches?

In a strict sense, no. But every concrete endeavor makes some compromise with reality; and in the case of transcendent therapy, a whole range of expedients have been devised to bring the mystical attitude into the services of therapy. It may be a weakened mysticism that is so employed, but its consequences remain practical ones.

What Then Is The Range Of Application Of Mysticotranscendent Approaches?

Obviously this varies with the type of approach chosen; and while this is too broad a field to be adequately summarized, a few examples will give an idea.

Meditation alone can have notable positive effects on a person, defined roughly by the phrase "centering of awareness." As noted above, this will improve neurotic feelings, but it is a strictly symptomatic approach and should not be thought the answer in itself to any neurotic condition. Its limits lie in the inability of any isolated individual to arrive at a critique of his life.

Meditation combined with psychotherapy has more or less the same range of application as the therapy itself. It is logically compatible with almost every form of therapy except classical psychoanalysis (see Chapter 3) and behavior therapy (see Chapter 14)—in the former case because it would violate the Basic Rule of verbalization, and in the latter because meditation involves what behaviorism rules out: subjectivity. Similar considerations hold with respect to the use of psychedelic drugs, alpha-wave conditioning and other consciousness-altering rituals—including *hypnosis* (see Chapter 14)—as an adjunct to another therapy.

In *meditative therapies per se,* there is no sharp boundary between therapeutic and religious practice. And since religion has so much more weight in the scheme of things, it would seem most advisable to recommend this treatment for people whose primary concern is spiritual fulfillment and not the alleviation of neurosis, since the latter could only occur to the extent that the former need were met. By the same reasoning, a complex neurotic problem, especially one that implicated the social environment, would be poorly served by a mystical therapy.

Is There Any Way To Choose, For Example, Between The Different Varieties Of Mystical Therapy?

None that I know of, for the reason that each variety is mainly the province of a gifted individual and a band of disciples. As a class the therapies clearly resist systematization, owing to their antiobjectivist quality. The only realistic guide is informed personal opinion.

What About The Role Of The Therapist-Guru? Is It Prone To The Kind Of Exploitation Discussed Earlier?

To an exceptional degree, owing to the ruling out of critical faculties and the stirring up of enormous infantile longing in the mystical setting. Whatever the independent transcendent base of the mystical experience, in practice it is very often associated with the arousal of all kinds of irrational transference feelings. These may simply be added on; but once present they offer a fertile medium for every kind of exploitation, which becomes all the more powerful for being religiously justified.

12

The Social Dimension: Group Approaches

We have surveyed some therapies that aim at an individual's mental state, as well as others that focus on the body, emotional catharsis or some esoteric realm of experience. An ingredient of each has been the social factor, whether seen in the neurosis itself or used as an instrument of cure. In some therapies this factor has played a prominent role—most notably in Neo-Freudian analysis; while in others—one thinks of biofunctional and transcendent therapies—it is more or less read out of existence. Still others—Gestalt and primal therapy, for example—use groups in some measure to further their goals of individual change. But in none of them has the social factor taken center stage. In this chapter and the next, we will consider therapeutic approaches that work *primarily* with the group as an agent of change. This chapter takes up artificial groups brought together for the purposes of therapy, and the following one considers the therapy of that elementary natural group, the family.

Of course all therapy must refer at some point to an individual's search for happiness, else no one could ever be motivated to go through the trouble. But the group orientation involves a qualitative change in scope—a way of looking at people not from the vantage of their individual subjectivity but within a system of relationships with others. We know that while our conscious thoughts go one way, and the life of the body another, we are also pulled by forces over which we have but little control, deriving from our attachment to the community. To ignore these forces only serves to flatten our perspective—it in no sense decreases their hold over us.

The three dimensions of body, mind and society to some extent run their own course. Yet they are just as clearly related to each other, indeed cannot be considered outside of their mutual inter-relation. Freud, though often accused of advocating a narrowly individual, mechanistic approach to psychology, wrote that "in-dividual psychology . . . is at the same time group psychology as well."[1] Whether we have a primary built-in "social instinct" is a moot point. What is not open to dispute is that everything worth noting about us occurs in the context of a social bond. We cannot define human life without reference to its social matrix. Hence, the most individualistic philosophy still has the group immanent within it, if only as the herd of others against whom the in-dividualist is asserting himself.

There is also biology within the group, even if not in the form of an elaborate social instinct. There is nothing more innate and biological than the helplessness and protracted dependence of the human infant—and nothing more impelling to the formation of social bonds. Culture itself is primarily there to regulate the ways of a creature that cannot do without others and needs them in every phase of existence.[2]

But although we begin with this view, it also must be recog-nized that the situation looks somewhat different according to whether we train our sights on the individual or on the group of which he is a member—and it seems to be necessary for us to look one place at a time, no matter how much credence is given to the holistic nature of things. From the individual side, we see subjectivity and fantasy, and we recognize the trace of the social world by its molding of instinctual drives, the internalization of values and roles, and by the whole collection of inner selves that go to make up our one person with an identity. Represented within oneself is an identification with the whole of the society of others with whom one has lived all his life.

From the group side, however, we see this person turning out-ward again: We observe his dealings, or *transactions*, with others; we study the range of *communication* in which he engages; and we observe that the self joins with others to form groups that appear to have laws of organization and behavior all their own.

The group dimension is everywhere in therapy. After all, the therapist and individual patient comprise a two-member group; they are communicating back and forth all the time, and whatever happens as a result—whether it is conceptualized as the movement of orgone energy, the recapture of "Primal Trauma," the revelations of a "true self" or the unconscious made conscious—occurs as a result of that communication. Behavioral scientists have been quick to point out that these communications are the one definitely observable aspect of the whole business. Those who are averse to inner constructions, such as "psychic reality" or the unconscious, prefer to deal with the empirical dimension of communication and the system within which the patient is embedded, rather than the system embedded within him.

Once we turn to this dimension, whole new realms of therapeutic strategy become accessible. Since every neurotic situation ramifies into the social dimension, working with social focus will affect the neurosis. Put some people together and pay attention mainly to the context within which behavior occurs, rather than to its subjective underpinning, and the conditions for sociotherapy have been created.

Of course this is only a beginning; beyond lies something of a free-for-all. It would be hard to think of an approach to human life that has not found its way into the group setting and been called "therapeutic," from multiple psychoanalysis to women's consciousness raising, satanism rituals, mass bioenergetic sessions, primals, nude marathons and heaven knows what else. Each must be saved in his or her own fashion; and the group, with its promise to restore the neurotically shattered bond, is a truly inexhaustible therapeutic resource.

It is also an economic necessity. Society cannot afford to have one-half the population treat the other half in individual, one-to-one psychotherapy, and few individuals can afford it either. This fact added to the staggering incidence of serious emotional disturbances and the need to do something about them makes it clear that group therapy of one form or another is destined to become the major mode of treatment, if it is not so already.

The group thereby becomes the means through which the focus of therapy widens beyond neurosis itself to include all the unfulfilled promises, the loneliness, the loss of meaning, the whole well of unhappiness. Just as the most fantasy-ridden neurosis is grounded in real social relationships, so do many manifestly realistic difficulties in everyday life have their neurotic component. Whatever the mixture, a group can be found that will meet it. The group will provide inner, subjective shifts that affect the neurotic balance, and will offer an infinite range of real social situations to compensate the patient for the deprivations wrought by his neurotic life. The question of whether therapeutic benefit consists more in achieving "inner" change (insight, flow of energy, awareness, "Primals") or in having good, corrective emotional experiences with real people can never be fully resolved. It is certain, however, that groups open the door to an amazing variety of new experiences. And as times change and new problems arise (e.g., returning veterans, gay activists, people in retirement communities, etc.), so will new forms of group therapy emerge.

It would be senseless then to try to present the range of what is inherently unclassifiable. In what follows, only a few representative types of group will be discussed to bring out themes of importance.[3]

TRADITIONAL GROUP PSYCHOTHERAPY

Usually associated with one or another of the psychoanalytic schools, groups of this type form the backbone of group therapy. The group may exist *sui generis,* or it may be composed of patients who are also in individual therapy with the group leader. At times there may be two (or more) therapists, the so-called *conjoint* therapy. This provides a greater range of interactive possibilities.

In group treatment, there is a division between practitioners who do psychoanalysis in groups and those who do group psychoanalysis. The former concentrate on the individual patients as they respond to the group setting, while the latter focus on the group as a whole and let individual themes emerge as they will. Obviously each faction has to cover both sides, since the individual's behavior and that of the group are at all times present in each other. The division, then, is a matter of emphasis and style, since only one side can be attended to at a time.

Thus the therapist who focuses on the individual can point to Mr. X, who is hogging the meeting, and interpret this as a result of a slight received from Ms. Y, who seems more interested in Mr. Z—and he may refer this back to what he knows of Mr. X's boyhood. In other words, he can use the analytic model of individual psychology, with its focus on psychodynamics and the personal past, as a guide.

If, on the other hand, he were the type of group therapist

who concentrates on the collective rather than the individual, he would comment on the *group's* passivity in the face of this triangle, relating to their collective need to remain helpless infants out of fear of their mutual hostility and jealousy. Thus he would be referring each piece of behavior to a lawful phase in their development as a group *qua* group—i.e., a development that will follow certain patterns irrespective of the individual nature of the members, although each group will go through this pattern in its own way depending on its particular makeup.

Although a great deal of important work has been done to define the developmental phases of a small group, there is no theory as yet that approaches the rigor and generality of, say, Freudian or Piagetian development theory.[4] This must have to do with the fact that group phenomena are harder to conceptualize and less reproducible, being closer to history than biology. Still, by calling attention to group life itself, the therapist can work powerful changes while remaining in touch with individual dynamics. No one who has been in a well-functioning group can escape the realization that forces of fantastic power can get stirred up—whether it be a therapy group or one of the many varieties of training groups (better known as T-groups) that have arisen in recent years.[5] The whole spectacle of history and the family is replayed in these artificial settings, all the more vividly for it not mattering in terms of the real, extragroup world. When one is enmeshed in group life, the outside world fades away, the constraints of reality vanish, and less adulterated forms of our inner selves clamber onto the stage. Loyalties reminiscent of groups in war, whose members would unhesitatingly die for one another; raptures comparable to those of the monastery; jealousies forgotten since age four; power plays worthy of a Borgia; tender intimacy one could never muster with one's spouse—it can all be summoned up within the group, whose intense, hermetic influence tends to dissolve the restraints that inhibit us in ordinary life.

Much of a group's development gets played out in reference to its leader. However, most therapists work toward eliminating themselves from the picture, in line with the therapeutic goal of personal maturation. Group members gain doubly thereby, both being less dependent on the authority and achieving identity with him by being able to help the other members. Although transference feelings toward the leader are mobilized more rapidly in group than individual therapy, they are often substantially easier to dissolve, owing to the presence of the other members. It is rather like being a member of a large family, with many siblings and extended relations, instead of an only child whose relationship is exclusively filial.

Why not eliminate the leader entirely then? In fact many groups have done this, while others have minimized the leader's influence. Obviously, this is a possible strategy to further reduce the bugbears of transference and dependency. The only problem is that it also reduces some of the therapeutic leverage. For unless the leader abuses the responsibility that has been placed in his hands (and group therapies, like all therapies, are easily exploitable), the distortions patients project onto them as a result of the transference—the slavish overidealization, the truculence, the provocation, the wheedling for favor, etc.—are nothing more or less than the gist of their neuroses. To deprive them of the chance to experience these attitudes and work them through in the company of others is simply avoiding the reality of neurosis. It would be like treating a red-hot boil with a fan.

The argument may be made that even the best of groups tend to dilute the intensity of individual therapy even as they make it more bearable. It is for practical purposes impossible to expect a group to delve into each of its members' psyches to the depth accessible via the individual approach. It is not just the limited time each can obtain in the session; more fundamentally, the whole attitude veers away from the subjective and toward the contextual—what each does in relation to the other rather than the accompanying chain of fantasies. The two spheres are connected, to be sure, but not identical; and whichever therapeutic advantage may be obtained from concentrating on each, it should be recognized that these are different advantages, each with its own distinct value.

Many therapists have taken the logical step of combining the approaches in hopes of getting the best while avoiding the worst of the individual and group worlds. Thus patients will have one or more individual sessions plus a group session each week. Whatever the potential gains, this expedient dilutes each therapy with the other—i.e., it prevents depth from developing in the individual sessions and evades risk-taking in the group. The point is moot, as it so often has to be in matters therapeutic.

A certain anomaly remains in group experience built upon the analytic model. If one's goal is insight, self-knowledge and exploration of psychic reality, then language, the tool of thought, is an indispensable instrument. Hence Freud's fundamental rule, to verbalize what one experiences. On the other hand, if the goal is, at least in part, corrective emotional experience with others, and if the focus is on context and not content, then words are less important, since there are many other modes of communication and relationship than the verbal. Verbalization now becomes one instrument among many; one, moreover, that may be valued as much for its expressive as for its reflective quality.

In addition, difficulties may arise in a group unless wider areas of communication than the verbal are established. Considering the numbers of people whose main relationship to reality is intellectualization, it should come as no surprise that many analytic groups bog down in sterile verbiage. It may in fact be easier to break through such defenses in individual than in group therapy, unless some other avenues of communication are included in the therapeutic protocol. This is not to say that proper handling of the group analytic model can't get beyond intellectualization, only that many patients and therapists alike have grown impatient with doing so. And with the increasing application of group therapy to problems of normal unhappiness, groups have become the *via regia* for all the expressive goals of the human-potential movement.

ENCOUNTER GROUPS

Here we come upon what W. C. Fields was given to calling an "equine of a different hue." Some of its basic principles have been described in the chapters on Rogerian and Gestalt therapies, and attitudes common to it have been noted in discussing the existential, transcendent and biofunctional approaches. It remains to touch lightly on the *group* aspect which gives the encounter movement its distinctive flavor.

If encounter groups cannot be summed up under one heading, it's because they grow wild, like weeds, thriving on their heretical approach to theory, order and systematization. Hence the resistance to scientific investigation that affects so much of therapy is here raised to a ruling passion.

Nor is it news that such groups constitute a major social phenomenon, albeit one that seems, like acid rock, to have peaked in the late Sixties. It had to. At the rate it was growing then, the movement would have engulfed all other forms of social organization by now had it not slowed. I recall being told during a visit to Palto Alto, California, in 1969 that that modest-sized town sported something like 360 ongoing groups. Most, to be sure, were written in water, and whether the slices of new experience they offered to the people who participated made any kind of long-range difference in their lives—for good or ill—will have to take its place with all the other unanswerable questions down through the ages.

Nonetheless, encountering lives on. And here, subject to even more of the qualifications about generalizing that have applied to the other therapies, is some of its flavor.[6]

The main point to consider is that people do not enter an encounter group as patients seeking help with their emotional disturbances (much less "illness"), but as normal individuals who want more joy, warmth, meaning, spontaneity, etc., in their lives. In other words, they come to add something positive, not to remove something negative. Most encounter-group experts make this distinction, and use it to rationalize the indifference of their methods to the usual therapeutic standards. The problem with this, however, is the same vexing one that dogs our steps whenever we consider therapy: namely, how to distinguish between neurotic misery and ordinary unhappiness, given the fact that each is generally interpenetrated with the other throughout the broad middle band of suffering common to the well-fed middle classes in contemporary America.

Once more we shall have to postpone the issue, except to note that the encounter movement poses a most serious challenge to the assumption that therapy is designed for what has been called "psychopathology," or "mental illness." The fact is that, whether we are neurotic or not, our ordinary life is conducted with a certain degree of tension. Short of the so-called peak experiences, of which orgasm is the commonest example, we are always holding back certain feelings. Even at the apices of life we are often aware that something is still being kept under control, that other feelings lie beyond. And these suppressed feelings always have the quality of being more exciting than everyday experience, hence the lure of the forbidden. In the case of neurosis, the forbidden feeling is rooted in the unconscious; while in normal suppression it is potentially conscious but forbidden by an external source or social convention. Obviously, one can be both neurotic and chafe under external constraint; and in either case one feels somewhat the same: tense, frustrated and bored.

The encounter group uses the group's powerful pressure to remove the ordinary constraints against what we feel to be forbidden. The group not only gives permission, it demands expression, by imposing its imperative of blunt frankness, or openness. To be open means just that: to open the gates that held back the impulse—whether that impulse was to disrobe, touch, curse or be held. And this is backed up by the whole range of reinforcing tactics which give the movement its immense variety: nudity, marathons, caressing, arm-wrestling, screaming, bathing and so forth. If something promotes expression of what has been held back, it will appear somewhere in an encounter group. Some groups, of course, are substantially tamer than others, but they all function by imposing a kind of liberating imperative.

Naturally enough, these maneuvers will shake things up, for the neurotic no less than the bored normal. To enact the forbidden and be told it's a virtue can have a tremendous effect. Impulses on the one hand and self-imposed prohibitions (what we may roughly call "conscience"; more technically, "superego") on the other are generally balanced, although we tend to have more respect for conscience. But since conscience has the thankless task of holding pleasure in check, behind this respect we usually harbor a good deal of hostility to it. But now the balance is reversed, so that the forbidden becomes the good. And who says so? The group. So the group acquires superego power and the individual bypasses his own onerous conscience by identifying with that of the group. Guilt feeling is down, pleasure is up, and narcissism expands to include all of one's cohorts. And it's all all right. No wonder encounter groups appeal.

It should not be thought, however, that the barriers come permanently down. Nobody except the utter fool (who occasionally crops up as an encounter-group leader) would claim that the degree of openness and intimacy achieved in the group setting is simply carried over into everyday life. No, prohibitions must remain, so much so that it is better that the contacts in the group be brief and, for all their intensity, impersonal. The encounter group in this light is a kind of bacchanal, the more vivid for being set off from the rest of the experience.

Yet although the person must return to the compromise of daily existence, the brief shift in his state of balance can have at least semipermanent effect—for the neurotic as well as the unfulfilled normal. Each piece of new experience adds a layer to one's life, and alters what has gone before. To be sure, to the extent that the disturbance arises from fixed unconscious sources—which is another way of saying, to the extent that a person is seriously neurotic—any new experience will have its effect muted. But new experiences, if a person is primed for them and the timing is right, can have a major lasting effect. Thus it is not hard to imagine a substantial breakthrough in neurotic patterns as a result of a relatively brief encounter experience. Sometimes people are just stuck; they need something to happen in order to get moving— much as an adolescent needs to get started with sexual experimentation if he is going to work out some of his conflicts. The effect shouldn't be overplayed, but it needn't be minimized either.

Unhappily, effects of this kind cut both ways. Encountering can turn sour as well as sweet. Individual conscience, seat of the harsh self-punitiveness of the neuroses, is only temporarily put into shadow by the bright light of the group. When this light dims, as it must, some fairly harsh psychological accounts can come due. More immediately, given the nature of what lies under our veneer, encountering in groups can lead to a lot of hostility. Combined with the unhappy tendency of groups to scapegoat, this means fairly often that some vulnerable soul is going to get more abuse than he or she can encounter intact.

No doubt better screening and more sophisticated technique on the part of the leader can diminish the likelihood of negative reactions, but it is precisely in the nature of encounter groups for such precautions to go by the boards. So when doyens like Carl Rogers proclaim how few people get hurt by encounter groups, they may only be saying that *they* run good groups. Or they may be saying nothing at all. A study by Yalom and Lieberman, for example, found that 16 of 130 Stanford University undergraduates who completed encounter groups (of 209 who began) could be considered " 'casualties'—defined as an enduring, significant, negative outcome . . . caused by their participation in the group."[7] This was a careful study, using selected, supposedly competent leaders representing most major therapeutic ideologies. Significantly—in light of the propensity of therapeutic ideologues to claim wondrous results for their techniques—the authors found that "the leader's ratings were a highly inaccurate mode of identifying casualties." Of note also is the fact that there was a low correlation between what a leader professed ideologically and what he practiced; further, those who practiced a highly aggressive, confronting approach (the one most generally associated with encounter groups) managed to accumulate the most adverse reactions, either by attacking vulnerable members or getting the group to reject them (e.g., for not being "open" enough).

Given the high rate of casualties and their seriousness (three students became psychotic), one should think thrice before endorsing encounter groups. This is not to say that disasters do not befall other therapies. They have to, from time to time (though, one might predict, less often), by the very nature of the neurotic balance. Nor does risk eliminate the potential gains of openness and frank expression.

It is another question, though, whether such gains are as singular as they seem. The problem is with the concept of frankness. Freud launched psychoanalysis by compelling the patient to be truthful—to say what comes to mind. But it was soon observed that something in the very nature of being human prevented the truth from coming out. This something worked at both ends of experience. At the expressive end the person could *suppress* his thoughts—not tell them—or lie about them and thus hide them from the objective world. And at the experienced end he could *repress* them—i.e., not even think them, hide them from his subjective self. The rule to speak the truth did not mean then, nor can it mean now, that the truth will automatically emerge if the person tries honestly to express what's on his mind. All that will emerge is what's on the conscious mind, not beyond consciousness. Thus Freud's Basic Rule served mainly to expose the fact of repression, clearing a path for work against it, so that psychological truth would be eventually developed.

Frankness, then, in no way guarantees a widening of mental horizons. It may in fact do just the opposite—narrow them so that the person remains frank and unrevealed as well. No one has an easier time being frank than the person with nothing on his mind. I once attended a talk given by a woman advocating the open, frank, speak-your-mind approach to group relations. It so happened that the group she was addressing was highly critical of her. Thus I was surprised to hear her say in conclusion that she had had such a wonderful time, and found us so supportive and accepting. My first thought was that she must have been kidding— yet she certainly seemed sincere. It then occurred to me that, no, she was not kidding but had probably purchased her honesty at the price of falsifying and limiting her perception.

No doubt a similar pathway can lead a therapist—needless to add, of any school—to tell us quite honestly how wonderfully his patients are doing and how little they have been damaged by his ministrations. And while everyone tends to behave this way when their interests are at stake, it is especially potent in groups, owing to their capacity to take over the critical faculties. Hence the possible tyranny of the encounter group—that it would impose an "awareness" that is heightened yet narrowly turned to the demands of the group. In his urge to reap the benefits of belonging (and in his fear of ostracism), a member can well conform to these demands, which he does most successfully by simply repressing any capacity for dissent. He will then have a clean mind, full of vivid feeling and wiped bare of critical, cluttering thought. In this state neurotic distress may well recede, and feelings of intimacy be heightened, with deep bonds of affection for co-members and veneration for the charismatic leader. The person may even learn something new about the social face he presents to the world. All this and fun too, in a relatively brief time, and at a reasonable price—in monetary terms, at any rate. Other costs remain to be calculated.

est

est, Latin for "it is" and an acronym for Erhard Seminars Training, is the creation of Werner Erhard, a former sales executive who changed his name (from Jack Rosenberg) and way of life and is in process of changing the therapeutic map with his innovation. Of all the therapies considered in this work, *est* is the newest and the least codified—at least I could find no systematic presentation in the literature. Further, people who have taken the *est* sequence, though they seem united in claiming remarkable results, are equally plain in being unable to describe exactly what went on. But for all its mystique, the training involved is perhaps the most highly organized and disciplined of therapies. This paradox probably accounts for its undeniable power in getting people to rapidly confront themselves.

Erhard may be the first major innovator in therapy to owe nothing to tradition. Whatever the significance of this development, it makes *est* hard to classify. Were it not so new, it would deserve more extended discussion in a chapter to itself. I have chosen to include it among the group approaches rather than as a variety of Gestalt or transcendent therapy because it seems, on the basis of my limited knowledge, that the group experience provides the energy for what happens in *est.*

Yet it is dramatically unlike other forms of group therapy. *est* is the first treatment to work with groups the size of a crowd. Some 200 to 250 people, having paid $250 each, gather together for two successive Saturdays and Sundays, essentially locked in a hotel ballroom, sitting on hard wooden chairs, unable to eat or go to the bathroom except once each day. There they stay for perhaps sixteen hours, being harangued, either by Erhard or one of his small cadre of trainers, on the *est* approach. This includes exposure to Erhard's philosophy of life plus a set of directed meditations (usually performed with eyes closed) on the current dilemmas of life. In addition there are periodic confrontations between individuals and the trainer. Expression can be at any level— from emotional sharing of inner experiences to arguments with the trainer—but no one is required to speak out. Thus although the experience is *in* a group, and doubtless could not occur without the group structure, it is not so much *with* the others in the group as it is with one's self.

The philosophy promoted by *est* is no more than basic human-potential subjectivism. To quote Erhard, "Consciousness is all there is, there *isn't* anything else."[8] We live mechanically, by belief and intellect, instead of trusting to experience, to being. We are responsible for our lives; what we see as necessity is really a choice. *est* strips off the pretenses we make to hide truth from ourselves, and puts us back in touch with being—and so forth.

What translates this rather ordinary—and arguable—point of view into something dynamic is Werner Erhard's insight that people can be moved by placing them in a group of such size for so long, with so little ordinary tension release (in addition to what goes on in the room, *est* exacts a pledge not to drink, smoke or take drugs for the duration of the training) and subject to the influence of a trainer who has neither doubt nor inhibition about telling them that their lives don't work. In sum, *est* has discovered how to compress and intensify the basic psychotherapeutic maneuver of breaking down defenses. From one side the tedium, haranguing and privation are battering resistance; while from the other the group experience leads a person to dissolve his or her individuality, and its stubborn arrogance, and to psychologically merge with the others in the room. The very size of the group, along with the technique of *est*, tends to keep those others in a rather undifferentiated state, hence promoting a sense of union with them. The result for the individual is a state of openness, receptivity—and weakened discrimination. Into the gap steps the *est* philosophy, embodied in the trainer and, behind him, Werner Erhard.

The most sophisticated judgment in the world is no match for such conditions—which indeed make their effect felt, not on the intellect, but on the soft space that yearning occupies behind the mask of reason. Numerous people who have undergone *est* tell of how they attempted to dispute the trainer, only to become confounded and yield. What such reports leave out is that the most powerful intellect necessarily becomes puerile under the conditions of the training. It is like playing tennis with your side of the court under water.

This fact does not make *est* pernicious; it only demystifies it and makes it comparable to, say, revival meetings or other large-group phenomena under the sway of a leader with a powerful ideology. The most titanic intellect may be the instrument of self-deceit, and could use some overhauling. And from all accounts, *est* is a potent force for putting people in touch with their deeper feelings and releasing personal energy. So long as it is not construed as a proper approach for severe emotional disturbances (in which instances changes could easily become uncontrolled—a danger of which *est* people seem aware, as indicated by their emphasizing their work as *training*, not therapy), or as a substitute for sustainedly working through one's conflicts, *est* would seem to be a positive addition to the range of therapies.

Once more, however, the problem arises of keeping some sense of proportion. No surer sign exists that *est*'s fundamental means of change is crowd psychology than the adulation afforded Werner Erhard. We are told that he shuns being worshiped and feels that *est* will be destroyed in essence if it becomes yet another institutionalized belief system. Those are fine sentiments. Yet the fact remains that he has *essentially* created yet another mass-psychological religious movement; and if he will not be its idol, someone else will have to take his place if the training is to keep its hold on the great body of spiritually deprived people searching for transcendence who constitute the therapeutic clientele in to-day's America.

If this seems extreme, consider the following: "And one man is the undeniable source of it all—the energy, plans, special *est* language, content of the training. All that happens springs from Werner. The staff member who has been with him the longest admits: 'If Werner died tomorrow, we'd disappear the day after.' On the other hand, all concerned are perfectly confident that Werner will not check out tomorrow, so in charge is he of his universe."[9]

Glad tidings—for all except the Arthur Janovs.

PSYCHODRAMA

Only the briefest mention shall be made here of this complex and highly developed procedure, with its elaborate system of directors, auxiliary and multiple egos, its stage settings and its philosophical superstructure. To describe it adequately would exceed my grasp of the matter.[10] Again, a few themes must suffice.

Psychodrama can no more be separated from the name of J. L. Moreno than psychoanalysis can from Freud. And while Moreno failed to make quite the same impact on civilization as did his Viennese elder, this gap was easily spanned by his titanic self-regard. Compared to Moreno, Arthur Janov is a veritable Uriah Heep of self-effacement. One does not, however, have to grant to Moreno his demand to be stood among the gods to recognize that he was a real innovator. His career was long enough to let people forget that he had virtually launched the emphasis on spontaneity and here-now experience that now dominates so much of therapy. Moreno is said to have coined the term "group therapy" itself, and his development of the concept of *role-playing* has had impact far beyond the perimeter of psychodrama.

Roles are expectable patterns of behavior belonging to a certain social context. To the extent that we live in a complex social world, so will we have to play a multiplicity of roles—child, parent, friend, teacher, lover, boss, customer, etc., etc. Reality forces us by and large to play these roles according to its dictates—i.e., nonplayfully. Even neurotic situations, insofar as they are grounded in reality, involve one or more of these roles, this time in conflict. Thus a neurotic youth may experience a need to play the role of a perfect, highly-achieving hero with respect to his mother, and an abject, passive failure with respect to his father. All neuroses can be conceptualized usefully in this manner. And although role psychology cannot possibly reveal the subtlety or range of mental functioning, it will do as a galvanic representation of the social state of affairs in which the person finds himself.

Moreno hit upon the idea of letting a person re-create the conflict of these roles in the here-now controlled therapeutic setting. Since a small society is being created, a group is needed. Here, in contrast to other forms of group treatment, the members devote themselves to the role dilemmas of each in turn. In the instance cited above, one member would play the mother, another the father, and one or more others would be auxiliary ego and play out one side of the conflict within the patient, while the patient (now called, appropriately enough, the "protagonist") played the other, then switched, and so forth. The situation is a little reminiscent of Gestalt, except that instead of the psychological focus on awareness, we have the psychosocial re-creation of problems in living.

Treatment proceeds by gradually redefining the key situation, letting the person attack it from a number of angles until a sense of mastery is achieved. The therapist has special tasks here, suggested by his new title of "director." He has to plan the shifting scenarios in accordance with what the protagonist reveals at any given moment. At the same time he interacts therapeutically with the protagonist and the rest of the group. These others, while waiting their turns to be protagonist, meanwhile identify intensively with the protagonist and his situation. After the dramatic session, there is generally a regular group meeting where feelings are discussed and the situations referred back to outside life.

The holiday from real consequence is what allows people to get so intensely involved in role-playing. As with theater itself, we can experience life all the more vividly when its focus is narrowed and removed from practical aims. Some of the multiplicity of the self is thereby unfolded, shifting the neurotic balance and allowing therapeutic work to proceed. Benefits in psychodrama and other forms of role-playing undoubtedly result also from the mutual helping and learning in the group. Where a group is involved in a clear task, as in psychodrama, the members can band together much more effectively and keep under control all kinds of conflicts that would otherwise complicate the life of a freely developing therapy group. This renders the group more cohesive and less likely to get into regressive patterns or into transference binds with the leader. It also, of course, deprives the members of an opportunity to work some of these patterns out within the group. But then, they have their scenarios in which to do so.

TRANSACTIONAL ANALYSIS

Transactional analysis is the undoubted smash hit among therapies. Eric Berne wowed them in the Sixties with *Games People Play*, while the Seventies belong to Dr. Thomas A. Harris, whose *I'm OK—You're OK* was number-one best seller for more than a year in its hardcover edition, vaulting the million mark in sales. Whatever else it is, transactional analysis has to be the therapy that fits best into modern American life.

At first glance, nothing grandiose meets the eye. TA appears to be a respectable, pragmatic therapy compounded out of a number of familiar elements. Its creator, Eric Berne, was no guru but a trained Freudian analyst who branched out into group therapy and developed a psychological shorthand for describing the transactions—i.e., structured reciprocal interactions—between people in groups. The psychology that emerged from this is less Freudian than Adlerian and Sullivanian, and quite recognizable. It emphasized environmental response ("strokes"), feelings of security, self-esteem and inferiority (the "OK" and "not-OK" postures) and analysis of the ego and consciousness (the Parent, Adult, and Child—"P-A-C"—ego states) rather than infantile sexuality and the repressed unconscious. ("Transactional Analysis focuses on the ego and on consciousness because these concepts explain and predict behavior more effectively than do psychoanalytic concepts," states a scholarly presentation.)[11] But there is certainly nothing remarkable about this trend anymore, sixty years after Adler set it going.

Nor is there anything dramatic about the group technique in which the therapy is grounded. TA is brief (usually small multiples of ten once-weekly sessions), to the point (a focal contract, faithfully obeyed, is decided upon during the first session) and educational. No nonsense here—no masturbating, screaming, rolling around, few whole-group comments by the leader, and no god-playing either; the leader stays close to the level of the members.

There is a lot of give-and-take by everybody, good humor is the rule and verbal exchange the means as the members analyze each other's "scripts" and "games"—the self-perpetuating (and defeating) patterns of transactions through which they have sustained their lifelong non-OK-ness. The goal is to give the adult ego state—the mature, realistic, ethical part—hegemony over the harsh, enjoining parent and the reckless, impulsive, selfish child. With this stance, the individual is said to become able to choose for the first time the TA *summum bonum* of "I'm OK—You're OK," and so breaks out of the neurotic trap.

What then can be so appealing about this therapy that promises no ecstasy, nirvana, orgasm, primal or superordinate self-knowledge, only the ascension of the Adult? Have Americans become so seized with a burning desire for maturity that they would storm the bookshops and keep Dr. Harris on top just to learn that they are merely OK? The answer has to be yes, but this only rephrases the question: Just what is meant by being OK, anyhow?

Pondering this question begins to give us some insight into the attraction of TA. For being OK means at heart that one is judged well by peers—is acceptable to them, belongs with them. It now strikes us that TA appeals precisely by staying away from the extremes of experience, and so unifying people, through its groups, with the compact majority in the middle. Its energy is directed to promoting an ideal of normality and developing means for getting people to rapidly identify themselves with it. Despite the appeal of special experience—deep analytic insight, orgastic potency, Gestalt awareness, mystic selflessness or the Primal Scream—when the count is in, ordinary acculturated ways will win out. The tortoise, remember, beat the hare. Many therapies make use of the appeal to normalcy, but TA best succeeds, indeed raises it to a veritable art form as it puts so many back into the fold of OK-ness.

One facet of Berne's genius was his talent for popular exposition. He did this by stripping his language bare of terms that referred to hidden mental phenomena, or were at a high degree of abstraction. TA aficionados like to claim that this demystifies psychology and gets it down to where people can use it. This is no doubt true; at least it establishes a set of symbols that can be readily employed by groups of relative strangers. It is also true, however, that by means of this strategy a critical dimension is lost, since linguistic usage can never achieve any distance from what is obvious. Further, the group will be bound together at the level of immediately evident, hence socially sanctioned, experience. A demystified language is one in which nothing baffling is recognized, no hidden meanings that can't be rapidly worked out by script analysis. Any mental regression, any drift toward the repressed unconscious, whether it be an erotic fantasy or some transference attitude, is thus headed off and diverted into the category of "game," or transaction.

A comparison with psychoanalytic practice may be instructive. Contrary to the allegations of TA writings, a well-trained psychoanalyst scarcely ever uses theoretical discourse in the clinical setting. Plain English is the rule, and the language of the patient's own life becomes the currency of the analysis. Theory is reserved for generalizations about clinical experience, which are made in another setting.

Berne's innovation was to use the theory of TA directly in the clinical setting. That is why it is commonly called "educational." The special terms—P-A-C, OKs, strokes, injunctions, hooks, etc., etc.—are taught in the first session and serve to define what ensues. Theory and practice collapse into each other. Hence we get a highly practical theory, close to everyday events, and an equally theoretical practice, with everyone analyzing everything: "She's hooked your parent"; "Now you're playing Rapo" (one of Berne's games); "You just gave out a cold fuzzy" (an insincerely affectionate "stroke"); and so forth.

Some interesting consequences follow. Mysterious dimensions of the mind are enjoined, as has been noted. Equally important is what replaces them. For in lieu of psychological depth we have the terms of Berne's theory. People *become* these terms; they turn into a collection of games and ego states, all going around together in the life of the group. And the terms are drawn directly from current consumerist society. People now become creatures with "rackets," who accumulate "trading stamps" with their neuroses so they can cash in later. They revolve in this merry circle, like characters in a TV situation comedy or game show. One almost hears the nervous canned laughter. This is positivism carried far beyond the mirroring technique of Carl Rogers's unconditional positive regard. Rogers's positive fact was the person's self-reflection—i.e., it was primarily psychological. Here the facts about people become reified—thinglike precipitations of living human reality, machines really, suitable for technocratic tinkering. Indeed TA succeeds in doing what all of science has yet to accomplish: It finds a direct link between ego and brain function. Harris, for example, refers to the Parent and Child as "tapes," programmed directly by early experience, unmediated by any wishful fantasy. The ego state is in fact nothing but an actual nerve network of memory traces in the brain.

Such dehumanizing implications as have been revealed in the foregoing analysis are, to be sure, a far cry from the professed intentions of TA proponents, many of whom regard their therapy as a great liberatory praxis. Of course they do not all agree on what liberation means. Claude Steiner, for example, wishes to use TA to promote some kind of social revolution (for Steiner, and other "radical" TA therapists, the Parent is differentiated to include the Pig Parent, an incantation against evil authority);[12] while Thomas Harris is down the line for Democratic Liberalism and Progressive Christianity.

Yet they all share a missionary zeal which seems to contrast at first with the homespun pragmatism of the therapy—until we recall that therapy in general shows little inclination to rid itself of the idea of salvation, which springs so naturally to mind as the pathway out of the neurotic trap. Thus it is pragmatic in the extreme for a therapy to promote allegiance to some great and good cause while at the same time flattening away all insoluble inner contradictions and joining its devotees in a flock with a few handy rules. So many religions have done it for centuries, there is no reason why therapy shouldn't try. Harris's success is due to his ability to pull out all the stops: "The problems of the world—and they are chronicled daily in headlines of violence and despair—essentially are the problems of individuals. If individuals can change, the course of the world can change. This is a hope worth sustaining." And, touching upon Paul Tillich's description of religious grace, Harris adds, modestly draping his thought with parentheses, "(I would like to paraphrase [Tillich]: Do you know what it means to experience I'M OK—YOU'RE OK?)"[13]

The key to this therapy is the direct imposition of a moral standard as the prime instrument of change. Moralization is an enormously common, and to some extent timeless, element of therapies. In some measure it informs all of them. Again, however, TA succeeds in doing the job with a special élan.

The Adult in TA is the element of moral change. But who is this Adult, if not the ideal principle of the bourgeois order? He is the individual whose change will do the trick, since there are of course no fundamental problems in the social order, itself. Cleverly opposed to the Parent, which as the repository of irrational morality serves as a kind of stalking horse, the Adult is able to stand for good rational morality, backed up by the group and sanctified by the high purposes to which the therapy aspires. Thus strengthened, the Adult will tame the Child—i.e., the impulses—and sustain repression to the point where from the practical standpoint neurotic suffering may abate; while from the theoretical end, the unconscious can be read out of Berne's universe. Repression is what civilization, for what it's worth, is supposed to accomplish in the first place. Its introduction here means that the virtues of society have to be taken seriously within the terms of the therapy. God, morality, the bourgeois ideal—all are invoked to hammer down the lid. And the Parent-Child so stifled becomes a puerile revolutionary, with his excessive criticism and irrational impulses.

By making superego and id theoretical abstractions, Freud was able to critically comment on the psychohistorical play of forces. By reducing them to banal concretizations—actual ego states—Berne, Harris and even Steiner, who professes radicalism, turn them into buffoons in a situation comedy. To be OK—I, you, everyone all together—all we have to do is accept the "adult" definition of reality; in other words, conform to the established order.

That therapy appeals most which is best in line with the advancing edge of the culture to which it belongs. If this edge happens to include game shows, situation comedies and technocratic fiddling—along with a confused idealism—then the therapy should embrace the whole mélange and apply moral pressure to mold patients into identity with it. That the results may become conformist, simplistic and mechanistic is unfortunate, but doesn't rule out the possibility of their being "therapeutic" as well—it only calls into question the values inherent in therapy.

The above considerations apply to group therapies in general, and to all the therapies since they include a social dimension whether they acknowledge it or not. TA at least has the virtue of being straightforward; many "psychoanalyses" have done the same for all their lofty rhetoric. The nature of the social process means that no small group can be regarded as primary—i.e., autonomous with respect to the larger society. Society is the only really primary group—the ocean compared to which all other groups are cups of water. Another way of putting this is that every therapy has a political content, which, given the nature of things, is liable to be concealed behind its manifest assumptions. And therapies such as TA, which are so potentially conformist, may be directly exploited for political ends. They have become, for example, instruments of corporations, prisons and the military for making people get along better—i.e., for stifling dissent.[14] The same applies directly to behavioral therapies, as we shall see in Chapter 14, and, indeed, potentially to all therapy. For any instrument of liberation can also be used for domination.

PRACTICAL SYNOPSIS

What Factors Favor The Choice Of Group Therapy In General Over Individual Treatment?

Group therapy is likely to be less expensive. It also offers both a readier access to interpersonal neurotic patterns and a different vantage on those patterns: We get to see ourselves as others see us. The group is more dramatic, more filled with intense feeling, action and risk-taking, thus it is likely to produce behavior change more rapidly. There are certain aspects of our lives that are barely touched upon in individual treatment but which can be exhaustively dealt with by the group—our dealings with peers being one obvious example. Other problems, such as conflicts about authority, that may be unworkable in the one-to-one setting may be worked out in the group owing to the more complex social field.

What Factors Favor The Choice Of Individual Therapy?

Group treatment cannot go as far or deep into a person's life as can individual therapy. The reason is not simply dilution of attention by the other members. Equally important is the fact of the group's identity. This depends on the composition of the group as a whole and exerts a powerful influence over everything that goes on in each member. Thus, in every kind of group, the particular difficulties in outside life for which one sought treatment may become sidetracked owing to an absorbing interest in the preoccupations of the group.

How Is Group Experience Modified By Therapeutic Philosophy?

Group work has been done under the aegis of virtually every school of therapy, including all the psychoanalytic schools. The only exceptions might be some forms of existential analysis, with their extreme cultivation of individual subjectivity. In every case some influence of the parent school will be evident with respect to goals, method, what is selected as fit for discussion, and so forth. Every group tends to develop a dominant ideology. Where a therapeutic school is involved, the world view of that school greatly influences the group's ideology, and all that takes place will be interpreted according to it. This will be so whether individual sessions are combined with group ones, or whether the treatment philosophy is applied strictly through the group. As noted above, there is no *a priori* way to predict whether mixing individual and group therapies adds up to a net gain, since enough might have been diluted out in the mixture to bring their sum below the level of either one alone.

How Does The Particular Structure Of The Group, As Exemplified, For Instance, In The Task It Sets For Itself, Modify The Experience?

Profoundly. To the extent that a group is given a mutually agreed-upon task—say, figuring out life scripts in TA, developing scenarios in psychodrama, or mutually considering their collective unconscious—it has been removed from the spontaneous development of the social ties between its members. This may make for more cooperative relations as the members band together against the common task—and this in turn has an emotionally supportive effect. However, as elsewhere, one gains at the surface but sacrifices a wider and deeper look at social relations. The situation is exactly analogous in analytic treatment of the individual: One both gains and loses by focusing attention instead of allowing free association.

What About Educational Groups, The So-Called Training Or T-Groups? Are They A Substitute For Therapy?

There are many workshop or training experiences in group relations, most of which offer abbreviated but intensive opportunities for a person to learn by actual involvement. The great majority insist that they are not offering therapy or a substitute for it but rather a special type of education in human relations. Therefore a person with a neurotic disturbance in living should not think of a T-group as an answer, and should only approach it on its own considerable merits. However, the matter cannot be that simple, since all therapy is educative, all people are more or less neurotic, and every group experience re-creates to some degree the basic terms of the neurosis, thus allowing some therapeutic gain to be made but also raising the possibility of worsening the conflict. Therefore, it would be self-deceptive for one to deny that some therapeutic interest is attached to T-groups. The important thing is to keep some idea of its boundaries and to seek a training experience that will responsibly try to keep to its professed goals.

How Can One Avoid The Tyranny Of The Group While Obtaining The Group's Powerful Supportive Help?

The dilemma here arises from the fact that the two are so intimately related. Tyranny in group life can come from two sources: very intense experiences within the group that dissolve one's powers of judgment; and conformism of the group as a whole to social mores. In either case the individual member may feel much better without having altered the neurotic problem that brought him or her for help.

Fortunately this combination need not hold; group experience, in other words, can supply an enriching closeness that does not violate one's freedom. The key factor is not so much the ideology of therapy as it is the qualities of the group leader. If the leader is inert, passive, confused, dull or whatever, then no emotionally powerful group experience is likely to ensue. At the opposite extreme, if the leader is highly confrontative, grandiose, verbally aggressive or manipulative, the experience is likely to be intense but tyrannical. It is important to sense what—for want of a more precise term—one has to call an "ethical" quality in the therapist, coupled with sensitivity and interpretive skill. This is obviously difficult, given one's original neurosis and the unpredictable nature of the group itself, hence many experiences either fall short of help or create a certain amount of havoc. But one can at least try.

What About Leaderless Groups? Do They Not Avoid The Authoritarian Trap And Better Promote Intimacy And Freedom?

Given the range of such experiments, no one can tell. A leaderless group can produce its own "Lord of the Flies" as easily as it can a communal breakthrough. No matter how inspirational, the experience will not provide the precise approach to neurotic difficulties that a skilled leader using a therapeutic system can offer. It is probably in the direction of leaderless group experiences that genuine innovations will be made, however, even if these not be along the lines of the classical therapies.

13

Family Therapy

The subject of this chapter is of a different stripe from what has been presented up to now. For family therapy is not so much a school of therapy as a basic redefinition of the therapeutic task itself. No individual steps forward to lend his name to this body of doctrine, values and techniques; and the many leading personalities in the field probably disagree among each other almost as much as do the various individual therapists about matters psychological. What they do not disagree about, however, is the conviction that, by redefining the object of therapy from the individual to the family, they have accomplished a major breakthrough.

Nor are we dealing here with a "dimension," like the existential or transcendent attitudes which, in commenting about the nature of therapy, seemed to move away into other areas entirely. Family therapy can stand by itself as a complete system; it is aggressive about changing people's lives in the most direct sense, and it prides itself on being able to deliver the best mental-health care for the majority of disturbed people.

In this regard the family approach has been making great headway within the profession. Quite young as approaches go (scarcely any family treatment was being done twenty years ago), family therapy has, without the heraldry of best seller or cult, been steadily expanding its grip on practice throughout the vast run of public mental-health agencies, while becoming an important mode of private practice as well.

The reason for this is twofold. One, family therapy is an effective and logical device for treating, if not all, at least a good portion of emotional troubles. And two, the family in modern America is falling apart; everyone feels it, and many rush to the banner of a technique that addresses itself to the crisis.

No doubt, if the family in America were as stable today as it was, say, a hundred years ago, there would still be logic to family therapy. It is inconceivable for a neurosis to exist without some root in disturbed familial relations; and it is thus quite likely that affecting the ongoing pattern of these relations will have a powerful effect on neurotic experience.

But this does not account for the zeal of the family therapy movement or the clamor for its services. The family therapist gets his authority nowadays only in part from his skill in dealing with disturbed behavior. The lion's share comes because he is willing to step into the breach of family chaos that afflicts advanced industrial society. He stands for the restoration of the primary unit of social life; and in a time when nothing in social relations makes much sense or can be taken for granted, this is no mean service.

Not that family therapists must work toward the sanctity of hearth and home. On the contrary, many are actively concerned with communes, group marriages, etc., all the forms of experimentation in human relationships that have arisen in response to the crisis of the family. The point is that they are concerned with *relatedness* itself, as against the inner, subjective life, and it is relatedness that so perplexes us, and seems to be running out of control. To be sure, the individual, too, is under attack. However, psychoanalysts had already staked this territory out, leaving, for all its contribution, a mighty gap to be filled.

Important areas of knowledge arise dialectically in response to historical crisis. The chaotic state of personal relations and roles is only the most direct of the challenges out of which family therapy has sprung. Equally important, and far broader, is the whole ecological predicament.

The idea of universal interdependence has been gradually gaining ground, spurred by the ominous recognition that human society is rather too much like a cancer on its host, the earth. A vast current of contemporary work—in biology, game theory, communications research, as well as ecology itself—has centered around the theme that what counts most in an entity is its formal organization and its interdependent exchange of information with other entities. Summed up broadly under the rubric of *General Systems Theory*, this point of view has found a logical extension to the area of emotional disturbance by way of that naturally occurring, ecological, informational and thoroughly impossible unit, the family. Following the lead of Gregory Bateson[1] and others,[2] the ecological or systems point of view has become the ruling philosophy of family therapy—and a good deal of social and community psychiatry as well.

Family therapy amounts to a fairly major break with tradition. For all their differences, therapies from Freud to Berne had sliced the individual one way or another, found a set of forces (drives, ego states, blocked Primals, orgone, or what have you) at play, and influenced behavior through these forces. Systems people may or may not take inner forces seriously; but they are as one in focusing not on the individual but on the pattern of relationships in which he lives. A thoroughgoing systems family therapist would even take exception to the proposition that neurosis is merely rooted in the family, and to its implication that the two—neurosis and family—are related as a plant is to soil. For them, the family is everything, alpha and omega, and neurosis an aberration within it that merely happens to select one vulnerable member for its expression. In some extreme variants of family therapy, the individual ceases to have much meaning at all, being regarded essentially as a gear within a watch.

Method generates thought. In other species of therapy the person is placed in a setting against which his inner life unfolds. The outside setting becomes symbol, and the inner self the reference point. In psychoanalysis the transference is projected onto the analyst; in Gestalt the self appropriates its own projections through dramatization; in biofunctionalism the body takes the stage; even in group treatments the others of the group become test cases, simulations of the actual key others in one's life. The very unreality of these settings gives the inner life its sway: Because the analyst is not the real father, the fantasy father can come out of hiding; or, pushed by the group and leader, the Gestaltist (or psychodramatist, or analytic group member) can let himself play at feeling, or being, or doing what the fantasy son in relation to this fantasy father would feel, or be, or do. And so what seems important to these therapies is the unfolding of the inner self.

In family treatment, however, the real father is there in the room, as are the mother, or the spouse, the child, the sibling, the grandparent—in some combination or totality. What comes to the fore then is the actuality, not the fantasy symbol. Both are always immanently there, but a method necessarily focuses on one and not the other; indeed, the more you hold one dimension down, the more the other comes up. When the real people are there in the room, added to only by the therapist (or, as likely, therapists) whose role it is to force attention to emotion-laden issues, then the situation takes on its social-systemic and not its fantasy-projection form. The family-system neurosis is the analogue of the individual disturbance, equally bizarre, but separated by the leap that occurs between individual subjectivity and social organization.

The statement that they are *equally bizarre* needs to be understood. As crazy—and stable—as the inner life may be, so crazy—and stable—will be the family analogue, expressed however in terms of its own set of laws. And the craziness in each case has to do with the conflicting claims of individual and group. There is a level in the individual that cares not for the real needs of the others in the family group; and there is a level in the group that cares equally little for the needs of the individual. No one in the typical family relates to the other simply in terms of his or her individuality; each sees the other not only as he or she is, but also as sucked into the vortex of the self, with all its conflicting passions.

Thus the mother becomes the lost unity for the child; the boy a rival to the father as well as the ideal being he never could become; the husband an inferior father for the wife; and her son the man she felt her own mother wanted her to become; the wife a mother to the father, whose son thereby sees him as a jealous sibling and, at the same time, an admired hero; and so on and on.

Moreover, this is only a small part of the subjective side. The observer sees something else, its objective form, played out, like any real drama, not just in words but in gestures and cues as well: The mother raises her eyebrows at the table as she passes the carrots; the son reaches across the father, who scowls to threaten the boy and slackens his jaw to draw forth nourishment from the mother, who accuses the son of greediness as she bends forward, tilting her breast to the father, who complains that the carrots are mushy as the son spills his milk, provoking a bitter attack from father for his clumsiness and an indulgent defense from mother, who pours him another, bigger glass, turning her breast now to the son and her backside to the father, who tilts his chair away from the table and stares off into space beyond the son, who is just now beginning to have the asthma attack that will be diagnosed as an allergy to carrots.

The systems family therapist will observe (in the office or at home—there being little reason except practicality against, and much logic for, seeing people in their natural habitats) until he is clear about the rules governing the behavior of the family system. He then intervenes, focusing not on subjective feelings but on the discrete behavioral operations between family members. The goal is to interrupt the circular feedback of pathological communications, then replace it with a new pattern that will sustain itself without the crippling limitations imposed by the rules of the original setup. If, for example, mother interrupts Sally every time the latter expresses any initiative, and father averts his eyes, and if this is followed by some piece of psychotic behavior on Sally's part, and in turn by father's becoming solicitous, mother grumpy, and Sally, calmer now, venturing forth once more only to meet mother's interruption . . . then the systems family therapist may instruct the family to let Sally write out her activities for each day in the morning and to have mother and father publicly agree, not just to let her follow them, but to together insist that she does. The important thing is to give everybody his or her due, and to impose a program that will not go beyond the effective capacity of the system (as might occur, for instance, if they were told that Sally was to be in charge of everything, or that she had to move out of the house before she or the others were ready), while at the same time altering the rules in a new, self-sustaining way.

Given the immense complexity of family life, a great premium has to be placed on therapeutic flexibility. Some very sophisticated judgment has to be used to develop programs that may seem simplistic but are in fact subtly adapted to the given situation: an alteration in seating arrangement; change in the tempo of communication; detailed attention to the manifest subject matter of what is said; even counterinjunctions such as those we use in dealing with children: "Go ahead, eat this whole box of cookies," instead of "Don't eat the cookies." A boy who compulsively soiled himself, despite all of the family's outrage and prohibition, stopped soon enough when the therapist ordered him to make in his pants and bring the product in.

The therapist who works in this vein can, and must, take a role rather different from the classic impersonality demanded of the analyst. The family therapist is right there in the front lines, heaving and hauling his way through the clutter of disturbed transactions. He has to be actively involved, for it is only the force of his influence that can oppose the weight of the system. The family therapist can't wait around for a "family unconscious" to rise toward him; he has to introduce new energy into a system that will otherwise roll right along on the path it has carved for itself. This, of course, is a recognizable and time-honored role, that of the wise man of the clan—the mediator, venerable, judge, or what-have-you.

I do not wish to give the impression that family therapists see eye-to-eye on all these techniques. There is ample disagreement here, much of it centering about the role of psychoanalysis.[3] Despite the ascendance of the systemic star, a sizable minority conducts family treatment with an eye toward some variant of psychoanalytic principle. For now, at least, they are swimming upstream; but the fact is, once we begin to look at the problem of emotional disturbance from the side of the family, more than just systems theory comes into view. Yet it also becomes quite apparent that any individual approach leaves much of the trouble out of the picture. Therefore, since people are often drawn to practice family therapy out of concern for precisely those things that the intrapersonal, subjective approach leaves out, they tend to be less than sympathetic toward psychoanalysis.

It is inherent in the analytic method to neither give directions nor impose values. Action is downplayed and at times considered a definite hindrance to gaining self-knowledge; and the real world is deliberately put into the background. Other forms of therapy (even group therapies), though they may frequently encourage activity and freely lay on values, share with analysis an inability to apply any direct leverage to a person's relationship with those closest to him. As a result we frequently see people who have become thoroughly "enlightened" by their therapy and yet make little or no effort to deal with their personal reality. A man may gain insight into the manifold unconscious sources of a lifelong inability to feel close to his father; and this knowledge may make a real difference in his life so that he will become calmer, less hard on himself, more productive, closer to other people. Yet he may still find himself unable to feel close to his father, even though he has learned that the breach between them is not as hopelessly wide as he had imagined it to be. So he simply continues to avoid the relationship.

It may be said by analysts that this means the man has not achieved full insight into the problem and is still sufficiently riddled with infantile anxiety to have to avoid dealing on a present-day basis with his father—in other words, he may need more, or better, analysis. But the fact remains that a great many analyses—and other therapies—stop far short of annealing family relationships. No doubt this has something to do with the therapist's lack of leverage with which to influence a person's dealings with the real world. After all, the analyst has forsworn imposing directives on the patient. Moreover, the essential goals of the treatment are said to be met when the transference neurosis to the analyst is resolved as best as it can be, and there is no reason why this optimum state has to wait upon perfection in family relationships.

More fundamental, though, is the fact that the family system itself, not to mention the other people in it, goes its own way and, behaving by its own laws, is only indirectly affected by what happens in the individual therapy—and then not always in the most harmonious manner. Countless marriages have broken up because one spouse changed faster than the other in individual treatment, or because both realized—separately—that they were never that happy with each other in the first place.

While this might be just fine for an individualistic ethic, and while many marriages were from the beginning dreadful mistakes from whose bonds everyone would be better off for being released, the claims of the family—including, especially, the children—would have it otherwise. From the value position of the family, might not have treatment as a couple, or family, have had a higher chance of keeping them all together more harmoniously? True, this might have forfeited a number of other possibilities, including deep exploration of one's unconscious. True, too, that such individual exploration might also have worked to yield greater strength in the relationship—a wife who learns to discriminate between what she wanted from her father and what she wants from her husband being more likely to live harmoniously in the here and now with her spouse.

But it's also true that neither Freud nor analysis ever promised to make people live more harmoniously together, only to make the unconscious conscious, and id into ego, and so to uproot the substratum of neurosis. Yet, no matter what the state of their inner minds, people also suffer from actual relationships which are expressed in the immediate transactions of family life. And since the family today is in a chaotic state as an institution, there are numberless people desperate as to how to set things right. As individual therapy isn't supposed to do this (except according to its most fatuous popularization), family treatment is bound to flourish.

But in their haste to cash in as messiahs, zealots who abound in the family movement often fail to realize that the conditions of life set some serious limits to what they can accomplish. Whenever a therapeutic school begins trumpeting itself as the answer to the riddles of existence, you may be fairly sure that some sour note is being drowned out. In the case of the systems wizards, what is left out is history. This is done from two sides, one of which we will touch upon now and the other at the end of this chapter.

The eagerness with which some family therapists read the individual, subjective, psychoanalytic unconscious out of existence is only partly explained by the understandable parochialism that comes from having discovered important new territory and by resentment at what psychoanalysis does not do. More pertinent is the fact that to include the unconscious would undercut the fond, sustaining hopes for perfecting human beings through current family intervention. Freud recognized that some major part of each of us is locked, not in our actual, current family, but in the fantasy family of the past; that our unconscious mind is actively turned away from the present by means of repression and is actively hidden as well. In a sense then, the unconscious relishes being ignored by students of human behavior.

But the power of unconscious thought does not mean that what is conscious, reality-based and current is unimportant. Quite the contrary; unless current, conscious reality counted in an important way, the unconscious would have nothing to hide behind. Hide it must, and likes nothing better than to have a sturdy present-day reality to mask itself in.

Thus, every family transaction has a multiple aspect, one part hidden and not belonging to the present, yet attaching itself to it. The Oedipal bond, for example, is not to the real parent—this aging individual who is carrying on the current family system—but to the young, firm man or woman of long ago, who lives on in memory, not even as he or she was back then in reality, but as transformed by infantile desire.

The family system meanwhile rolls along in the present, as systems theorists rightly insist, with its cues, rules and feedback loops. But precisely because it is a system of its own, the family is disjunctive from another system, the wishful one behind repression. And this split is what generates emotional conflict.

The sticking point is that the mental system Freud discovered doesn't want anything to do with the conscious, reality-based system. It won't communicate with it—a great sin to family therapists. You can fiddle till the cow jumps over the moon with who sits where and how mother twitches when Sammy interrupts father—and Sammy will keep yearning for the lost monumental mother and father archived in his unconscious thoughts. His life may improve, he may feel stronger and better able to repress his nagging demons, everybody may function better—yet his tangled repressed wishes will remain, and be a part of him that family treatment—at least as it is generally construed—can scarcely touch.

But while family therapy, like all therapies, is a limited endeavor, it still remains a powerful modality. It is particularly well suited for the management of severe emotional disorders such as schizophrenia, where the individual patient is so difficult to reach, the handling of everyday reality itself is so much in question, and the family unit is usually so obviously in need of help. This is not the place to discuss schizophrenia, except to note that the manifestly psychotic patient is quite generally found to be embedded in a family matrix whose members cannot truly individuate themselves from each other. Straightforward individual treatment in these instances either has to stay on a superficial level (where it can effectively be combined with drugs) or run the high risk of getting mired in a quicksand of transference. For these reasons, family treatment has a special value here.

We can see the systems-theory logic of family therapy unfold in the vast number of situations where an individual is trapped in a net of multiple factors—social, biological and psychological. And it should come as no surprise that the net tightens as one descends the social ladder. Hence family-systems treatment will often be a first line of approach to the emotional problems of the poor,[4] countless numbers of whom have been pointlessly subjected to ersatz psychodynamic treatment when they need immediate material support and practical intervention to keep going. It is the most obvious point in the world, yet somehow easily forgotten, that psychological dynamics require a fed body if they are to have any energy.

Family therapy is also a possible recourse, needless to say, for many instances of marital disharmony or overt generational problems, such as various disturbances of childhood and adolescence. Further, it would be a logical choice for some conditions, such as certain cases of alcoholism, which are intertwined with marital discord and where the individual is not well motivated for other types of treatment. Unfortunately, alcoholics are often not motivated for any kind of treatment, least of all being confronted by a spouse—but this takes us into problems of special application that usually have to be decided on the fine points of an individual case.

Being anything but hidebound, family therapy has been subjected to modifications far too numerous to relate. Indeed family treatment can be adapted to almost anything except the (quite common, of course) situation where no family is present or where the individual insists on being seen for himself alone. One of the more promising modifications is the multiple family group,[5] which combines the two principal modes of sociotherapy and is especially suited, if only for economic reasons, to the therapy of schizophrenia.

Another quite logical extension is the family-network treatment of Speck and Attneave.[6] Here the extended family is brought together, not just the nuclear unit. Key individuals from outside the family structure itself may also attend. From forty to sixty people may fill the room, focusing at times upon problem members, but ultimately on the question: What is the entire family all about? Where has it been? Where is it going? And what can the members do about the present crisis? Although this therapy obviously requires heroics of organization and stamina, it is undoubtedly an intriguing venture.

One part of its program is of particular concern. If the whole extended family can be brought in, along with key outsiders, can we draw the line anywhere? Isn't all of society the logical network? Some family therapists are not loath to take up the challenge, believing that their field will prove to be the Rosetta Stone for a unified approach to all levels of human organization.

But here comes the other level of historical amnesia from which the family approach suffers. Not just the personal history twisted into unconscious fantasy, but the history of society, too, stands as a barrier against any naïve extension of the family system across the whole human landscape. The family is just as much a plaything of society as is the individual. If the family is breaking up in contemporary America, it is through no simple inner contradiction of its own, and certainly not because we haven't had enough instructional manuals, courses in family dynamics, family-therapy workshops or family-network gatherings. Nor is it a matter of communication. It is fundamentally because of the demands of the social order imposed by monopoly capital.

I say "fundamentally" because the forces society sets loose on the family system do not appear as immediate givens, any more than do the demands of the personal unconscious. They act rather as larger-scale dislocations and prevailing currents of influence, as the jet stream, say, determines climate. Class society built upon profit has always been ruinous to family relations among those excluded from power. This trend continues full swing, especially in urban ghettos; and the modern development of monopoly capital and the consumerist economy extends the trend to middle-class families as well. The family is pulled asunder by currents that appear in everyday life as impersonal economic (and therefore supposedly "rational") imperatives, such as the need to separate work from the home by great distances; to have a highly mobile, interchangeable work force; indeed, to do dehumanizing, alienated work. An equally powerful aspect descends as the ethos of consumerism—which is not just to buy things, but to sell one's self and so make the person into a commodity, enjoyed for the moment and then discarded. Here too is a system, but one for which fidelity in relationship is anathema, as is steadfastness, discrimination, or too much integrity—except as it relates to delivering the product at a profit. Moreover, consumerism forces each generation to disparage the previous one. Without this attitude, the craving for new goods could not be generated.

But the family is also useful to monopoly capitalism—useful as a piece of bourgeois ideology to build a TV series upon, and materially useful as a breeding ground for reliable workers and consumers. Hence even as it gets torn down as so many sand castles against the waves, a clamor arises to keep the family from dissolving completely.

The family therapist is caught in these crosscurrents as well as in the winds blowing from the personal unconscious. Viewed as a system all its own, the family looks wondrously stable; but when regarded as an uneasy mediation between the radical demands of the individual and those of society, its existence becomes much more tenuous, although still necessary to both its masters.

Small wonder then that so many family therapists take refuge in their particular systems, venturing into social theory only so far as would be compatible with the goals of social work. Even Laing and his group, who have done the most to implicate the larger world in family pathology, stopped well short of bringing any genuinely radical political/economic analysis to bear.[7] Indeed, since Reich's Sex-Pol studies in the early Thirties,[8] precious little has been done in this direction, and the best of it comes out of feminist critique.[9]

The result is that most training programs for family therapists are even more unaware of in-depth social analysis than of depth psychology. And thus, although these therapists can be of considerable help to individual families, their pronouncements on the family as an institution are often conformist and confused. Indeed, the therapist who thinks that his technique can be extended to the care of society, or even to the rescue of the family as an institution, is not simply whistling "Dixie." By drawing attention away from where the real struggle lies, he may be perpetuating the problem instead of helping to resolve it.

PRACTICAL SYNOPSIS

What Are The General Advantages Of Family Therapy?

One advantage is that it tends to be relatively less expensive and briefer than individual treatment, at least that of the analytic kind. It also enables a person to focus more directly on the real behaviors that affect life with those closest to him. Certain aspects of the emotional world that appear right away in family treatment may remain inaccessible to any form of individual therapy, or even other group therapies. At the same time, the transference factors which beset so many individual and group therapies can be substantially blunted in a setting where the real family members are the object of concern. In no other form of treatment does the therapist have more rationale for acting in an ordinary social way.

In addition, family therapy allows for a more comprehensive approach to other kinds of environmental problems besides the interpersonal. And finally—if this is one's value—family treatment tends to promote more responsible attitudes toward other people, in contrast to individual therapies whose emphasis on the self may pass over into selfishness.

In sum, family therapy may be considered the most pragmatic of all the therapies.

What Are The Main Situations
Where It Is Useful?

These have been noted above, but to recapitulate: Family treatment is useful for schizophrenia, where people in the family are not that well individuated; for all those instances where the family unit itself is jeopardized and people are more concerned about its security than about their separate development; for families where a host of social and economic problems complicate psychological ones; and for many types of intergenerational conflict, including a wide range of emotional disturbances in children.

What Is The Status Of Children
In Family Therapy?

This partly depends on whether the treatment will focus on the parental couple or the whole family unit. Both are legitimate varieties of family therapy, and in every case children will be affected insofar as their parents are affected. Indeed, the bulk of emotional disturbances in children is transient, and often much of it can be modified if parents work out their own behavior. Needless to add, this can—and should—happen when the parent is in individual treatment, as well as when the couple is treated.

But it happens to a greater extent when the children are directly included in family treatment. Here, of course, the matter is qualitatively different, as the child's behavior itself enters the concern of therapy. This approach makes sense in cases where the child's interaction with other people in the family is part of the problem, and also in those cases where the child seems to be the principally afflicted one in the family, the so-called designated patient. Often the child's symptom—say, some behavior disturbance such as a phobia about going to school—is like a fever chart for trouble within the family as a whole. On the other hand, parents all too often displace their own problems onto the children and become defensively preoccupied with them. In this case, including children directly in the treatment may make it more difficult for the family to come to grips with the very problems that may be really troubling the children.

It should be stressed however, that judgments of this sort are not easily made. Thus in general a consultation with a clinician trained in child psychiatry should be sought whenever a child's behavioral disturbance becomes notable.

Isn't Sex Therapy A Form Of Family Treatment?

Much sex therapy is a variant of family treatment. See Chapter 14 for further discussion.

Does Family Therapy Compromise Goals Of Personal Growth That Might Be Found In Other Individual Therapies?

Obviously it has to alter these goals. But alteration needn't imply compromise, only a different value structure and a different path out of the given neurotic situation. Family therapists argue, with considerable logic, that a very genuine individual growth can be achieved under the aegis of their treatment. Until people examine their family relationships fully, they are likely to remain enslaved by them. The promotion of a more mature mode of relationship within the family offers a definite version of a rather universally held vision of emotional well-being within our society—that of individual freedom coexisting with interdependence.

How Close Can The Goals Of Family Therapy Be Then To A Psychoanalytic Treatment Goal?

Since Freud's psychoanalysis was from the beginning a study of the family within the individual, there is a logical connection between psychoanalysis of the individual and a psychoanalytic version of family therapy. For obvious reasons this cannot be conducted as a psychoanalysis, hence different sorts of self-knowledge will be gained, having less to do with deeper unconscious wishes and more with the way those wishes are played out in a hidden way within the family. There would be less to do then with fantasy and the body, and more with the complexities of dependency and power. Because of family therapy's firm grounding in social reality, it would be unwise for a person to expect from it the particular goals of individual treatments, whether these be the self-reflectiveness of psychoanalysis, the breakthroughs of Gestalt, or whatever.

What Are The Hazards Of Family Therapy?

In general it entails fewer risks than the individual therapies, simply because the family itself is adapted for security. Of course stormy feelings can be stirred up, and upsetting confrontations and shifts in power relations might occur, but these would have to be classed among therapeutic effects. However, there is a trend associated with this that should be watched for. Since the feelings within the family unit are so intense, and the structure of the family itself intrinsically conservative, it is easy for simplistic and conformist solutions to leak into the practice of family treatment. Too many family therapists find it congenial to act like a kind of superparent. This would be the other side of that pragmatism which is one of the treatment's main assets; and insofar as it amounts to a shortselling of what a person can get out of the therapeutic encounter, it amounts to a definite drawback.

14

Behavioral-Directive
Therapies

When all is said and done, therapy of every sort comes down to people influencing other people in a controlled way, and adding new, learned behavior to their repertoires. A set of assumptions is always formed about the "real" nature of the emotional problem; and a set of procedures is carried out accordingly. All therapy thus involves some set of directions by the therapist and some process of learning by the patient, shaped by the directions. Subjectively speaking, we say that a new layer of learned experience is placed over what had happened before; while from the objective side the same can be said for observable behavior.

All therapies, then, are learning therapies. Only some, however, deserve to be called "behavioral-directive." This distinction is reserved for therapies whose assumption is that the *essential* emotional problem lies in something observable. The treatment then sets out to influence what it has decided to observe.

In behavioral-directive therapies the therapist engages in a certain activity focused on the observable source of the emotional problem. He thereby separates the problem from the patient. The problem becomes some attribute of the person, something he *has* rather than what he *is*. In the psychoanalytic therapies, by contrast, the whole person is under concern—the neurosis is me, or, at least, in me; in Gestalt the neurotic sphere is the self's awareness; in biofunctionalism, the body—which is not separate from the self; in TA, in a game-playing ego; in family therapy, in the family in which I exist. In each case, the whole person is involved.

In behavioral-directive therapy, however, the person and the problem are at different levels. The problem becomes objectified, while the person stays out of range. The person "owns" the problem, so to speak; he brings it into treatment, makes some kind of agreement with the therapist to have "his" problem looked into, and meanwhile leaves some part of himself in the waiting room. Since the problem is never construed as part of the whole self, the therapist is given license to attack it aggressively and without heed to subtleties of relationship. He can be rather more like the dentist who freely assaults one's mouth with hammer and tong, having entered into the implicit contract that it is the physical, possessed mouth on which he is working, and not the possessing, oral self.

A moment's reflection will reveal that where other therapies tend to drift off into religions—i.e., they eventually get involved in questions about the ultimate purpose of life—behavioral-directive therapies, by delineating the problem as something observable, move in another direction entirely. Here the slide is to medicine and empirical science, and to a biology that pursues, not the absorbing wholeness of nature mysticism or biofunctionalism, but rather the discrete physical-chemical body, object of experimental investigation.

Behavioral-directive therapies need not go all the way into biology, however; they may well focus on social interaction or some psychological factor, even on moral content. In each case though, the problem lies in something that can be delimited, directly observed and immediately affected by therapeutic influence.

The behavior-directive approach is immensely appealing and undoubtedly accounts for the vast bulk of naïve correctives routinely applied down the ages: "It's only your nerves"; "You're tense because you've been working too hard—take a rest"; "Stick this pin in this voodoo doll"; "Forget about it—it's only your imagination"; "What you need to do is turn over a new leaf"; etc. All of these are unlettered examples of the behavioral-directive approach. If we recognize that such bromides would not be so immensely common did they not afford some gain, and appreciate the potential amplification of that gain by more sophisticated variations on the theme, then it may be agreed that this last of our topics is by no means the least, but may well inherit the therapeutic earth. Here is a skimming of variations.

SOMATIC THERAPY

It is not my purpose here to take up the immense, elaborate and as yet only partially understood component of emotional disturbance that can be studied by biological science and influenced by biological treatment such as drugs, shock treatment, psychosurgery and the like.[1] We will have to rest with the bald assertion that there has to be such a component. It has been fairly well proven that a distinct inherited somatic predisposition exists for schizophrenia, while some forms of severe depressive illness are clearly inheritable. And since emotion has a somatic leg in the nervous and endocrinological systems, affecting that leg will alter emotional input and, with it, emotional disturbance of all sorts. To ignore this level in the interests of a pure psychologism or environmentalism is simply to fly in the face of truth. An ostrich is an ostrich whether he belongs to the tribe of pure naturists or that of the nurturists.

What we have to ever-so-briefly consider is not the element of somatic truth about emotional disorder but rather the therapeutic strategy that uses it as a source of authority—in other words, a behavioral-directive approach that, by seeing the physicochemical body as the heart of the problem, offers to the therapist a perspective from which his directives can have a primary organic hue: somatic therapy.

First of all, somatic therapy is big business. Nothing can relieve a guilt-wracked and confused family more quickly than being told that their psychotic child is primarily suffering from a bodily disturbance that is no one's fault and beyond their control. Nor will anything clear a harried physician's mind—or fill his pockets—faster than dispensing a biological directive ("You're suffering from nervous tension") and backing it up with a glossy, multicolored pill or two to put the patient into a pleasant and obscuring fog for a while.

Secondly, there is the even bigger business that embraces this shamanism—our fabulous drug industry, of whom it has been justly said that it has a virtual license to print money. Such is the working of consumerist culture in the modern age that the drug industry has been able to effectively colonize large areas of consciousness within both the medical profession and the general public. The former territory is secured by the heavy financing of professional associations (only look at the volume of ads in their journals) and the inundation of every physician with such a flood of dubious and shallow free literature as to constitute an ecological hazard to our forests no less than a blight on the mind. Meanwhile the general public (doctors included) is swept up by the general ingestive ethos of consumerism and the special torrent of patent-medicine commercials. When we combine these forces with the tendency of many psychologically active drugs to become at least mildly addicting (by means of the powerful psychological reinforcement that comes from having one's problems blotted away, only to depressingly return once the drug wears off), it will be readily apparent just why the discreet form of pushing that passes under the name of pharmacotherapy flourishes so.

Again, there is a rational ground for the use of drugs. Everyone goes through times, for example, when anxiety and tension are such that a sedative is in order. For the use of a sedative in such circumstances to make sense, however, the crisis had best be brief and the main cause an external one. In instances of sustained emotional agitation a more psychological and social approach is the wiser course, and the sedative drug would tend to obscure this need. However, at the further end of the spectrum, drugs other than sedatives are definitely useful in the management of certain severe disorders—phenothiazine for schizophrenics; lithium for mania; tricyclic antidepressants for so-called vegetative and psychotic depressions; and so forth. The same could be said for electroconvulsive therapy which, for all its odium, is in certain instances all that a reasonable and concerned psychiatrist can offer. Some of therapy's more zealous advocates find it convenient to ignore the fact that in the real world things get so bad for so many people that, whatever the "ultimate" cause in disturbed social relationships, the suffering individual has to be helped by organic means, or not at all. Ignorance of this reality may make for a glossy, sweet theory that is little better than pills.

But if the base for organic treatment is to be rational, then it also has to be limited. The rational use of organic treatment would never be paraded as therapy in the sense we have been developing the concept here, with ideological value or social influence. Nor would somatic treatment pretend to be other than what it was—a humane and limited expedient, indeed a last resort in a world that too often can afford no better.

Hence the problem with somatic therapy is that, like many approaches, it so easily slips past its rational bounds. The need to reduce moral, psychological and political dilemmas to an organic base is just too strong. It meshes too well with the entire technicized drift that characterizes modern forms of oppression, whether these masquerade as soviet "socialism" or the technocratic wizardry of our own state. In each case (much more pronounced in Russia) labeling some deviant "biologically disturbed" is a surgically neat way of removing him from the body social. By eliminating the human dimension and substituting for it a trumped-up imperative of objective science, such labeling clears the way for quashing dissent, whether by psychosurgery, some clever chemical, or by the mainly psychological modes that we shall touch upon later in this chapter.

In any case, the danger inherent in the behavioral-directive reduction needs to be grasped, even though it may only dimly apply in the vast range of therapeutic instances. To return to more everyday applications, consider a behavioral-directive therapy that combines a physiological-behaviorist analysis with psychological counseling to approach one of the most perennial of problems.

SEX THERAPY

In the years since William Masters and Virginia Johnson brought forth their major studies, *Human Sexual Response* and *Human Sexual Inadequacy*,[2] their program for an objective approach to sexual ills has become the basis for a widely practiced and growing therapeutic strategy.

There is certainly no lack of a clientele. The peculiarity of the sexual force in humans is that, while it is the strongest source of pleasure and the very glue of relationships with others, it is endlessly plastic and not essential for the maintenance of individual life. As a result sex is at once the most easily disturbed of functions and the one whose disturbances are the most easily put aside. Nothing fascinates people more, and nothing is a greater source of misery once basic survival needs are met.

Since sexual dysfunction can be associated with the widest spectrum of causes, ranging from simple ignorance to intractable psychosis, it is only natural for an equally wide range of treatment approaches to have arisen. Indeed, what held back the development of sex therapy was not so much a lack of rationale as widespread shame and reluctance to feel entitled to greater sexual happiness.

That has largely changed with the so-called sexual revolution. Whatever its tangled roots, the new attitude toward sexuality explicitly includes the recognition that erotic pleasure should be had by everyone. And the sex therapies are an attempt to realize that expectation. Quite pragmatically, they stay in the here and now; regard sex as an objectively attainable, demonstrable procedure that can be speedily treated; and prescribe a relatively precise set of directions designed to bring about rapid change. In short, they are behavioral-directive therapies: A person *has* a sexual problem, it can be specified, techniques can be developed for overcoming it; and if a person can follow directions, the problem will get better.

Since the great bulk of its practice is with married couples, sex therapy should be considered a special type of family therapy (see Chapter 13). In fact it makes use of the two modalities—behavioral and family—in a mutually supporting way; harnessing the social power of the marital tie, yet keeping it limited by focusing on the objective side of sexual functioning.

Although sex would be nothing but dull reflexes without fantasy's secret yearning and its dissolution of the separateness between lovers, the objective side is no less necessary. Indeed, it is the ever-changing tension between the actual and the imaginary that keeps the sexual fires going. Without actual and gratifying copulation, sexuality eventually burns itself out in hopeless frustration.

And this is exactly what is still happening in a horrendously high proportion of marriages. The pattern is too familiar: In the earlier years, guilt and shame—in part socially induced, in part stirred up by a neurotic developmental conflict—are dealt with though avoidance or inhibition of sexual function. In the marriage itself—which may have been too hastily pursued because of sexual anxiety ("Better to marry than burn" still sticks to the Western conscience)—the inhibition shows itself as unsatisfying performance; and instead of the patient, loving process of mutual adjustment necessary for good marriages, the difficulties in performance become the occasion for a self-perpetuating cycle of embarrassment and recrimination. Often sex is jettisoned to save the marriage, and the couple settles down warily to live in low-grade bitterness. In former days people often lived out their lives in such quiet desperation, making do with good works. Now, all too often the marriage ultimately goes down the drain.

Clearly something had to be offered for this sexual misery. Just as clearly, conventional psychotherapy, though it may work well in many instances, is not the answer on a broad scale. Aside from questions of time and expense, psychotherapy cannot effectively limit itself to any one particular area, such as sex; for another, its view of this area is too limited, leaving out the crucial actuality of the sex life between the marital couple. Thus traditional psychotherapy is both too ambiguous and too subjectivistic to get at the problem in any generally effective way. Biofunctional therapy (see Chapter 9) on the other hand, while addressing the problem directly, was not subjective enough; further, by cutting off the social dimension it makes it impossible to get at the real facts of the matter; and finally, it was simply too radical a treatment to appeal to more than a limited clientele.

Into this gap stepped Masters and Johnson. Their great contribution lay in staking out a middle ground that encompassed the biological, psychological and social factors in disturbed sexual relations. More important, they were able to keep each factor in the proper proportion for therapeutic success in a great middle range of cases.

Who are these cases? In general, sex therapy is for couples whose sexual life is significantly marred by frustrating practice, yet whose relationship remains fairly intact, at least intact enough to sustain them through a mutual examination of their difficulty. They are people who suffer from the effects of inhibition or ignorance at a previous stage of development but have since matured enough to benefit from relearning. It should not be expected that such marriages be free of neurotic factors, or even that these factors be solely the result of poor learning or frustration. The only criterion is that neurotic elements should not have become overwhelming—in short, that there is the capacity for communication, the will to work and some specific behavioral defect to be worked on. And just as the sexual failure can amplify the neurotic tendencies that may have given rise to it in the first place, so is sexual success capable of lulling a neurosis to sleep through a combination of heightened self-esteem and the discharge of tension.

Since there are so many possible sexual incompatibilities, and so many factors to be considered in each of them, we can do no more here than suggest some of the practice of sex therapy. The key in every successful case, so far as I can tell, is an artful mixture of psychotherapeutic, behavioral and physiological methods. The behavioral-physiological part of the treatment, based to a large extent on Masters and Johnson's pathbreaking experimental studies of sexual functioning, includes various directed exercises for enhancing erotic arousal and diminishing unwanted behavior. The former is called by Masters and Johnson the "sensate focus"; while the latter includes techniques such as that discovered by Semans in England for diminishing excitability in the prematurely ejaculating male.

It would be a great mistake, however, to conceive of the therapy simply as the passing on of a few technical hints for better sexual performance. This was certainly not Masters and Johnson's intention, nor does any effective sex therapist practice it as such. What makes the physiological and behavioral techniques effective is rather the psychological setting in which they are carried out.

Sex therapy aims at creating an emotional climate whose first and foremost role is to demystify sex, to make it more matter-of-fact. The treatment usually begins with an elaborate and specific examination of medical and sexual functioning. Thus from the beginning the couple's attention is shifted to objective fact and away from fantasy. They are encouraged to see their sexual problem as something outside themselves that they can attack together. This strategy tends to immediately reduce the mutual recrimination that has been souring their relationship, and to introduce cooperation in its place.

But the whole venture would still most likely come to naught were it not for the influence of the therapist—or therapists: Masters and Johnson consider it best to work as a team. They believe, quite correctly I think, that an indispensable feature of the treatment is to give each spouse an equal share of the responsibility and therapeutic opportunity; and that for this purpose it is advisable to have a male/female treatment team. In this way each partner has a therapist of his or her own sex to identify with, and won't feel too threatened and/or seduced by the therapist of the opposite sex. (Obviously the situation could get much more complicated, but this arrangement remains a useful ideology.) Since in the sex-therapy clinics that have sprung up across the nation this strategy is not always followed, it should be pointed out that its advantage is not an absolute one and that the same goals can be pursued by one sufficiently skilled therapist of either sex.

However the therapy be organized, it stands or falls on the ability of the therapist(s) to instill an attitude of confidence and, most importantly, a moral conviction that the couple is entitled to a better sexual life. Learning new techniques is an essential arm of the therapy, both for its own sake and as a way of putting to rest the neurotic fantasy structure that is always at least potentially present. But this repression of noxious fantasy cannot really be carried out without the authority of the therapist. In effect—and at times actually—the therapist has to urge each spouse to be selfish, to allow him or herself to do things that inhibition and morality have long forbidden. At the same time each partner must be made to feel that his or her own pleasure is for the greater good of both. Unless this ethos is imposed with therapeutic activity and finesse, all the technical details of sex therapy are just calisthenics.

The chances of sex therapy working are best when the difficulty has a clear behavioral aspect, such as premature ejaculation or vaginismus (an involuntary spasm of the vaginal muscles, making penetration impossible). To the extent that subjective factors are also present, the success of sex therapy becomes more problematic. Spite, self-destructiveness, revenge and other neurotic attitudes call into question the couple's motivation or ability to work in the behavioral mode, and in such cases other forms of therapy are more likely to be of help.

It should also be pointed out that, despite all that has been learned recently, sex therapists, like psychologists in general, have an easier time understanding male than female sexual behavior. Consequently it is generally simpler to treat men than women in a sexually behavioristic way. Nonetheless, ample numbers of people of both sexes have been helped by the demystifying techniques of sex therapy, and, so long as its limits are kept in mind, it remains one of the most distinctive advances in the recent history of therapy.

One of these limits has already been implied, and it is well to conclude this section by making it explicit. By demystifying sex, Masters and Johnson brought it into the scope of objective science. But they also had to lessen the importance placed on the dimension of fantasy. By making fantasy less important one can, in a sense, make it go away; and for the purposes of a therapeutic strategy which values pragmatic results, this may be a sound approach. However, individuals or couples entering sex therapy should bear in mind that they are being asked to forget as well as forgive. It may be practical wisdom to do so, but it may also entail loss of self-reflectivity, not to mention that sense of madness which makes sex so interesting. Finally, a person should bear in mind that what may be practical in one sense may be mechanistic in another. Sex therapy abused can "heal" by trapping eros in the technology which has been both the pride and bane of our civilization.

DIRECTIVE THERAPY

Perhaps we should call this "directive therapy *proper*," since it is based on the idea that, if the relationship with the therapist is so important in therapy, then it is logical to ground technique on the simple application of his authority to neurotic ills. This is indeed the most elementary kind of therapy and undoubtedly the oldest. It will often do in a pinch, as when a physician I knew, weary and disgusted with the endless work of a New Year's Eve in the hospital emergency room, was confronted by an obviously hysterical woman who had come in shrieking, "I'm blind! I can't see!" Drawing himself up to his full height, he pointed an imperious finger and in his deepest and most convincing voice solemnly intoned, "You are not blind! You can see!" Whereupon—you guessed it—the woman ecstatically cried, "I can see! I can see!" and rushed back out into the night. A complete cure, purely directive.

Directive therapy is behavioral without having to postulate an observable locus of behavioral disturbance, such as the brain, one's "nerves" or faulty sex technique. Simply leaning on therapeutic authority accomplishes the same. Each directive is, perforce, directed at something; it creates a target simply by virtue of being aimed. The target becomes the patient, who is there, expectant, yearning for the sense of order that can be conjured up by the therapist's word. And the patient directed becomes, for that time at least, an object for the therapist.

The most fundamental mode of directive therapy is suggestion, the process by which the therapist guides the patient's awareness toward accepting a version of truth about his condition. Suggestion—and direction itself—is a part of every therapy. The questions are: How big a part, toward what ends, and by what means?

Hypnosis or *hypnotherapy* is our current term for the original,

Mesmerian psychotherapy, which became part of Freud's route to the founding of psychoanalysis. Although Freud dropped it because its results were too limited, transient and artificial—or were they just not interesting enough?—hypnotherapy itself went right on and shows no signs of dying out.

The essential feature of hypnosis is that it induces an altered state of consciousness by means of a technique that affects attention, such as repetitive suggestion.[3] This gave Freud a window on the unconscious, and it can still be used for such purposes. In hypnotherapy proper, however, the patient's passive, altered state is seized upon for active countersuggestion by the therapist: "When you wake up, you will stop having those spells" (or smoking cigarettes, etc.). Much of the patient's life is excluded, and what is affected teeters along the edge of a rather hazardous repression, as Thomas Mann demonstrated in *Mario and the Magician*. Hence, hypnotherapy tends to work within rather narrow bounds. Some therapists use hypnosis in conjunction with other forms of therapy, which may expand its range—although the hypnosis may just as easily compromise the other therapy as be enriched by it.

In any event, the hypnotic subject is being directed to assume a state of mind in which mature discriminations are excluded and childish dependence upon the hypnotist is encouraged. As some people are pleased to be in a state where life seems narrowed down to an easily manageable level of closeness with a powerful guiding parent, hypnosis is in no danger of extinction, despite its limited therapeutic potential.

Other directive therapies have sprung up using a slightly more mature model of relationship—the moral. Essentially the application of a set of norms and injunctions to neurotic behavior, moral treatment has been part of the cultural scene throughout much of the modern era. Today we have Dr. William Glasser's so-called *reality therapy*.[4] Dr. Glasser's reality is that if a person behaves more responsibly, his neurosis will go away—i.e., he should conform to the established order, be a good citizen and shape up. Since neurosis consists of the breaking through of profoundly antisocial impulses, the moral approach is bound to have some efficacy. Moral imperatives do not work too well in themselves as an aid to repression—if they did, we wouldn't have to make *new* resolutions each New Year's Day. But backed up by a suitable authority, they may do the trick and hence provide the security that comes from knowing one is in the bosom of the community, such as it is.

In any event, reality therapy will remain popular with clergy, law enforcement agencies and other representatives of reality, and variants will doubtlessly spring up as reality advances.

Indeed this has already come to pass in the form of Dr. Albert Ellis's *rational-emotive therapy*.[5] The genial Dr. Ellis imposes *his* directives from the sphere of hedonism and practical philosophy, assuring himself of a solid base of support from progressive units of society by aligning his therapy with the human-potential movement. The patient is encouraged to "analyze" the conscious assumptions of his behavior, to become more assertive and to realize positive, sensible plans for having fun and getting ahead in life. "Encouraged" may be too weak a term here, since Ellis relies heavily on confrontation and encounter techniques to achieve his goals. While some may find this unpalatable, even mindless, others cannot help but be drawn to such energy and verve. At any rate, the therapy has prospered. Needless to add, rational-emotive therapy interdicts anything hidden, unconscious, from the past or involving transference.

Ellis's central idea is a common one throughout the world of therapy, although no one else has pushed it quite so far. It is, simply put, to narrow the gap between therapy and education as much as possible. By emphasizing the cognitive, problem-solving aspects of treatment, seemingly intractable emotional ambivalence —and most problems in living—can be argued down to size, then crushed by therapeutic authority. Ellis's aim is to eventually penetrate the educational establishment with his framework of treatment. If he succeeds he may well become the new Alfred Adler.

BEHAVIOR THERAPY

Many behavioral-directive strategies are too close to voodooism to satisfy the scientific mind. Either they rely on too crude a reduction, as in the organic biotherapies, or are too grossly moralistic or shamanistic, as in reality therapy or rational-emotive therapy. The real thing, the pure form and the official success among this genre is behavior therapy itself, a behavioral-directive approach that is strictly psychological. Behavior therapy is definitely the choice of the psychiatric and psychological establishments as the rational alternative to the psychodynamic treatment informed by psychoanalytic principles, which is the main form of psychotherapy practiced today.

Nearly all therapies we have discussed so far have arisen outside of, and in many cases in opposition to, academic centers. Freud's work was no exception, at least so far as its origin is concerned. However, while remaining beyond the pale in Europe where it began, psychoanalysis became, quite contrary to Freud's expectation, a major influence on the American academic scene. Adulterated as it may have been in many instances, psychoanalysis was the main orientation of psychiatric education in the United States during the middle third of this century. And where it did not make its mark directly as psychodynamics, it became, as we have seen, seedbed and benchmark alike of almost all other approaches.

Almost . . . for alongside the development of dynamic psychiatry, and rather independent of it, grew the academic tradition of behavioral psychology, distinguished by an attention to observable, testable, quantifiable, reproducible—ultimately *objective*—behavior in contrast to the psychoanalytic (and existential, and transcendent) concentration on subjective "psychic reality." It was only logical that a therapeutic canon would spring from behavioral psychology. For one thing, subjectivist therapies are notoriously ambiguous and inefficient. For another, it had been shown that precise manipulation of environmental operations can markedly affect carefully chosen "target" behaviors. The whole weight of experimental psychology was there to back up behavior therapy, along with an academic hierarchy—indeed whatever in modern society gravitates toward a strictly objective control over events.

With so much behind it, the fledgling discipline has grown by great bounds. Behavior therapy is now considered by the American Psychiatric Association to be the second major force in therapy. Journals are founded right and left to keep track of its proliferation, and new and interesting practices are thought of every day to make use of its method. With such a plenitude from which to choose, we must select for discussion here only a few main themes and techniques, and leave to the reader the job of further investigation.[6]

True to its membership in the class of behavioral-directive therapies, behavior therapy proceeds by first analyzing manifest behavior into some target symptom, such as a particular fear, then applying a set of directives aimed at altering the behavioral lesion. Thus, specificity is the key to the whole method. In complete contrast to the emphasis on spontaneity that pervades other therapies from classical psychoanalysis to the most florid encountering, behavioral therapy begins by *narrowing* the problem and so putting it under control. If it is *this* and not *that* which needs treatment, then clear-cut, experimentally testable goals can be established and a precise set of operations defined. Of perhaps greater importance from the patient's standpoint, treatment is already well begun by advance elimination of so much with a wave of therapeutic authority.

This stricture on the object of therapy may seem to exclude from the grasp of behavioral treatment everything but discrete cases of symptom neurosis. Not so. Although the treatment works optimally in cases such as enuresis, stuttering or certain phobias, where a sharply delineated aberration dominates the picture, true believers in behavior therapy would never settle for such crumbs. They want the whole loaf; and since scientific analysis can plunge into the murkiest caves and bring out specimens of something, there is no pot of human trouble that behavioral zealots have not been able to boil down to manageable proportions. The most leaden depressions are seen to contain a hidden phobia that is the real problem; the subtlest forms of masochism are beheld as a lack of "assertiveness"; while addictions turn into "unwanted habits," and difficulties with the social world become "behavioral deficits."

It is true that many behavior therapists are more modest than this, and explicitly deny that their treatment is for feelings of alienation, purposelessness, lack of identity, impoverished relations with others and so forth—in short, for the great run of nonspecific neurotic-social disorders that burden people today. But it is also true that there is no problem too amorphous to yield at least some discrete crystals of behavioral disturbance on which behavior analysts can go to work. And where there is opportunity in therapy, someone will seize it.

Once the problem is circumscribed, treatment can begin via a number of techniques, only some of the more prominent of which can be discussed here. It should be kept in mind as we go through them that a competent behavior therapist doesn't apply his techniques ritually, but tries to fit them to the situation. If one procedure fails, he tries another, guided by the indisputable advantage of being able to readily check his results, since only that which can be observed and measured—e.g., how far one has to stay from a phobic object—is treated. Compared to behavioral treatment all other therapies work in the dark. Even if one believes that the best therapy lies outside the net of quantification, it has to be granted that there is something to envy in the behaviorist's positivism.

Techniques consist mainly of applying control over some manageable piece of behavior and then building stepwise until the target problem is under control. One of the simplest techniques is *progressive relaxation,* which uses breathing exercises and the suggestion of pleasant scenes to steadily introduce a state of calm. Note that the behaviorist works here with thought as well as action. This is quite commonly the case. The allegation that behavior therapy has no use for subjective states of mind is not true; quite to the contrary, almost every maneuver relies upon some report to and/or by the subject of what is going on. Mental states are welcome into the camp of behavioral treatment—so long as they can be controlled and reported. Of course this is a major qualification, which makes the subjective into something of a slave (who, like a real slave, might be prone to hide much from his master). However, a slave is quite a necessary element in certain kinds of social systems.

One of the most important behavioral techniques is *systematic desensitization,* created by Joseph Wolpe for the treatment of phobias.[7] It has since been extended widely, and can be applied whenever overt anxiety is part of the picture. The point of systematic desensitization is to find a graded hierarchy of danger situations, beginning with something the patient can behaviorally manage and proceeding all the way up to the target symptom. In sex therapy, for example, a sexually frightened couple might be instructed not to do anything more erotic than simply lie close to each other the first week; remove articles of clothing the second week; kiss on the lips the third week; fondle breasts and genitals the fourth week; and so on and on, until the two are so fired up and eager to get on with it that they could copulate on a crowded subway train.

One of the clever nuances of this technique, whether applied in sex therapy or elsewhere, is to set tasks beneath the patient's ability. This not only builds confidence, but creates a climate of counterinjunction,[8] as the patient soon comes to feel he wants to do more than the therapist is asking of him. Since there is a level at which every feared object is also a desired one, at some point the therapist becomes a restraining influence who can be defied, and the hitherto feared object something that can be appropriated.

Another main current of behavioral treatment, with vast social applications, builds on Skinnerian *operant conditioning* mixed at times with the Pavlovian approach. The main difference between these two dominant systems of behaviorism is that in classical Pavlovianism (which dominates Soviet psychiatry) the stimulus is applied *before* the behavior; while operant conditioning deals with stimuli applied *after* the behavior—to reward it, punish it, generalize it, reinforce it, extinguish it, etc. Since Skinner's approach starts with the individual's self-initiated behavior, then influences it and puts it in a chain of consequences (the response to one piece of behavior releases the stimulus for the next behavior, and so on),[9] it is particularly well suited for social programs of all sorts. For example, couples therapy can be readily adapted to a behavioral model.[10] Each partner can be shown what he or she does to reinforce the other's negative response, and that the other's response reinforces his or her reinforcement, etc. The similarity to systems family therapy should be noted. Like much of family therapy, behavioral couples therapy gains considerable leverage from being able to pin the problem down to something precise and observable while avoiding the darker side of feeling.

Operant conditioning is enthusiastically applied to behaviors in institutional settings and to those that run afoul of society's norms, such as perversions, addictions and criminality. Many state hospital wards are now being run on "behavior-modification" programs, one example of which is the so-called token economy.[11] As behaviorists have astutely noted, the most effective reinforcer known to mankind is money. Among other positive reinforcers, sex is too disruptive; while from the negative or aversive side, torture and fear of death are too gross and, worse, self-defeating in the long run. Money, however, is just the thing to bring people into line. So tokens that can be later exchanged for goods are awarded for correct behavior, and taken away for bad, and— lo and behold—many a chronic schizophrenic perks up. At the least, they're getting attention beyond the custodial; no doubt they also profit from the realization that they are being reincluded in society's deepest ritual.

Chronic schizophrenics tend to languish if left untreated in a state hospital, so the token economy in this case offers the clear benefit of giving them something to do. More difficult is the case of the antisocial individual, who does too much of a bad thing. Here, as the American Psychiatric Association Task Force Report on behavior therapy cannily observed, "some types of inappropriate behavior appear to be maintained because their natural consequences are reinforcing for the individual, such as addictions and sexual attractions to inappropriate stimuli."[12] In such cases behaviors have to be taken away, a task that may call for some therapeutic ingenuity in the art of aversion.

Hopefully these programs are to be worked out in the context of consent, as in the case of an individual who is thoroughly fed up with, say, his exhibitionism, or other perversion. But even if carried out on consenting individuals, the reader will have surely reflected by now that behavior-modification programs—indeed the whole range of behavior therapy and the behavioral-directive approach in general—suffer from some deep complications.

The problem with behavior therapy is not on the level of efficacy, even if it may have a rather more restricted range of application than its promoters claim. For where it has a rational application—as for example in cases of stuttering or childhood enuresis where the symptom itself is crippling, and depth-psychological methods too slow—treatment of this sort may be a humane expedient, as electroconvulsive treatment can be for intractable psychotic depression.

Nor is there much sense to the bugbear, raised so often against behavior therapy, that the symptoms will come back—"substitute"—the way a weed crops up again when you only pull its stalks and leave the roots intact. For one thing, it has been shown empirically (there is that strength of behaviorism again) that this does not happen. For another, there isn't even any theoretical reason to expect it would happen, unless one has an extremely simple-minded view of human beings. A symptom, after all, is no weed, growing separate in the soil of personality; it is too much part of the whole person for that. And the person is in contact with the environment, which reacts to his behavior, and influences him by its reaction. Any neurotic symptom is therefore fed from the two systems, environment and psyche, and does not simply spring from within. Neurotic symptoms lead to many secondary losses—shame, feeling of failure, tying down of energy, and so forth—which weaken a person and make it more likely for the neurotic imbalance to be maintained. Thus neurotic patterns tend toward self-perpetuating feedback loops. Conversely, when the symptom is removed, even at the level of overt behavior (think of an enuretic child), a real alteration in the whole balance of forces occurs. Therefore there is no *a priori* reason to assume that neurotic toxins will well up again (although of course that could happen too, especially insofar as people have an unconscious need to suffer somehow).

Nor is the main difficulty with behavioral therapy its moronically simplistic view of therapeutic process, which allows in just enough of the mind and the intricacy of therapist-patient relationship to make everything look like a well-oiled machine, but is blind to the subtle dialectic that in fact transpires.[13] That is a problem, but not the *serious* problem. After all, superficiality itself is no crime. On the other hand, superficiality yoked to power for ill is another, much more serious matter.

The real complication with behavior therapy, then, is not that it is the wrong therapy but that, unless scrupulously controlled and limited, it is wrong, period. All therapies use reinforcement techniques as a means of influencing. The analyst, for example, positively reinforces free association and inhibits resistance, while the family therapist reinforces more open communication. But only behavior therapy fetishizes the process of reinforcement itself. And by making behavior into an idol, it turns the human subject into an object of manipulation while correspondingly inflating the behavioral standards of the given social order.

All therapy stands poised between the two alternatives of telling a person what to do or promoting his ability to choose on his own whether to do it or not. No therapist, not even the most disengaged existentialist, can avoid some dictation of what "reality" is, or should be; the simple attention to various behaviors of the patient, and inattention to others, imposes a certain world view of the situation. But in the great range of therapies, from analysis to family treatment, some tension is provided between the imposition of a view of reality and the freedom of the patient to develop his own responses to it. An essential ground of any such freedom is recognition of the subjective dimension as something clearly distinguishable from the objective. It is true that the invisible spheres of unconscious terror and desire occupy some of this dimension, that they give rise to neurosis and much needless suffering, and that we would be better off if they were mastered.

But without the subjective sphere we would also be victims of the environment, without the capacity to resist oppression. And so any therapy that builds its edifice on the ruins of subjectivity, or that seeks to reduce it to the status of a slave, had better be watched.

We should not take this to the extreme of blaming behavior therapy for dehumanization. If token economies, for example, are dehumanizing, that is because of the social situation of state hospital patients, which certainly had little of the human in it for decades before behavior therapy came along. Indeed the behavior therapists are often sincere reformers who cannot be faulted for stepping in where other psychiatrists have feared to tread. But Skinner et al. are more than fools, for all the vacuousness of their planned environments.[14] They have also done us the disservice of lending the prestige of science to social engineering of a pernicious sort, thus debasing both science and society.

It may be said of behavior therapy then that, by emphasizing proclivities for being passively manipulated and minimizing the realm of fantasy, spontaneity and imagination, it shows contempt for people. And it has to be added that this is the contempt that blends too well with political authoritarianism. And as there is no way within the terms of behavior therapy to limit such an ultimately fascistic drift, it follows that limits have to be imposed on behaviorism itself.

Indeed, if behaviorist psychology be the only path of science, then science deserves the brickbats hurled at it by the counterculture. Surveying behavioral psychiatry is like dragging heavy furniture across the floor—much of it is an oafish concoction of ponderous concepts. By confining important human phenomena within what is obvious, behaviorists have made their science an exercise in elaborating the obvious—witness the following from the APA Task Force Report: "The most effective way to eliminate inappropriate behavior appears to be to punish it while at the same time reinforcing the desired behavior."

More than simple examples of rampant intellectual inflation, such offerings sound a very serious claim to power. They are the mustering of the technocrat as enforcer. It should lead one to inquire: What reinforces the reinforcers, and what about punishing the punishers?—and enlist science in the service of an answer. Happily, science has more to it than the puppetry of behaviorism. Science is the application of creative reason and the rules of evidence to phenomena. But although a phenomenon has its objective side, it is no fact floating separate from an observer. It cannot be overlooked that every phenomenon is not passively "out there" but has to be selected by an active process. Indeed, the act of selection is an ultimately political choice. We only deem worthy of scientific investigation that which we care about. Thus each psychology gets the mentality it deserves, and begets the social order it finds necessary.

PRACTICAL SYNOPSIS

Under What Conditions Is It Best To Regard One's Problems Behaviorally?

The question might be more usefully framed in terms of the conditions under which one's subjective side should be minimized, for that is the essential condition of all behavioral treatment. The answer cannot, of course, be generalized beyond saying that it becomes advisable when it is in one's interests to do so.

There are two types of situations when this is so. The first is when one simply values that kind of view of oneself—in other words, one chooses to believe in the unimportance of the subjective world. The second, which we may term a "behavioral reduction," consists of those instances where practical considerations dictate a temporary shoving aside of the subjective. The simplest example would be when one is anxious, can't sleep and faces a critical task the next day. Here, brooding about the deeper causes of the anxiety is probably a less intelligent response than drinking a glass of warm milk and trying to forget. A more complex instance when behavioral reduction might be warranted would be a discrete, limited yet disabling symptom, such as an involuntary grimace; or an unwanted habit, such as smoking; or something that has to be learned, such as sexual technique. Finally we have the more severe emotional disturbances where some kind of objective physiological state is implicated, such as the psychotic depressions. Here the subjective approach, while still important, cannot get at the organic root of the problem, hence somatic-behavioral treatment is warranted.

In all the above instances the behavioral reduction, if it can be sustained, allows a focused attack on the problem, and such an attack may sweep it aside. The functional gains that result can then serve to maintain the change.

How Is One To Know Whether Reducing One's Problem To Behavioral Terms Can Be Sustained?

By its very nature the behavioral reduction involves a deliberate foreshortening of perspective on oneself. None of the problems noted above, for example, can really be grasped without reference to the whole of a person's life, for the understanding of which inclusion of subjective fantasy would be necessary. However if the problem is delimited enough, and one is determined enough, then some behavioral focus can be maintained. Indeed, countless people, analysts and behaviorists alike, have simply decided to give up smoking without any special technique.

What Are The Potential Hazards Of A Behavioral Reduction?

There are numerous instances when a person chooses to reduce matters to behavioral terms in order to avoid a deeper problem. One of the unhappiest and most common situations finds a person taking a sedative drug in order to master a focal task (perhaps because a physician hasn't time or skill to deal with the psychological issues), and readily finding that the drug dulls some emotional pain, he keeps on taking more. Since the pain always returns, the individual is soon hooked, and has succeeded only in adding a new problem onto his old one. For all the vast expenditures of the pharmaceutical industry to promote their thousand-and-one delights, one thing is certain: that the bulk of the nervous tension they purport to relieve has not diminished one bit.

Another kind of complication arises from the openness to emotional exploitation of the person who is trying to convince himself that it's "only nerves," bad habits or whatnot. Such people have secrets to hide and are hence ripe for manipulation by the behavioral therapist, who has been pretty much given a license to do or suggest anything to a patient who is, so to speak, foresworn not to speak his mind or find out what's going on.

What Safeguards Can Be Taken Against
The Hazards Of Behavioral Reduction?

The only genuine security comes from a clear mind and full knowledge of the nature and limits of the procedure being undertaken. In other words, patient and therapist must share a compact as to the boundaries of the treatment. Obviously, some knowledge of the therapist's reputation would be helpful here. One should also give wide berth to therapists who simply lay on moral injunctions as a means of stamping out neurosis, a practice that is both mystifying and oppressive to the patient. This quality in a therapist is frequently masked by some kind of pseudoscientific jargon, but it hints at an underlying megalomania that will inevitably show through.

Part THREE

*For The Customer
And Citizen*

15

Guide For The Perplexed

If nothing else is certain by now, the idea that therapies are not easily compared should be. The causes for this are many—the basic complexity of neurosis and its continuity with normal functioning, the saturation of therapeutics with value judgments, and the slovenly state of definition and conceptualization being but the most prominent. Yet some general notion is needed if a person is to make a rational choice. If we review what has been written up to now about the various schools, the outline of a common principle can be glimpsed through the murk.

All therapy offers some model of neurotic disturbance, gets the sufferer to relive his neurosis in the terms of its model, and exerts some kind of influence on this state of affairs to move it toward some goal. On so much they all agree. The rest, however, is pretty much in dispute—just what kind of model, how the person is to be fitted into its procedure, how influence is brought to bear and what goals are to be sought. All therapists agree they can help some people, but they don't have the same people in mind and they don't share the same view of what is wrong or what constitutes help.

Not only do they speak at cross-purposes, they don't really use the same language, even though many words are the same. Some work with concepts in the terms of which absolute cure is inconceivable—e.g., neurosis defined as a defect in self-knowledge. Others, by focusing down to observable behavior such as the manifest orgasm, set up a situation where positive "cure" becomes a reasonable goal. Still others, by attending to self-evaluation—e.g., feeling "OK"—make it possible for almost anybody to feel a sense of improvement. And others yet, like Gestaltists or some of the transcendent therapists, think in terms of consciousness itself— which once again changes the terms of what can be expected.

Therapies differ in all these ways—and yet one also senses that they're pretty much of the same cloth. All therapy tries to put the person in touch with something that has been lost or split off; it uses human relations to do this (whether therapists admit it or not); and it seems to fit, somehow, into the present state of society.

Given the babel of therapies, how is a person to know what is going on? Of course one can consult the "experts"; but it should be clear by now that almost all of them will give advice that is self-serving to some degree, while none will be in possession of more than a small part of truth. More important, the one value that can be emphasized in the selection and conduct of a therapy is the pursuit of free, autonomous choice. Neurosis enslaves; and there is a hidden potential for enslavement in every therapeutic situation, no matter what the school. The only solid ground from which to begin then is through active and informed choice. And if well begun is half done, the other half will come about through active participation in the treatment process.

Choice in therapy begins with deciding whether to begin and who to begin with, but it continues throughout the process of treatment and on into evaluation of the outcome. As a guide to this development, some topics relevant to the various stages are taken up below. The aim is not to give pat answers—which would be contrary to the spirit of autonomy—but to help the reader frame the right questions.

Can Everybody Be Helped By Therapy?

Everybody can be helped by some therapy if appropriate goals are set for his particular situation. By the same token, some therapies are wrong for everybody. Either the values of the therapy clash too much with their own, or it makes demands that they are un- prepared to fulfill. A common way people have been misled is by the mistaking of the emotional reaction to severe social privation for neurosis. Many people have been thrust into psychodynam- ically oriented therapy when the real dynamics of their situation called for material support or some degree of actual control over their lives. This is not to say that they could not have profited from therapy—only that a necessary precondition for emotional treatment is the meeting of material needs. Given this, then some- thing can be done for everyone who needs it, even though the result may fall short of perfection.

Does Therapy Involve A Necessary Loss Of Self-Reliance?

Many people have refused to seek help on the grounds that therapy encourages dependency, which they equate with weakness. If this is a freely held value, then there is little more to say except to point out that it is one which runs against the program of all civilization, since everything we are as humans is a social product based on mutual dependence. Too often, however, the value is not held freely, but is rather a neurotic overcompensation. Some people are so beset by unconscious conflicts about passivity and dependency that they compulsively flee any situation, such as therapy, wherein they may experience the forbidden feelings.

Nevertheless, there is a grain of truth to the complaint in some circumstances. Therapy, when it becomes too readily gratifying, in fact tends to sap a person's self-reliance. Since indulgence makes one feel better, it may be experienced as "therapeutic." Unfortunately, a person's most insistent cravings tend to have a dark side, which gets stirred up too, thus intensifying the neurosis. Love is never enough where neurosis is concerned; but needless to add, it is ever-tempting. Hence many a therapist has exploited his patients and compromised their autonomy by setting himself up as an all-giving god or a perfect breast.

Can Therapy Ever Work If It Is Carried On Under External Compulsion?

To deal with this question adequately would take us into areas, such as involuntary commitment, beyond the scope of this work. Here I am only discussing compulsory psychotherapy. It is easy to see why treatment of this kind—whether forced by a judge who gives some deviant the choice of treatment or jail, or by a wife who threatens to leave unless therapy is undertaken—is not the right way to go about things therapeutically, and besides has nasty political implications. But such matters are never simple. What is dubious from the political or ethical standpoint may still bear fruit in terms of changing behavior. Desperate situations force expediency on people.

A moment's reflection will also reveal that even the most seemingly motivated person harbors hidden resistances toward therapy, and certain reluctant ones may secretly want to be coaxed, perhaps even compelled. "External compulsion," therefore, cannot be easily defined. Certainly pressure is not applied only by judges or desperate spouses, but can be applied via a whole range of subtle patterns.

Still, to the extent that a person enters treatment of his own volition, so will the chances for a good outcome be improved. And where the treatment is relatively involuntary, the therapist had best not be a double agent representing the enforcing power as well as the client.

Taken All In All, Is The Quality Of The Therapist More Important Than The Mode Of Treatment? And How Can One Judge His Quality?

The answer to the first question would have to be yes, particularly in view of the fact that the really dangerous effects of treatment are transmitted through the therapist. What we call "weaknesses" in therapies are more a matter of openness to abuse than of ineffectuality. Therapy that doesn't work leaves matters pretty much as they were—except, needless to add, that the patient has missed an opportunity, and has lost time and money too. But therapy that harms is a cruel hoax. Though it has countless manifestations, harm in therapy usually occurs as a result of too-rapid dissolution of defenses against deep anxieties. These anxieties are rooted in hidden desire; thus they can come to the fore when the therapist, for whatever reason, undertakes to play on the patient's self-destructive wishes. The fact that self-destructivity usually masquerades as pleasure (consider the alcoholic) makes the situation of therapy one of great moral delicacy. The most reliable safeguard against this is the integrity of the therapist, as it is less the inept therapist than the gifted, exploitative one who does the damage. Ineptitude, after all, carries a self-imposed limit as to how far defenses can be dissolved.

From another angle, it is not therapies as such that are ineffective. They all have their limits—practical, theoretical, moral and otherwise—but within these limits they are all designed to work, if they are properly applied. And as all of them have to be applied by the person of the therapist, it follows that, no matter what the form of treatment, for therapy to work at all the therapist must possess certain characteristics. He or she should be able to sense what is going on psychologically within another person; be attuned to communications, both as receiver and sender; form balanced rational judgments while keeping himself open to feelings; be able to flexibly adapt to changing circumstances without losing identity or purpose; and, most essential of all, *maturely* care for the well-being of the patient. By "maturely care" I mean the therapist should wish for the patient's growth as a person for the patient's own sake, not the therapist's. I would hold that all therapies—behavioral, family, psychoanalytic, bioenergetic, whatever—need practitioners of this sort if they are to work, even within their limits. Indeed, the therapies can only be compared on their intrinsic merits if it is assumed that therapists of genuine caliber are there to practice them.

Unhappily, no such assumption can be made on a general basis. In fact, it is impossible to avoid the observation that ineptitude is more the rule than the exception in the world of therapy. Think of an undesirable trait in a therapist—rigidity, superficiality, impulsiveness, inertia—or an undesirable practice—prescribing drugs far beyond their rational indications; assuming it's all in the mind when real environmental problems are screaming to be heard; or imagining that a little tinkering with reality will plug up a deep well of spite and passivity—name it, and if it is against the goals of good therapy, you will find the practice widely followed.

I do not wish to overstate the problem of the real limitations of therapists. There are plenty of good ones around; and just as no one is perfect, so are few without some redeeming virtue. But there are plenty of poor ones around, too. It may be that the task is too great, or the demand too enormous, or the training too inadequate. But whatever the reason, the low level of therapeutic competence is a painful reality to be faced.

This problem is especially vexing since the forces locked up in neuroses lead one to lose clear judgment about the therapist in both positive and negative ways. One either tends to overvalue the therapist as an omnipotent parent, or disparages him as just another slob who can do no good for one's precious self—or one can swing back and forth between both attitudes—no matter what the real traits of the therapist.

Given this predicament, the best that can be offered in answer to the second question is to bear in mind the possibility of self-distortion, and then go ahead to judge as best one can. And of all criteria for judgment, the most important are to sense in the therapist a basic desire to help and a basic ethical respect for one's personal integrity. Without a trusting feeling of this kind, no treatment can begin.

What About Professional Qualifications?
Is It Best That The Therapist Be A Physician?

Since it is so hard to know in advance whether the traits mentioned in answer to the preceding question are present in the therapist or not, the next-best criterion is level of training. It may be assumed that physicians have a certain degree of competence and personal strength, since they have had to go through so much to get where they are. Further, the postdoctoral training which prepares a physician to become a psychiatrist is long and comprehensive enough to provide a reasonable foundation for good care, especially if the training center maintains good standards, as a high percentage do. There is also the fact that the physician's training includes real experience in caring for people in life-and-death situations. And finally there is the practical consideration that many insurance programs only recognize care by licensed physicians as eligible for benefits.

However, other professional groups—clinical psychologists and social workers—have also received an intensive training, one that pays as least as much attention to psychological factors as does psychiatric education. Moreover, since *all* professional training tends to winnow out free spirits, there is no guarantee whatsoever that the basic and necessary human traits required for good therapy will be found only amongst their ranks. Finally, it scarcely needs to be emphasized that, for all their individual merits, physicians as a class have not distinguished themselves for their human qualities. Indeed there is reasonably good evidence that the physicians' hegemony is as much the result of monopoly control of health care as it is a product of real merit, which tends to be something of an incidental. There is no question that the doctor's immense authority—based partly on monopoly power and partly on responsibility for physical life and death—can be readily extended to the care of the emotional life, where it gives treatment an added transference push. Many people find the physician's aura irresistibly appealing, but to me it seems rather a needless perpetuation of authoritarianism. Therapy can and should be conducted on a freer basis.

In fact the real training for most therapists takes place outside their regular degree-granting education. Most schools of therapy maintain training centers where the canons of the craft are taught. The range of these training programs is much too great to be presented in any detail here. Unhappily, it is also too great to provide much guidance for the prospective patient wanting realistic information about the credentials of a therapist. Therapists and therapies as such are not licensed by the state, and there is little or nothing that can stop anybody from passing himself off as one.

This, of course, is where the possession of an advanced professional degree offers some minimal assurance. Most training programs require a prospective therapist to undergo the treatment he or she is later to practice, to take some course work and to treat a few cases under supervision. However, the level of training varies enormously, from the classical Freudian schools (organized nationally under the aegis of the American Psychoanalytic Association), which make extraordinarily stringent, Jesuitic demands upon their (mainly physician) candidates, all the way to the most wildly haphazard programs imaginable, new ones of which spring up every day.

As with professional training in general, the kind of training a therapist has received can only establish a certain probability of skill and integrity. Training in itself does not guarantee the promotion of virtue—indeed a long-standing debate has raged within psychoanalysis as to whether or not the exacting training program is itself stifling. Nor, however, does lack of established credentials rule out merit. By the same token, although by and large a therapist grows through continued experience, there are many instances in which a younger, less experienced person might strike up a better relationship with a patient than an old hand.

In sum, the prospective client should take nothing for granted where the qualifications of a therapist are concerned. The most essential consideration is to be able to form a proper working relationship; all other factors should be examined in this light.

What Of The Social Stigma Attached To Therapy?

There is no question this stigma exists, although the degree varies greatly. By and large it is a product of the need by a particular group, whether a family, corporate office or community, to isolate the deviant and thus maintain its own image as pure. (I do not mean to imply by this that the converse—ready acceptance of therapy—implies enlightenment.) Whatever the cause, the stigma forces one to weigh the possible gains of therapy against the possibilities of ostracism. A perfectly reasonable expedient in some situations is to conceal the fact of therapy—although this may lead to further unpleasantness, which in turn has to be weighed against the possible gains of therapy. Often, however, the choice is not weighed reasonably, since the community's intolerance may be used by an individual to rationalize his own fears of self-discovery. The case is analogous to the conflict about therapy—and self-reliance discussed earlier, in that a dilemma at a moral or practical level may be subtly turned to the purposes of one's neurosis.

What About Cost?
And Is Private Care Better Than Public?

Again, this is a topic too big for thorough discussion here. Therapy is part of a market economy no less than it is an instrument of help. Its contradictions tend to be as serious as those of the market itself, and there is no use in pretending them away, as practitioners often try to do. The fact is, whatever else they want, therapists are out to make a living and they tend to charge what the traffic will bear. In therapy one hires another's time and usable consciousness, which turn out to be valuable commodities, given how much people suffer from their neuroses. And like most other valuable commodities in our society, they become the property of the well-to-do. Interestingly enough—although it should be little consolation—the very rich often get shortchanged in therapy, because their power insulates them from disillusionment. Hence they often hire, at great expense, sycophantic, drug-pushing psychiatrists instead of somebody who might deal honestly with their problems but possibly shake them up.

Since most therapists either belong or aspire to the upper middle class, it is to this class that their attentions are basically directed. The less affluent person seeking help usually has to turn to some kind of clinic or public facility, where he will have substantially less choice over who treats him and with what method, and will likely work with less experienced therapists who tend to turn over fairly quickly. He will also have to put up with the interposition of the institution between the therapist and himself, with its red tape, compromise of confidentiality and so forth. A deeper problem yet is the inevitable tendency of the institution to compel the therapist into some kind of divided loyalty between the patient and itself.

Many of the innovations in the world of treatment—especially the group and family therapies, and certain types of brief psychotherapy—have been devised in the hope of finding a lower-cost treatment than the classical therapies, especially psychoanalysis. But briefer treatment, group treatment, etc., should be for kinds of *problems* that warrant it, not for poor *people*. What is needed is a rational selection of treatments for the tremendous range of problems that afflict people, not a ritzy department store with a bargain basement.

There is nothing sacrosanct about the fee and no reason why equally good treatment cannot be given in a clinic or public facility—as in fact happens in numerous places. Indeed there is good reason for public care to become an ideal goal to replace the present manifestly unjust system. The problem, however, will have to be approached at a fundamentally different level from the kind of tinkering that has been attempted up until now. The new level must be one that shifts value from the marketable commodity to communitarian ends. Until that happens, contradictions will be rife in the practice of therapy; and when, or if, it happens, the terms of neurosis will be so different from what we recognize today that the entire concept of therapy will require rethinking. In the meantime, however, the emotionally troubled person will have to exercise individual resourcefulness in matching his means to the available ends.

Confidentiality Was Mentioned Earlier. What Is Its Importance In Therapy?

However neurotic experience is elaborated, it invariably involves much about which the individual feels afraid, ashamed or guilty. Every therapeutic situation, then, entails exposure of things that could be a source of humiliation, and the power of the therapist follows from the trust which the patient must feel if he is to reveal even the outer shell of this side of himself. There would be no surer abuse of that power than for the therapist to violate that trust.

Confidentiality is in every instance an ethical value in therapy.

How absolutely that value is applied depends on how great a role the revelation of personal secrets plays in the conduct of treatment. At one extreme there is psychoanalysis, in which strict confidentiality is so crucial that analysts have gone to jail rather than disclose any detail about their patients—even, in one case, when the patient requested disclosure. At the other end are types of directive-behavioral treatment where subjective experience is probed no more than it is in routine medical care. At this end also are types of group treatment—for example, psychodrama— where the essence of the therapy is to publicize one's hidden thoughts. In every case the patient has a right to confidentiality, though the lengths to which this is pursued varies with the situation. In clinics offering analytic psychotherapy or psychoanalysis, there is bound to be conflict owing to the public nature of the institution and the private nature of the treatment. The conflict can be particularly acute when, as is often the case, the clinic is part of a training program, so that some disclosure is inevitable. The irony, which only reflects the basic inequity of our society, is that such clinics usually offer the best in low-cost care. In any event, the patient has the right to be assured that every reasonable effort is being made to preserve confidentiality.

What Other Rights Should The Patient Expect?

He has the right to know the basic assumptions and methods of the treatment being undertaken; to make sure that he and the therapist share the same goals for himself; to have a clear understanding of his obligations, both in the conduct of the treatment and with respect to fees, etc.; and to feel free to terminate the treatment at any time.

A word of amplification may be in order here. While the above are definite rights and should be carefully guarded, the nature of neurosis, and especially neurotic transference to the therapist, makes it hard for people to apply them. Either one tends to go along unreflectively with anything (due to neurotic submissiveness), or one forgets (due to a need to appear stupid) or tries to change the rules in midstream (neurotic rebelliousness) or needs to feel cheated (masochism), and so forth. In short, the person who could exercise these rights fully wouldn't be neurotic in the first place. At the same time, no one is so far gone as to not appreciate them at all. And the need to appreciate and enforce one's rights is more than ethical; without them a person would not have the realistic nucleus of autonomy which lies at the heart of all genuine therapeutic efforts.

What Rights Does The Patient Not Have?

Basically, the patient does not have the right to compel the therapist to deviate from his chosen role so long as this is a legitimate one. And if agreement can't be reached on whether it is or not, the therapy had best be terminated.

No therapy is perfect, but all have been thought out, and all require a certain role which the therapist chooses as appropriate for the goals in mind. In other words, a therapist can't just be "himself." If he behaves in ordinary ways, then so will the patient, who thereby remains as neurotic as before. Every neurosis resists resolution; and resistance regularly takes the shape of trying to get the therapist to change the rules of the treatment: to be more "giving," or flexible, etc. Judgments of this sort are rarely all wrong, since therapists *should* be flexible, giving, etc. But it is only by being flexible and giving within *limits* that any therapeutic work gets done. One is free to argue about these limits, but the therapist has to reserve the right to maintain them.

What About Sex With The Therapist?

This is a special case of the issues raised in the answers to the last three questions. Although it is more talked about than done, sex between therapist and patient is no rarity. And no mystery either, considering the intensity of infantile sexual wishes locked up in neurosis and their inevitable mobilization by treatment. Certain savants have gone to some length to rationalize sex in therapy as necessary to overcome alienation and loneliness or to bring a patient into touch with his or (almost always) her "real" feelings.

Even if this were true it would still be a shabby screen for other motives not too difficult to imagine. But the argument turns out to be false. For neurosis is played out in the imagination. No external event will jump the gap between the repressed and reality; and while sex may indeed get things moving, when it is sex with a figure onto whom one has projected the most intense infantile images and in whom at the same time one has placed one's trust, then the direction in which things will begin moving is likely chaos.

To What Extent Does Belief In The Therapist Play A Role In What Happens?

In the majority of cases, to too great an extent; and in every case, to some extent, for therapy can never be freed from suggestion, at least not so long as neurosis entails suggestibility. A necessary core of nonrational—but not irrational—faith has to be present if any treatment is to matter. All the intellectual conceptions in the world will not compensate in therapeutic effect for the elemental sense some therapists inspire of hope in a future goodness. The task is to ground this faith in something thoroughly worthwhile, and such a basis must include primarily a respect for the autonomy of the patient. Therapists who attempt to lay on values, no matter how excellent these may be in their own right, are in every case falling short of the one paramount value of autonomy. Moreover, the indoctrination that occurs in therapeutic settings is basically spurious. No one is in a position to adequately judge the merits of, say, a political belief when he is lying on a couch struggling with his need to submit to father. Needless to add, the intellectual weakness of a person in the grip of his neurosis has not deterred many therapists from setting themselves up as great philosophers to their patients.

It should be realized, however, that the goal of autonomy applies to a lessening degree to people who are more greatly disturbed. The care of many chronically psychotic people would be seriously compromised unless therapists laid down rather firm guidelines. Becoming an auxiliary ego is one thing however, and acting like a god another, the effects of which would be as pernicious here as elsewhere.

What Effects May Be Expected On Family Life While One Is Undergoing Therapy?

It is hard to generalize because of the complex balance of forces. Therapies—from psychoanalysis to primal therapy—that involve the uncovering of hidden conflicts usually lead a person on a journey that involves reliving old suffering. Although the goal is eventual mastery, it is safe to expect some periods during which one both feels and acts worse than ever. In the best of circumstances a tolerance for increased moodiness and demandingness is required of other family members. Understandably, they often cannot sustain such a lofty attitude and become so jealous and upset by what is going on that they too enter treatment. In still other instances a spouse in therapy may pass through a phase where, in reliving old sexual conflicts, he or she may act them out, either by seeking affairs outside the marriage and/or inhibiting sex within it.

Whatever the manifestation, individual treatment always introduces some tension in life with others, simply because of basic contradictions between individual and social interests. In many instances things settle down, and the family unit is reconstituted on a more solid basis. But in many others, divorce or some other rupture is the consequence. For individual, exploratory treatment to be effective, no preconditions on its outcome can be set. The potential hazards have kept many people from seeking analytic treatment or have led them into family treatment—and indeed may be regarded as one of the sources of the family-therapy movement itself.

It should not be assumed, however, that family therapy has to have the goal of patching up conflict. Here, too, the treatment may come upon the irreconcilable, though family therapy is somewhat less likely to stir up the kinds of antisocial impulses that the deeper individual therapies do.

As for children, they are always affected by treatment, whether or not they directly participate. It has been my experience that people can be mobilized to work more effectively in therapy on issues concerning their children than on other areas of their lives. Neurotic parents generally care for their children; indeed the problem is often that they care too much, regarding their offspring not as individuals in their own right but as extensions of the parental self. Whatever the deeper complications in parental overprotection, there is often some mature regard left over for the child as a separate person, at least enough to motivate the parent to let him be—a course of action that rarely fails to have beneficial results.

To be sure, there are limits set by the neurosis itself on how much people can be allowed to grow and individuate themselves. In their counterattack, one trick the neurotic forces play on family relations of people in treatment is to insert an intellectual image of the therapy or therapist in the place of spontaneous family feelings. "Now what would Dr. Scheissvogel say?" goes the thought, as emotional action withers away into a caricatured interpretation along the lines of what the good doctor might in fact say: "Sammy, why aren't you eating your oatmeal? Is it because you're mad at me?"

Communications of this kind, which were virtually unheard-of before the age of therapy, are more than parody; they become the ground of new varieties of neurosis. A refined colonization of Sammy's mind is what in fact occurs, and the child will indeed become mad if it continues—but not in the sense the parent has in mind. Some of the newer nonverbal therapies—Gestalt for example—have been developed in response to the threat of neurotic intellectualization, but they have contradictions of their own, one being their unsuitability to deal with the complexities of real human relations.

The questions of how or when little Sammy actually goes mad, or whether he needs help of his own, get into matters beyond the scope of this work. As noted before, consultation should be sought when there is some doubt. Whatever the problem, the parent is best served by recognizing the temptation to underplay the individuality of our children (especially when we are boasting about how "special" they are, which mostly means how wonderful *we* are). A last stronghold against a world of ruthless administration is the recognition of a child's autonomy. Therapy well used helps secure this, just as therapy abused becomes a new form of administration.

Why Should Sexuality Play Such A Special Role In Therapy? Isn't There An Overemphasis On Sex, And A Downplaying Of Other Key Issues In Much Therapy?

The importance of sexuality in therapy is mainly a function of method. Jung used to say that different people had different "psychologies" and should go to different types of analysts—Freudian, Adlerian or those of his own school. The implication was that, for some people, unresolved sexuality lay at the root of their neuroses. These people needed Freudian treatment, just as those with power conflicts should see Adlerians, while those having conflicts of the spirit should turn to him.

His point only makes sense however if put in terms not of "psychologies" but of predilections or self-images. The methods of the different analytic schools—and the same holds for all other approaches to therapy—necessarily lead to different conceptions of what counts in neurosis and health. Freud's discovery was of a method: If one free-associated without being able to perceive the person to whom one was talking, then a certain world of subjective fantasy would be entered, the desires in which were sexual and led back to basic neurotic conflicts. What was implicated, however, were not recognizable *adult* sexual impulses but lost remnants of infantile wishes, wishes impossible to fulfill from the outset. As these wishes worked their way back to the surface of actual life—including but not limited to the life of sexuality— so developed the neurotic disposition.

Freudian psychoanalysis retains the method that leads back to fantasy of the repressed infantile sort. Other methods of treatment approach the problem at other points of the pathway between the invisible spheres of deep repression and the actual surface of the objective world. And so they arrive at other images of the whole— conscious awareness, feelings of security and self-regard, interpersonal relations, bodily functioning, even, to be sure, *adult* sexuality. Each image, like any representation of reality, is simpler than what it represents; and contact with any portion can have a beneficial effect if a person succeeds at that point in re-creating some part of the neurosis, then mastering it.

If the sexuality Freud discovered retains any special status among these images, it is because it remains the most subversive, startling and anxiety-provoking element of human experience. The other parts of the whole that have been made accessible to therapy since Freud—whether relations with reality or higher states of consciousness—were also accessible before, even if not in the overall context in which they now find themselves. But the Freudian map added to the ensemble a decisively unifying territory: repressed infantile sexual fantasy.

To claim that the change in sexual mores has eliminated infantile sexuality, or the need for any special technique to uncover it, is a colossal piece of nonsense. The whole sexual revolution has only added new layers of conscious experience and value. The new ways of behaving have doubtless altered the overall state of the mind—and may even have changed some of the contents of the unconscious—but haven't in the least altered the fact of repression or its powerful effect on the psyche. Today as always, conscious experience and fantasy lead back into the unspeakable, nameless realms of terror and desire. If a person regards this area of life as unbearable, or sees other regions as more pressing, he will find therapies to meet his needs. But he should not think thereby that he has legislated repressed sexuality out of existence —just as the person in analysis should not think that the external world has somehow been made less significant by his plumbing of the subjective depths.

How Do Drugs Affect The Course Of Psychological Treatment?

The number of drugs, the complexities of their action and the range of individual idiosyncrasies of response are so vast that no definitive statement about the way one feels while taking psychoactive drugs can be made within the confines of the present work.[1] Put simply, psychoactive drugs generally have four types of effects: they sedate, or lower the general level of consciousness (e.g., barbiturates); or they excite consciousness (e.g., amphetamines); or relieve anxiety without much altering consciousness (e.g., phenothiazines); or they counteract certain types of severe depressed feelings, again without major alterations in consciousness (e.g., imipramine, or Tofranil). But this outline barely touches the range of feelings stirred up by drugs.

Indeed often enough one feels nothing at all, either because the dose taken is insufficient for one's level of reaction or because of habituation to chronic use. In the latter case, effects are felt from *not* taking the drug, and usually run counter to the drug's action itself—excited, anxious and restless when habituated to sedative drugs, and depressed and sluggish when habituated to excitant drugs.

Whatever drugs do, they do not approach the psychological or social causes of emotional disturbance. They are mainly helpful when the problem is in a significant way organic or where some emergency situation arises. Drug companies like to claim that their elixirs facilitate psychotherapy by making the patient less anxious. But except in cases where psychotic anxieties (which have an organic component) are rendering someone incommunicado, the assertion is plain garbage. Whenever a person takes a drug as an adjunct to psychotherapy, he is necessarily limiting the area in which he accepts responsibility for his thoughts and hence his life. This limitation may conceivably be offset when the drug taken is a so-called mind-expanding one, as Claudio Naranjo (see p. 155) has claimed. But Naranjo's argument remains quite problematic, and certainly does not apply to the standard nostrums dispensed by the billion, courtesy of the U.S. pharmaceutical industry. The reader should especially beware of physicians who casually dispense feelgood cocktails containing mixtures of drugs.

How Can One Tell Whether Therapy Is Working?

In treatments where the goal is clear-cut and the approach specific and limited—e.g., behavioral sex therapies—there is no problem. Either the behavior is changed or it is not—a determinable quality of such therapies that appeals to many people and most researchers. In other treatments, however, things are less determinate and more difficult to evaluate. In some instances of psychoanalytic treatment, the goals can be so elusive that years can go by while analyst and analysand are trying to figure out whether the goals are being realized.

The potential for such extreme uncertainty is a real hazard to a therapy such as psychoanalysis. But in many ordinary instances in therapies of all sorts the same problem arises. Because neurosis mystifies and deceives, therapy works in the dark toward the light. But darkness always seems the same—a night is just as dark at 3:00 A.M. as it is at 11:00 P.M.—and the night of neurosis has no assigned beginning or end.

The problem becomes even more tangled when the relationship between therapy and pain is considered. As noted earlier (see p. 235), when one deals with conflict, getting better may involve a period of feeling worse. Our neuroses were set going long ago in order to ward off anxiety over forbidden wishes. Thus overcoming a neurosis means reexperiencing the anxiety, facing the wishes and giving up some of the pleasure they promised. Though the source of anxiety may be only imaginary, and will fade when exposed to the light of day, the patient doesn't know this, no matter how sophisticated he may be; and so he or she will fight the treatment and howl in pain as it is being realized. Moreover, no one ever outgrew a neurosis except by modifying the desire for something cherished, albeit destructive. Humanist psychologies may march under the banner of adding joy without sacrifice, of both having and eating the cake, but the extent to which the ideology is practiced only signifies how little of deeper neurotic functioning has been touched—and how much, conversely, of middle-class boredom and anomie. Analysts earn the nickname "shrink" honestly. To appropriate the unconscious entails a painful giving up on its realization, whether the hurt stems from relinquishing a hidden tie to parents or is simply the pain of disillusionment. This is not a matter of Calvinist ideology—strong medicine being necessary to prove one's worth in heaven—but rather a reflection of the actual amount of pain a person has buried down here on earth. If there has not been much pain in the past, there will be that much less in the treatment. The actual amount, though, will be determined by one's real history, not wishes that it be otherwise.

However, there is in many people a whole side to neurosis which relishes suffering and misfortune. Like prisoners grown fond of their chains, such people seek to prove that one can be as miserable with therapy as without. Thus we seem to be in a quandary: Getting better may involve feeling worse, but feeling worse needn't mean one is getting better; it may only mean one is a masochist. How is one to know whether the turmoil will eventually lead to self-mastery and *joie de vivre,* or whether it will circle round on itself like a dog pursuing its tail?

The question hinges, it seems to me, on whether or not the goals of the treatment are experienced as an ongoing *process.* In other terms, one should not look so much for "improvement"— which can be such a vain, illusory business where neurosis is concerned—as for *discovery.* In analytic work one should expect a progressive unfolding of feelings, ideas and memories that had been previously unrecognized; or a sense of heightened interrelatedness between seemingly disparate areas such as work and sex; or a deepening of the relationship with the analyst, or simply a developing tension between actuality and goals. In other forms of "uncovering" therapy a similar process would have to be felt according to the terms of the treatment. Thus in Gestalt one would look for developments in awareness and a sense of the whole; in bioenergetic treatment, for alterations in the way the body is experienced; and so forth.

The sense of discovery indicates that the neurosis has been engaged at one of its points. It should be thought of as necessary—but not in itself sufficient—for the therapy to be of help. For real benefit to occur, the therapeutic process must involve life outside the session in a thorough and consistent way. The experiential changes in therapy are like the pseudopodia of an amoeba, tentative extensions into new areas of functioning, and they have to be followed by movement of the entire organism if the way is to be prepared for the next step.

Note that a working therapy proceeds by steps. If dynamic therapy is to take hold, it is in stages: Changes developing within the treatment make possible some movement outside, which creates in turn the conditions for further developments within, and so forth. Each session should be a comment neither on outside life nor the previous session, viewed in isolation from each other, but rather on the dialectical movement between session and outside life. Therapies that minimize the dialectic in the interests of exclusive attention to one end or the other are liable to miss out. By working only with reality outside the treatment, they settle for the limited (but real) gains of counseling; while by concentrating excessively on changes within the office, they become prone to enthrallment and brainwashing. Obviously a brainwashed or enthralled person is not going to be in much of a position to recognize what is happening to him. Some clues may be afforded, though, if the therapy becomes an end in itself, or if prolonged obsession with the therapist takes place, or if—what comes down to the same thing—a narrowing of interest occurs instead of an expanding sense of discovery.

It turns out that even the best treatments do not follow any neat progression; rather, periods of stagnation, or even backsliding, are to be expected. Freud termed the reverses "negative therapeutic reactions" and ascribed them to an unconscious sense of guilt that barred improvement. While there is good reason to believe that his insight was well founded, work over the years has made possible a somewhat more optimistic assessment of the possibilities of overcoming an unconscious sense of guilt. Still, periods of stagnant despair can be expected in many eventually successful treatments. Often the matter turns on such ineffables as hope, or on subtle and poorly understood qualities of relationship between therapist and patient.

What About Winding Up Treatment? What Is The Long-Range Prospect Of A Therapeutic "Cure"?

Again, when symptoms are defined as the issue—as for example in sex therapies—then success is readily determined. In such therapies long-range improvement can be expected to the degree that the symptom was uncontaminated by deeper neurotic issues.

For treatments which set subjective goals, however, termination can never be defined in an absolute sense, but only as a shady point beyond which the effort and expense of treatment seem greater than the likelihood of further beneficial developments. If this point is reasonably close to the goal—whether it be analytic self-reflectivity, Gestalt awareness or intrafamily communication, —then the treatment can be called successful.

In every instance, no matter how successful, a person should expect some turmoil during the termination phase. Having to give up the attachment to the therapist and treatment process, with its inevitable hopes of perfectibility, is simply too great a wrench to be taken calmly. Toward the end one may expect a reliving of the history of the treatment itself, including a return of the original distress. Often, however, the deepest gains are made right at the end, in the heat of separation. And if the treatment has been well conducted, a person may expect to continue its constructive work on his own after it is over.

All treatments, symptomatic or otherwise, only touch part of a person's being, and only in one phase of life. To the extent that the treatment gets at neurotic roots, and to the extent that its functional benefits set in motion a positively reinforcing cycle of increased self-esteem and environmental adaptation, the therapeutic benefits will be lasting. But times change—one grows old, or on, sustains losses, faces new challenges, gets swept up by life—and in the process new problems of a neurotic sort can arise requiring a fresh assessment for therapy. One would hope to minimize the extent to which new neurotic problems crop up; however, the claims of therapeutic hucksters—e.g., that so-and-so, after a period of magical ministration, remained "well" for many years after—are to be regarded as an unreliable guide for assessment. It's best to just congratulate so-and-so on his miraculous restoration to the bosom of health, then get back to the business of dealing with one's own complex personal reality.

What About Creativity?
Doesn't Therapy Stifle This
By Reducing Neurotic Conflict?

It might—the more so as the therapist tries to impose some positive goal of "mental health" or "normality." On the other hand, therapy well used can free creative forces which had been bogged down in neurosis. Creativity is generally one shade removed from neurosis, and bound up quite closely with it in the real individual. Each state turns on the outcome of conflict between erotic and destructive forces—and each depends as well upon poorly understood innate factors such as talent or susceptibility to neurotic breakdown. Like neurosis, creativity is a highly idiosyncratic solution to life's paradoxes. And while creativity is the antithesis of neurosis in that its laws are those of freedom rather than compulsivity, it is also a close relation, since the freedom or compulsivity in each case describes the disposition of unconscious forces that have broken loose from repression. Viewed from this angle, every neurosis can be seen as a struggle toward freedom, but a struggle that has stumbled into a self-laid trap where it lies chained in compulsivity. Therapy, then, becomes an opportunity to get out of the trap in either a forward or backward direction.

Normality is what neurosis has broken away from in the first place; and the positive goals of therapy are a return to normality, which implies the reinstitution of repression. The idea of normality does not allow for anything dark and possibly destructive; while to be positive means to be certain. Unconscious conflict is minimized, and the given, common-sense reality is restored as the basis of truth. The promotion of such a state of affairs will necessarily tend to stamp out creativity along with relieving neurotic distress.

It must be emphasized that every variety of therapy is prone to such use, although some types—e.g., the behavioral-directive approaches—are more likely candidates than others. Whenever a therapist seems overly eager to impose ready-made and conformist goals, or when he does not take the trouble to truly listen and find out what a person's special reality—inner as well as outer—may be, then some kind of anticreative influence is at work in the treatment.

Is It Not True That Defining Life's Problems In Psychotherapeutic Categories Has Ill Served Those Who Suffer From Real Loss Of Power? In Particular, Has Not More Harm Than Good Been Done To Women, Whose Legitimate Struggles Were Redefined And Undercut By The Male-Dominated Institution Of Therapy?

As a lot, therapists are no better than anyone else. And as an institution that has become intimately involved at a number of levels with the material relations of society, therapy cannot be expected to stray much from dominant ideologies. Thus many therapists, whether through thickheadedness, or reactionary-patriarchal attitudes or both (all of which, needless to say, can be present in women as in men), have ill served women patients by psychologizing away oppression and pressing conformity on them in lieu of real help.

Unhappily there are pragmatic grounds for such an approach. Many anxieties can be stilled by fostering acceptance of the established order of things. The therapist, then, who subtly or not-so-subtly suggests to his female patient that she would feel better if she accepted her submissive role is, at least in the short run, not necessarily being nontherapeutic, though he *is* being reactionary. Similarly, the therapist who summons the specter of "penis envy" as a biological given is also not necessarily being untherapeutic; he is only being mystical in his biological way, and mystery backed up by authority can put to rest neurotic fears as well as stifle an emerging political consciousness.

But the matter is not so simple. There is a crude feminist ideology, equally "therapeutic" in fostering a group-sustained paranoia, which places the whole difficulty in the lap of the male oppressor. Any subjective compliance of women is read out of existence. Since the compliance is unconscious, it is easy to make it seem nonexistent—but another matter to make it go away.

The point is to neither situate the difficulty entirely in the mind—which exonerates social relations—or entirely in society—

which removes responsibility for one's own life—but rather to give each sphere its due, and appreciate their interrelations with each other. Then therapy can proceed on the basis of a genuine respect for an individual's autonomy and social aspiration, while still attacking neurotic distortion tooth and nail. And although many women choose to feel that only another woman can understand their situation, this need not be the case—even if it may allow for somewhat more accessible gains in self-regard via identification with the therapist. The best therapists, women or men, have an almost Tolstoyan capacity for envisioning what another's inner life is like. And this, coupled with real concern for the other's personal worth, is the only truly legitimate basis on which therapy should be built.

The same line of reasoning holds for blacks and other victims of racism, indeed for anyone who has suffered oppression. So long as it is not considered an antidote to history, therapy properly applied can be of real benefit in dealing with the neurotic distortions that can befall anybody, no matter what side of the social divide they happen to be on. And again, the right therapist could conceivably be of any identity. To assume otherwise is to read society too directly into the individual.

But wait a minute. There are contradictions all over the place here. The above sounds fine on paper, but in practice is bound to conflict with any number of "social aspirations." In order to get the "best therapist," doesn't one have to pay through the nose, hence have an upper-middle-class identity that will not be so readily relinquished? Furthermore, can any therapist help but select material that he regards as crucial, and thus impose his or her own values on the patient? And, given the transference and neurotic confusion, can authoritarian qualities really be removed from the therapeutic setting? What does this do to your precious "autonomy"? Finally, doesn't that same attention to the subjective world, which you claim characterizes therapy, at its best tend to inevitably draw attention away from taking command of the real situation? As we find all the ambiguities within ourselves, do we not become one with Hamlet, for whom "the native hue of resolution is sicklied o'er with the pale cast of thought"? In other words, for all your qualifications about this therapy promoting enthrallment or that therapy being dehumanizing, are they not all pretty much conformist by virtue of being Therapy itself?

These are valid questions, but we'll need a wider perspective if we are to deal with them. For this purpose we have reserved our final chapter.

16

Hysterical Misery
And Common Unhappiness

There is no question that therapy as an institution has to stand within bourgeois society. If neurosis is a splitting within the self, and healing consists of some degree of reunification tendered by therapists who have to live in the real world, then the product will have to stand within the given, bourgeois order of things.

But as such, the proposition is not a very interesting one; since all institutions, even the most revolutionary, have to connect with the social order to which they refer. Marx himself was the foremost exponent of this view. In his system any new order is born out of the actual contradictions within the old. Marx held that no revolution can be grafted onto a society from without; and the seeming novelty of revolutionary ideas like Marx's—and Freud's—only reflect the depth within the social order at which they were discovered and the alienation—or repression—which had hidden them from view.

So the broad social significance of therapy is not a matter of whether it is part of the bourgeois world but, rather, which side of that world's contradictions it takes. In other words, does therapy move people in a progressive direction or does it further stagnation, conformity or even reaction? Admittedly, these categories are exceedingly difficult to define in any case; and when they have to be related to something as haphazard and poorly delineated as the therapies, the problems seem virtually limitless. One starts with the clear understanding that in actual practice every therapeutic modality can be used in a number of political directions and can play a great variety of roles in social life. Bearing the above in mind, it might yet be possible to cast a little light. Let us begin by defining four main ideologies concerning the politics of therapy.

The first is that of Freud. It became the credo of psychoanalysis in general and has been endlessly restated, but never so clearly as in its initial formulation. At the threshold of his psychoanalytic discoveries, Freud depicted an imaginary dialogue with a patient who protested, "You tell me yourself that my illness is probably connected with my circumstances and the events of my life. How do you propose to help me, then?" To which Freud replied, "You will be able to convince yourself that much will be gained if we succeed in transforming your hysterical misery into common unhappiness. With a mental life that has been restored to health you will be better armed against that unhappiness."[1] In short, Freud proposed bracketing out the events of real life, which had undoubtedly played a role in creating the neurosis. Bracketing here meant taking into account but with a certain suspension of judgment. The analyst was neither to interfere nor judge but only to interpret and facilitate the patient's self-formative process. Meanwhile the world, whether it be the family or the state, was allowed to go its own way.

The second ideology proposes to deal with real circumstances as they immediately effect the individual, but to make no pronouncements about the general societal matrix in which they occur. Included here would be the great body of supportive or relational psychotherapies, much family therapy, symptom-oriented behavior therapy (including sex therapy) and so forth.

The third ideology extends the second by adding a positive pronouncement in which the therapy itself becomes a source of value and a remedy against "common unhappiness"—at least that part which stems from social alienation. Included here would be therapies as diverse as Jungian analysis, transcendent therapy, primal therapy and reality therapy, and, by definition, the whole human-potential movement, with its emphasis on joy, spontaneity and intimacy.

The fourth ideology goes one step further within category three and rejects all the rest. It is called "radical therapy." This movement flared up in the activist Sixties and has since somewhat subsided, but not without leaving its mark on theory and practice.[2] The central slogan of the radical therapists was "Therapy means change—not adjustment"; and although they, like radicals everywhere, could not always agree on what kind of change they thought best, they were unanimous in rejecting (as "Band-Aids for the bourgeoisie") most of the changes espoused by other therapies. Their particular scorn was reserved for Freud, in part because of the manifest elitism of psychoanalytic practice; but more significantly because Freud's dictum (stated above) seemed heartless in face of the obviously powerful role social oppression plays in the development of neurosis. Further, it led to a practice, analytic therapy, that necessarily encourages reflection at the expense of action.

The main concern of the radicals was to shift emphasis to visible oppression, whether this be of women by men, blacks by whites, patients by psychiatrists, or everybody by capitalism. Therapeutic modes such as transactional analysis or other group means could be drawn into the radicals' program, but only on condition that the categories by which behavior was to be explained be translated into directly political terms—i.e., terms that shifted the brunt of explanation from psychodynamics to sociodynamics on the broad scale. In sum, therapy was to be delegitimized as an institution. And since regarding human troubles as correctable by psychological means, or by individuals, saps the urge to unite as a class against the common oppressor, the delegitimization of therapy would deprive capitalism of one of its handiest props.

Surveying these ideologies, a few things stand out.

First, none of them could ever be applied in pure form by any therapist. Freud, for example, was quite prone to dispense advice (and on at least one occasion fed a hungry patient), and every psychoanalyst since has realized the necessity of conveying some reality to the patient, even if only in terms of the kinds of choices he made in dress, appearance, mannerism or location of office. Further, the kinds of responses made by the analyst invariably convey some sense of what he is interested in pursuing, as well as his style of thinking. And finally, there are many occasions when account has to be taken of concrete problems of living. At the other end, the most militant radical learns that if he practices therapy he has to appeal to some kind of inner emotional attitude if any change is to occur. Even if he chooses (as a number have) to drop therapy and try to accomplish the same ends by supposedly pure political means, he soon recognizes that the same subjective states play a large role in the way political realities are translated into the terms of everyday life. And the intermediate ideological positions are no less subject to compromise of one kind or another.

The second point is that compromises of ideology are forced

upon the practitioner by necessity. In short, ideologies have to be simpler than reality; indeed they distort reality and are in constant tension with it. In the present case the reality is the dialectical intertwining of the subjective and objective worlds, each with its hidden warping, each with its own laws, but each ultimately dependent upon the other. That is, neurosis would not exist did not the social world impose impossible contradictory and destructive demands on the growing individual—but once it does exist, it takes on a life of its own due to repression. Similarly, the social world is reproduced by and for people who have internalized destruction and contradiction—but once set going, it, too, takes its own course owing to the laws of political economy. Therefore all therapeutic ideologies are impossible to realize.

The third point, however, sets the matter back on track again. For the function of ideology is not to replicate reality but to guide it in a desired direction. Tension, imperfection and incomplete realization are necessary for all ideological positions, each of which expresses an "ought to be" on the part of the holder, and works to realize it. In this sense, then, therapeutic ideologies are authentic precisely as they strain against realization in practice. Therapy is worthless unless it gets us to aspire to something we might not ordinarily attain.

Further, all therapy is ideological, and no therapy is ideological. Wherever there is choice—whether to get treatment or not, whether to work at it or not, or whether to do anything or not—ideology necessarily exists, imperfect, perhaps implicit, yet always political. Reality is unformed, existing as a set of potentialities until human choice transforms it into a new, and still unformed, state. Ideologies may be efficacious or not according to how closely they approximate the actual dialectical state of reality. For example, the ideology of the Provisional Revolutionary Government conformed to the state of Vietnamese society while that of the Americans didn't. Consequently that society was transformed in a communist direction. And once transformed, new conditions and new ideologies are required—e.g., "permanent revolution," and so forth.

Similarly, Freud's ideology and method corresponded to the state of Western culture at his time. However, the ideology and practice of therapy can never be considered as static. Therapy is in an ever-dynamic relationship to the condition of society as a whole and has to be continually re-evaluated as new historical developments occur. In light of the current state of American society, then, what would be an adequate ideological position for therapy? Here, subject to all the limitations, is one observer's view.

It seems to me that the realities of neurosis in advanced industrial society have to be faced squarely, both as to their magnitude and causes. In this respect the radical therapies have made a notable contribution by pointing to the truth that neurosis springs not from some mysterious estrangement from nature, nor from "immortal ambivalence," nor from suppression or mystification in the family, nor from somatic constitution, but rather from the total societal organization—in this case, advanced capitalism—as it imposes contradictions upon *all* the forms of personal life.

So long as we have a dominative society with division of labor, alienation and class distinction, its splits will devolve onto family life and, given the natural susceptibility of human infants, will produce neurotic characters of one kind or another. It may well be that the susceptibility of infants to trouble is such that even within a truly free socialist society—i.e., one different from the ventures so far initiated—certain neurotic tendencies will arise. But that is an experiment which has to wait its turn. In the meantime we are stuck with a social system that generates colossal amounts of neurosis from every corner. Any effort to grasp the problem at a lesser level is going to be futile.

A large body of emotional crippling occurs, now as before, from the endless variety of traumatization which befalls people caught up in the lower classes of society, and from the direct brutalization that is bound to occur at all levels. It is of considerable importance to note in addition, however, that in the present state of advanced industrial society the very attempt to rationalize the conditions of life (within which would be included many "mental health" programs) is bound to increase neurotic tendencies. This is because such rationalization—e.g., as discussed above, the psychologizing away of the oppression of women—is in the interests of reinforcing a basically irrational system of social relations.

More than a century ago Marx predicted that, with the increasing autonomy of the production process, the development of a new form of "social individual" would occur as a means of production.[3] He might have added, had he been inclined to look in such a direction, that such an individual could not help but be neurotic. The relations of a social individual caught in an irrational society include, but are not limited to, the special inhumanity of modern work. They extend as well into the area of consumption, which permeates family life and filters downward to each person—in a way too complex to be more than dimly suggested here—as the cultivation of infantile desire along with the usurpation of parental authority by media, work relations, education, etc. The child is asked to develop his or her rational faculties in order to fit into an instrumental bureaucratic society that alienates real personal control over life. At the same time the individual is soothed with promises of personal fulfillment and happiness—without, to be sure, any solid communitarian base from which this is to spring.

The result is not the classical neurosis where an infantile impulse is suppressed by patriarchal authority, but a modern version in which the impulse is stimulated, perverted and given neither an adequate object upon which to satisfy itself nor coherent forms of control. In either case the impulse is inherently unrealizable; but the pattern of its disposition in the objective world changes. The disorder which is the hallmark of neurosis persists, as does the intrusion of unconscious desire and fear; but the entire complex, played out in a setting of alienation rather than direct control, loses the classical form of symptom—and the classical therapeutic opportunity of simply restoring an impulse to consciousness.

Beyond this point, however, the radical critique, at least as it has been made with respect to therapy, fritters itself away into mindless sloganeering. What the radical therapists forgot in their analysis was the distinction between the ultimate cause of a phenomenon such as neurosis and its actual manifestation. The harsh truth is that once neurotic repression sets in, whether at the behest of a repressive parent or by the alienated child's own effort to stem his feeling of inner chaos, the ensuing neurotic structure takes on a life of its own, becomes invisible. As a result any real connection to the world, such as can be gratified in action, is replaced by a symbolic linkage between a fantasy which goes its own way and a reality that represents it while being subject to laws of its own. I am not disputing the fact that concerted political action, especially that which unmasks the real external source of oppression, can have a beneficial effect on morale, etc., that goes will beyond simple material improvement. It may be that this is the most essential step, especially toward the prevention of neurosis. But it does not address the activity of neurotic functioning in the here and now. Thus radical therapists—whether they be feminists, gay liberationists or straight Marxists—who fancy that a direct appeal to visible oppression will unsnarl the inner invisible twisting are simply tilting at windmills. And despite their intentions, the extra cubit or two of false consciousness they are adding can only increase the degree of self-alienation which looms so large as a factor in neurotic despair.

The actuality of neurotic suffering in today's society is such that the therapies cannot be turned aside. This need not detract from the goal of abolishing the need for the services of therapists. For reasons stated above, however, I am skeptical that this goal can be realized within the confines of capitalist society. Such rationalizing efforts as come under the heading of "prevention of mental illness"—e.g., public-education measures; counseling within various arms of the bureaucracy, such as police, schools, family court, etc.; pastoral counseling and so forth—have their place, which cannot be explored here. But whatever they do, it will not be to stamp out "mental illness," even if the entire defense budget be turned over to them. And however much further socialism can go, we still have an immense mass of neurotic misery to deal with in the meantime. Nor should it be overlooked that, as Wilhelm Reich was the first to point out, the neurotic character structure itself impedes people's awareness of the actual nature of domination, hence extends that "meantime."[4]

Thus, whether one wishes to sustain the society but is nevertheless embarrassed by how much neurotic misery it churns out, or whether one wishes to transform it and is frustrated by neurotic inertia, therapy will have to be included as an institution for coping with neurosis. The questions remain, what kind, and how not to pervert it?

The general principle to follow, it seems to me, is to use therapy rationally without inflating its value. Consequently I am strongly opposed to any form of *totalization* within therapy. This principle has a wide-ranging application. It means, at one level, that no one system of therapy should prevail as the universal form of treatment, and that no professional body should exert hegemony over the realm of therapeutics. At another level, in the actual conduct of therapy, it means avoiding labeling, categorizing and behavior control insofar as possible. And at yet another level, it means avoiding the rigid application of the principle itself in dealing with certain people. I refer here to some types of chronically psychotic individuals, whose disorders have brought them to a level of objectification at which drugs, directive therapy, etc., are rational means of treatment.

The truth of the matter is that great numbers of people throughout history have been crushed by the brutalization of life in a dominative society. They never develop a definably neurotic character structure in which the subjective life, for all its twistedness, can be held up to therapeutic influence. It is hard to classify such people—certainly their existence is not a simple matter of social class—and harder yet to formulate ways of dealing with their myriad troubles. But whatever the answers to their emotional difficulties, they will not be found in simple psychotherapeutics.

The principle to avoid totalization is not unrealistic, in that advanced society has brought about an amazing diversity both of troubles and of means for dealing with them. Nor is it unscientific, as Jung was when he blandly claimed that people had different psychologies, hence needed different kinds of treatment. Being scientific in the present case means recognizing that the study of psychology must take into account the fracturing of the self which has occurred *pari passu* with the alienation of reality under capitalism. It is as though a mirror had been splintered by a blow. One can account for how it cracked, even describe the optics of the matter and the behavior of the molecules of the glass. And for this, psychoanalysis remains indispensable as a scientific critique capable of describing the formation of the self, whether whole or fractured. But the mirror is still broken, and the image it forms remains fragmented. And no therapeutic prescription, psychoanalytic or otherwise, can be made except as the subject recognizes some part of himself in the glass and seeks to build on it.

Moreover, the avoidance of totalization in therapy puts ideology in the proper political place. Therapy has to be taken most seriously within the terms of the neurosis it addresses. When, however, therapy begins to acquire a superordinate value—that is, when the treatment promises liberation, transcendence or the answer to the riddles of life; indeed, when it becomes an end *in itself* offering the hope of happiness—then we may know we are being duped, and distracted from more valid goals. This can happen in any type of therapy, although some schools are more susceptible than others, as I tried to indicate earlier. It can arise from the worship of introspection in itself by psychoanalysts, or of orgasms, or of primals, or of sexual technique, expressiveness, *est*, consciousness, OK-ness, communication, reinforcers—name it, and it will be made into an idol by some therapist who knows that his idolization will reap therapeutic gains simply by giving people something to grasp in the void.

It would perhaps be more precise to call the process *"fetishization,"* since the idol belongs to an earlier, religious phase of value, while the fetish is the creature of capital.[5] Fetishized therapy enters the world of commodity relations, hence tends to succeed. And there it joins hands with the rest of mass culture, which works to colonize a person's subjective life in order to keep him in line. Mass culture defines a cultural world bounded by capitalist relations. When fetishized therapy pretends that an inevitably limited personal reconciliation is adequate as a source of happiness, it is also necessarily implying that society as it exists provides adequate conditions for happiness. Such a goal is no rational one but only a rationalization for the established order; hence fetishized therapy rides the mass-cultural bandwagon. Under such terms therapy becomes a game; and games, therapy. It merges with "human relations" and sidles into the halls of big business and the military; while the therapist become a kind of folk expert in values and a monger of the proper conduct of life.

As part of mass culture, fetishized therapy becomes a fresh source of neurotic alienation. Its endless stream of moralizing slogans—"Be your own best friend"; "Stamp out sexual boredom"; "Stop hating yourself"; "Get it all out"; "Be free," etc.— does more than parody the original critical thrust of psychoanalytic thought; it sediments into a sludge of false consciousness that pretends to realize unconscious forces while in fact covering them with a thick layer of ooze. The promised payoff is in line with the ideology that we are to be happy with consumer society as it essentially is, thereby implying that we have no history to bedevil us.

But the unconscious is nothing but the claim made by lost fragments of personal history, and behind them, the history of a people. Hence fetishized therapy only changes the form of neurosis: Repression fails once again, the repressed returns, and the new, alienated self is led to turn to yet another therapeutic reassurance. Several of the newer therapies—for example, Gestalt or bioenergetics—arose in response to the fact that the sludge of false consciousness has in large part been composed of the intellectualized Freudian insight which resulted from the fetishization of verbal therapies. As such the new therapies were pointed at a real need. But often they, too, were fetishized from the moment of their birth. Promising fulfillment within the given society, they became as much a part of consumerist culture as ready-mix pastry, leaving room behind for the next "breakthrough" and fad.

If therapy is to arrest neurosis and not advance it, the role it must assume is a modest, defensive one, without pretense or any kind of totalistic claim. In sum, therapy has no business imposing upon people either political categories they are unprepared to accept or spurious values of instant transcendence they are only too willing to swallow.

Here the reflective therapies, including but not limited to psychoanalysis, have a special opportunity—and a special potential for perversion. The opportunity lies in their imperative of truthfulness. Fidelity to the untidy truth about ourselves necessarily opposes totalization. Honestly pursued, it cannot but lead to resistance against mass culture's colonization by false consciousness. But to honestly pursue the goal of truthfulness is to suspend ordinary judgments of ideology and value, all of which, no matter how "correct," inevitably twist reality in the direction of wish. Therefore, to honestly pursue reflective therapy one must bracket out values, including political ideology, which point toward objective changes in the world.

Such a course is logical in view of the fact that a person's subjective side is never in phase with either the way things are outside the self or with the way one wants them to be. Further, influencing a patient within the therapeutic session, in matters pertaining to the conduct of life outside, is always a doubtful venture, since the patient may well be under the sway of a transference that reflects the inner roots of domination, and not his mature capacity to judge. But to bracket things out means only to set them aside for the nonce; it does not imply neglect or the pretense that what goes on in the analyst's office is the "real" reality. The latter illusion leads to the very fetishization of psychoanalysis which has made it into the conformist institution it is today. For the inflation of analytic insight serves the same function as that of behavioral modification: In each case it is a bid for authority and control, a quest for power, not truth.

The truest function of psychoanalysis lies in its capacity to preserve an authentic realm of the imagination. While the imagination holds the greatest terrors to which we can become subject, it also provides the wish to be free. Indeed it is what makes us distinctively human, containing in its unconscious recesses the seeds of the best as well as the worst in us.

The domination of consciousness by late capitalist culture makes its preservation a precious goal—and one subject to elitism. Psychoanalysis has cultivated a fidelity to the processes of self-formation which, for all the innovations in therapy, remains a unique testament to the worth of the individual. Yet at the same time, psychoanalysis has not been able to avoid becoming locked into upper-bourgeois class interests, a fate which has exerted an inexorably stultifying influence over its theory and practice, and may be sounding its knell as a vital element in contemporary society.

While much will have been lost in such an eventuality, I do not think we need fear the final extinction of the impulse to preserve what is life-giving in the imagination—or even the loss of its power in therapy. For not only is this impulse too deeply grounded to wither away just because an offshoot should lose touch with its own roots; but it continually reappears as one of those contradictions capital stimulates out of its own makings, then tries to quell as an intolerable threat. Hence capital does not create the imagination; it only draws it into a new level of struggle.

Indeed, although continually modified by real historical circumstances, the force of imagination is in a deep sense transhistorical. It is generated in each child out of the human givens of infantile sexuality and object loss, factors that have been necessary for civilization itself and long predate any particular phase such as capitalism. The record of the imagination, in fact, goes back as far as art itself. Freud added a scientific dimension to what had been embedded within art and so amplified its power as critique. But a century before Freud, Blake, who of all poets was most in touch with dialectics, made the same claim. Listen to a version from *Milton:*

> But turning toward Ololon in terrible majesty Milton
> Replied. Obey thou the Words of the Inspired Man.
> All that can be annihilated must be annihilated
> That the Children of Jerusalem may be saved from slavery
> There is a Negation, & there is a Contrary
> The Negation must be destroyd to redeem the Contraries

> The Negation is the Spectre; the Reasoning Power in Man
> This is a false Body: In Incrustation over my Immortal
> Spirit; a Selfhood, which must be put off & annihilated alway
> To cleanse the Face of my Spirit by Self-examination.
> To bathe in the Waters of Life; to wash off the Not Human,
> I come in Self-annihilation & the grandeur of Inspiration. . . .[6]

The Negation—in contemporary terms, false, colonized consciousness, encrusted, passive and given to accepting the order of things as eternal and natural—has to be eliminated in order to face the true clash of opposites, Contraries. "Without Contraries is no progression. Attraction and Repulsion, Reason and Energy, Love and Hate, are necessary to Human existence," wrote Blake in *The Marriage of Heaven and Hell.* The sufferings of what we call "neurosis" represent a partial breakdown of the Negation of false consciousness. Closer to the impulse, with love and hate fused, then the flattened consciousness of official reason, each mental "disturbance" poses a dialectical opportunity. For the neurotic is both turned away from everyday reality and greatly inclined to submit to it. That is why we see neurotic people alternately rebelling and submitting: acting impulsively to free themselves, but winding up more enslaved than before.

The neurotic, in sum, is brought closer to Contraries but cannot face them. By reliving and mastering them, the neurotic disposition will be reversed. And this work can be begun but not completed in psychotherapeutic terms, for Contraries are not to be overcome within one's head. Their true location is between the subjective and objective world: The Energy opposed to Reason "is the only life and is from the Body"—the material body, with its erotic striving, and the material body of politics as well. Blake never doubted that the struggle had to include concrete revolutionary practice. As David Erdman writes in his excellent study of Blake's politics, *Blake: Prophet Against Empire,* for Blake, "at the limits of empire, Contraries begin."[7]

Contraries thus are situated in history—in real classes and the very material "dark Satanic Mills." The function of the critical imagination, whether in art, therapy or politics, is to clear away false, Negated, consciousness so that the work with Contraries can begin. In political terms: After liberation from the old order, true revolutionary work begins. And in therapeutic terms: After Self-examination, on with the business of dealing with the contrariness of real life.

We may recast Freud's dictum in Blakean terms—and, as he might have seen it, in Mosaic ones as well: Neurosis is grounded in everyday reality but breaks with it. Much will be gained if we succeed in mending that break by restoring to you the full power of your critical imagination. In that way you will be less neurotic and less dependent as well on Negations. You will be better prepared to deal with Contraries, closer to reality and more able to reverse the tide of common unhappiness. But I, your therapist, because of the special nature of neurotic distortion, and because I hold for you the goal of freedom, refuse to lead you further into the vision of a new community necessary to resist common unhappiness.

Therapy so viewed only hopes to mobilize our imaginative powers to deal with the real contradictions of life. There may be little solace in such a view, which promises no "True Self," gleaming with authenticity, striding out from the rubble of neurosis. But therapy so viewed does hope to restore to people some of their capacity to love and to choose, and to begin making real demands on a world shaped by the lies of history. In this way they may begin to determine for themselves in which direction the true self lies.

GLOSSARY

Actualneurosis: a term, now anachronistic, used by Freud to describe a neurosis produced by "actual" frustration—i.e., where the damming up of tension caused the neurotic behavior. This concept of neurosis became the basis of Reichian theory. (See **biofunctional therapy, orgonomy.**)

ambivalence: the basis of psychological conflict; simultaneously holding two opposed feelings or wishes—e.g., love and hate. Implied in the concept is an imperfect or falsified consciousness of this state of affairs. (See **defense.**)

analytical psychology: the theory of mind developed by C. G. Jung according to which psychological phenomena were to be ultimately explained by their relation to a collective unconscious, or universal mind, that made itself known in human life.

anxiety: a concept with many meanings, from the **existential** awareness of "being-in-the-world" to the **Actualneurotic** concept that anxiety is the result of sexual energy transformed through frustration. As used in the text, however, "anxiety" basically refers to a diffuse sense of approaching danger, when the content of that danger is unknown. The danger can be then from either **objective** or **subjective** sources, as from a partially repressed impulse. (See **defense.**)

behavioral-directive therapy: a group of therapies that work with the assumption that a neurotic problem can be objectively separated from the rest of the self—i.e., can be treated as external, and with direct instructions.

behavior therapy: a main category of the above, which isolates discrete "target behaviors" for change, then attempts to alter them with specific operations derived from learning theory. Implied in this is a downplaying of the subjective side of behavior.

biofunctional therapy: a type of therapy deriving from the work of Wilhelm Reich. It regards neurosis as an interruption of the natural functioning of the body and uses movement, massage, emotive expression, etc., as agents of change. (See **nature, orgonomy.**)

compulsion: narrowly, a type of neurosis in which repetitive acts are performed against one's will; broadly, the sense of unfreedom inherent in all neurosis.

contact: a **biofunctional** and **Gestalt** term for a state of completeness, manifested by heightened awareness, between a person and his bodily processes, or between two or more people, or between parts of a psychological pattern.

defense: a general term for the means by which a person alters consciousness in order to exclude unwanted ideas, feelings or impulses. Defenses are generally employed as a result of **anxiety.** (See also **ambivalence, projection, repression.**)

depression: a state that is to be distinguished from sadness, grief and mourning in that the person does not simply miss something but also feels badly about himself—burdened, self-critical, weary, all the way to suicidal.

encounter: a loosely structured and brief form of group therapy in which emotional change is brought about by the expression of strong feeling between members of the group.

est: an acronym for Erhard Seminars Training; a brief but intense large-group experience the object of which is to get in touch with one's responsibility for one's being. Means to this end include physical privation, guided meditation, and confrontations and indoctrination by the group trainer.

existential analysis: a group of approaches united by their cultivation of **subjectivity** and immediacy and an avoidance of intellectual explanations; varies from pessimistic European schools to optimistic branches of the **human-potential movement.**

family therapy: therapy that treats the family as a group, rather than isolating one member as the patient. It usually works with communications between family members.

Freudian psychoanalysis: see **psychoanalysis.**

Gestalt therapy: a therapy deriving from the school of psychology of the same name and developed principally by F. Perls, in which a person seeks heightened awareness through dramatization of split-off parts of the self. (See **projection.**)

group psychotherapy: any one of a number of approaches, usually derived from **psychoanalysis,** in which psychological problems are played out and worked through in a small group over an extended period.

human-potential movement: also called "humanistic psychology," "Post-Freudian psychology," etc.; a broad front of psychological approaches which coalesced in the Sixties about the themes of spontaneity, heightened awareness, emotional freedom and so forth. (See **existential analysis,** *est***, encounter,** and **biofunctional, Gestalt, Rogerian** and **mysticotranscendent** therapies.)

hypnotherapy: the original psychotherapeutic technique in which suggestion and an altered state of consciousness are combined to produce behavioral change.

identification: an **unconscious** alteration of the self to resemble another person, or a part of that person, such as his or her value system. (See **superego.**)

infantile sexuality: a complex pattern of fantasy and wish, discovered by Sigmund Freud, through which the developing person creates his or her erotic being out of bodily impulse and perception on the one hand, and family relations on the other; mainly **unconscious**, and as such to be distinguished from adult sexuality, which is the conscious, behavioral end stage of its development, manifested as felt lust and sexual activity.

mysticotranscendent therapy: a group whose central technique is meditation and whose paramount purpose is to cultivate heightened and refined **subjectivity**. It is often but not necessarily associated with Eastern religions and the search for higher knowledge.

narcissism: love of the self; a normal phenomenon, although invariably drawn into neurotic functioning in a distorted and compulsive way; the hitch being that when narcissism is disturbed, regard for the self has to be restored mainly through submission to or domination of another person.

nature: as used here, that which exists outside our will and history—e.g., the stars, or our deaths. In all human situations some natural element exists in a dialectical relation to our values, intentions and historically given setting.

Neo-Freudian psychoanalysis: See **psychoanalysis**.

neurosis: any pattern in which unwanted and **compulsive** thoughts, feelings and/or actions occur without producing a major, sustained disorganization of personality or the loss of a sense of reality.

objective: having a material quality; used in referring to those elements of a situation that can be described in spatial and temporal terms.

obsession: a form of neurosis in which unwanted, stereotyped thoughts occur involuntarily; also **obsessional**, a type of neurotic person whose main style of defense is to accentuate thinking rather than feeling.

orgonomy: Wilhelm Reich's particular development of **biofunctionalism** based upon the assumption of a universal, **objectively** measurable life energy, the orgone.

phobia: a form of **neurosis** in which **subjective** dangers are **projected** onto some event or object, which then has to be avoided in order to control **anxiety**.

primal therapy: a therapy developed by Arthur Janov in which the concentrated expression of deep infantile pain is promoted as a cure for neurosis.

projection: a **defense** in which **subjective** qualities are assigned to the **objective** world, as when we are angry at another person yet have the experience that he is angry at us. Projections may or may not be factually true; what counts is their role in falsifying awareness.

psychoanalysis: a theory of the mind and a mode of therapy developed by Sigmund Freud on the basis of his method of free association. The central tenets of Freud's theory are **infantile sexuality, repression** and the **unconscious**. Freudian psychoanalytic therapy makes use of the technique of free association to promote conscious appropriation of split-off unconscious traces of personal history. Central to the treatment is work with **resistance and transference**. Neo-Freudian psychoanalysis is a heterogeneous group that still relies on hidden forces within the mind, but downplays the role of infantile sexuality and repression, places a greater emphasis on steps taken to achieve self-esteem and security and uses a more direct interaction between analyst and patient as a means of treatment.

psychobiological: refers to those approaches which regard mental events as primarily determined by natural—i.e., nonsocial—factors. (See **biofunctional therapy, behavior therapy, mysticotranscendent therapy, somatic therapy.**)

psychodrama: a therapy developed by J. L. Moreno in which the elements of one's neurosis are dramatized as **roles** and enacted in an effort to overcome them.

psychodynamic: a term applying to any treatment or theory that relies heavily on the interplay of forces within the mind. (See **subjective.**)

psychosis: a state characterized by severe disorganization of the personality and the loss of a sense of reality—i.e., the inability to discriminate between **subjective** and objective worlds. (Compare **neurosis.**)

psychotherapy: broadly put, synonymous with therapy itself; more specifically, any therapy that relies on psychological means; more narrowly yet, a modification of **psychoanalysis** so that the patient sits up, has less-frequent sessions, focuses on current life problems as against free association, etc.

psychosocial: used in referring to those approaches that regard mental events as primarily determined by social—i.e., non-natural—forces. (See **family therapy, group psychotherapy,** etc.)

rational-emotive therapy: a therapy developed by Albert Ellis which stresses a problem-solving, positive approach to emotional problems and relies heavily on the imposition of values. (See **behavioral-directive therapy.**)

reality therapy: a therapy developed by William Glasser which relies on developing responsible, moral behavior as a means of overcoming neurosis. (See **behavioral-directive therapy.**)

repression: the basic **defense** by which thoughts are kept **unconscious.** It includes both an active forgetting, and a forgetting that we have forgotten—i.e., it occurs silently. Usually combines with other defenses. (Compare **suppression.**)

resistance: in Freudian psychoanalysis, any maneuver by which the patient blocks the unfolding of his **unconscious** thoughts; includes **defenses** insofar as they interrupt the analytic process, but also **suppression** of what is known, missing sessions, etc. The same concept can be generalized to any dynamic therapy.

role: behavior structured by expectations of the social environment, including that of therapy. (See **psychodrama.**)

sex therapy: a variant of **behavioral-directive therapy** and, usually, **family therapy** in which adult sexual disturbances are dealt with in an objective, matter-of-fact way, and managed by educational methods. (See **infantile sexuality.**)

somatic therapy: all those therapeutic approaches which apply physical means

—drugs, electric shock, etc.—to the body, as a strategy for altering an emotional state. (See **behavioral-directive therapy, psychobiological.**)

subjective: also known as experiential, psychic reality, etc.; used in referring to those elements of a human situation which do not have an **objective** basis and are describable as thought, feeling, wish, value, fantasy, etc. Every emotional state is necessarily subjective as well as objective.

superego: in psychoanalytic theory, a mental system involved with the guidance of behavior by norms and value; includes conscience and ideals but is largely **unconscious**; formed out of **identification** with parents, hence invariably implicated in the **transference** aspects of all therapies.

suppression: actively withholding from communication thoughts that are conscious.

systems theory: a body of thinking, widely employed in science, that regards entities—systems—as defined by the interrelationship of their parts. Each part may be a system in itself, and each system may be a part of a larger system. Very influential in **family therapy.**

transaction: a structured interaction between people that has a specific quality and is extended in time; as when wife nags → husband drinks → wife nags, etc.

transactional analysis: a group therapy developed by Eric Berne and others in which **transactions** between people are used to define and analyze so-called ego states within the individual—the Child, Parent and Adult—with the goal of moving toward Adulthood.

transference: the **unconscious** repeating of an earlier relationship in a current setting. It is strictly defined for **psychoanalysis**, where a transference edition of the original childhood neurosis is developed toward the therapist and overcome. But it applies in any therapeutic setting—indeed any kind of setting where a difference in power is an issue.

trauma: the result of an overwhelming situation in which a person is flooded with more stimuli than can be mastered; in childhood, the nuclear setting for the development of **neurosis.**

unconscious: used in referring to a system of mental processes occurring outside awareness. Variously defined in many psychological theories (see **analytical psychology, Neo-Freudian psychoanalysis**), but the meaning employed in the present work is Freud's: the unconscious primarily as a radically **repressed** system of lost fragments of actual experience, erupting in **neurosis**, always making demands on reality, and never appeased. (See **infantile sexuality.**) In addition to its use in describing a mental system, the term is also used to describe the quality of a thought according to which it is excluded from conscious awareness.

NOTES

Introduction

1. For a somewhat different approach to this dimension, see Seymour Halleck, *The Politics of Therapy* (New York, 1971). And for an excellent brief introduction to the necessarily social role of the therapist—along with an ample bibliography—see Benjamin Nelson, "The Psychoanalyst as Mediator and Double Agent: An Introductory Survey," *Psychoanalytic Review*, 52, no. 3 (1965): 375–90.
2. Philip Rieff, *The Triumph of the Therapeutic* (New York, 1966).
3. Russell Jacoby, *Social Amnesia, A Critique of Conformist Psychology from Adler to Laing* (Boston, 1975), p. 121.
4. Of the first type, consider Adelaide Bry, ed., *Inside Psychotherapy* (New York, 1972). Of the second, the best-known is Ruth Monroe, *Schools of Psychoanalytic Thought* (New York, 1955). A more recent venture, emphasizing the European schools, is Dieter Wyss, *Psychoanalytic Schools from the Beginning to the Present* (New York, 1973). An exceptionally scholarly and careful analysis that covers more ground than the above studies is Donald H. Ford and Hugh B. Urban, *Systems of Psychotherapy, A Comparative Study* (New York, 1963). Finally, a wide-ranging study that aims to find the common ground underlying psychotherapy is Jerome Frank, *Persuasion and Healing* (New York, 1963).

Part One. NEUROSIS AND THERAPY

Chapter 1. The Contours Of Disorder

1. A valuable study that explores the social roots of the concept of mental illness is Peter Sedgwick, "Illness—Mental and Otherwise," *Hastings Center Studies*, 1, no. 3 (1973) : 19–41; also in *Salmagundi*, Summer–Fall, 1972.
2. Included here is something that lies outside the scope of this work, the question of inherited predisposition to emotional disturbance. There is no question that people tend to exaggerate the effects of biological and constitutional factors as a way of avoiding certain emotional insights. However, this should not be taken to imply that constitution is unimportant—only that it is irrelevant for present purposes, since it is a given, and we are concerned about what to *do* with the given situation.
3. See Selma Fraiberg, *The Magic Years* (New York, 1959); Theodore Lidz, *The Person* (New York, 1968); Anna Freud, *Normality and Pathology in Childhood* (New York, 1965).

4. A useful discussion of clinical entities may be found in John Nemiah, *Foundations of Psychopathology* (New York, 1961).
5. A good introduction to the issue is Nicholas Kittrie, *The Right To Be Different* (Baltimore, 1971).
6. For a general introduction to schizophrenia, see C. Peter Rosenbaum, *The Meaning of Madness* (New York, 1970).

Chapter 2. On Therapy And Therapies

1. It is for this reason that efforts to evaluate therapeutic outcome are so often suspect. There is nothing wrong with being scientific about therapy, but the science in question should not be of the positivistic kind that splits facts from values. Indeed, the evaluation of therapeutic result is so fiendishly complex that the best studies usually come up with no clear conclusions, while those that insist on definite answers (e.g., H. J. Eysenck and S. Rachman, *The Causes and Cures of Neurosis* [San Diego, Calif., 1965]) do so by working with a model of therapy that is virtually unrecognizable in human terms.
2. Claude Lévi-Strauss, "The Sorcerer and His Magic," in *Structural Anthropology*, trans. Claire Jacobson and Brooke Grundfest Schoepf (New York, 1963), pp. 167–86.
3. See Henri Ellenberger, *The Discovery of the Unconscious* (New York, 1970).
4. Michel Foucault, *Madness and Civilization*, trans. Richard Howard (New York, 1965).
5. See Ellenberger, *op. cit.*
6. The literature on Freud is both too vast and too controversial to allow for a critical bibliography. The key biography, for all its one-sided adulation, is still Ernest Jones's three-volume study, *Sigmund Freud: Life and Work* (New York, 1953–57); see also Richard Wollheim, *Sigmund Freud* (New York, 1971), and O. Mannoni, *Freud* (New York, 1971).
7. The Ellenberger study, *op. cit.*, also contains an elaborate survey of the history of psychoanalytic schools through the first half of the century. This book is useful because of its encyclopedic nature, although in my opinion it has little critical value or real historical analysis. Also see Wyss, *op. cit.*
8. Rollo May, Ernest Angel and Henri Ellenberger, eds., *Existence: A New Dimension in Psychiatry and Psychology* (New York, 1958).
9. There is still an amazing shortage of good work on Reich. For some interesting autobiographical reflections, see Wilhelm Reich, *People in Trouble* (Rangeley, Maine, 1953); for some other personal notes, see Ilse O. Reich, *Wilhelm Reich* (New York, 1970), and Ola Raknes, *Wilhelm Reich and Orgonomy* (New York, 1970). For the work, see Constantin Sinelnikoff, *L'oeuvre de Wilhelm Reich*, 2 vols. (Paris, 1970), soon to be translated.
10. Frederick Perls, Ralph Hefferline and Paul Goodman, *Gestalt Therapy: Excitement and Growth in the Human Personality* (New York, 1965).
11. See the autobiographical essay by Rogers in Arthur Burton, ed., *Twelve Therapists* (San Francisco, 1972).
12. For surveys of the range of group therapies, see Harold Kaplan and Benjamin Sadock, eds., *Comprehensive Group Psychotherapy* (Baltimore, 1971).
13. See Clifford Sager and Helen Singer Kaplan, eds., *Progress in Group and Family Therapy* (New York, 1972); Ivan Boszormenyi-Nagy and James Framo, eds., *Intensive Family Therapy* (New York, 1965); Andrew Ferber, Marilyn Mendelsohn and Augustus Napier, eds., *The Book of Family Therapy* (New York, 1972).
14. Arthur Janov, *The Primal Scream* (New York, 1970).
15. Eysenck, H. J., ed., *Behavior Therapy and the Neuroses* (New York, 1960); Joseph Wolpe and Arnold Lazarus, *Behavior Therapy Techniques* (New York, 1966).
16. See Melanie Klein, *Contributions to Psychoanalysis* (London, 1950).
17. See Harry Stack Sullivan, *The Interpersonal Theory of Psychiatry* (New York, 1953).
18. See Introduction, note 4.

Part Two. THE VARIETIES OF THERAPEUTIC EXPERIENCE

Chapter 3. Freudian Psychoanalysis And Psychoanalytic Psychotherapy

1. Though writings on psychoanalysis as a therapy are legion, the general reader cannot do better than Freud. As an opener try chapters 27, "Transference," and 28, "Analytic Therapy," in *Introductory Lectures on Psycho-Analysis,* volume 16 of the *Standard Edition of the Complete Psychological Works of Sigmund Freud* (henceforth referred to as *S. E.*) , ed., James Strachey. For a comprehensive recent synthesis, see Ralph Greenson, *The Technique and Practice of Psycho-analysis,* vol. 1 (New York, 1967).
2. See Sidney Tarachow, *An Introduction to Psychotherapy* (New York, 1963); Paul DeWald, *Psychotherapy, A Dynamic Approach* (New York, 1964).

Chapter 4. Neo-Freudian Analysis

1. See Monroe, *op. cit.,* and Ford and Urban, *op. cit.,* for detailed analysis of the different schools.
2. See Ellenberger, *op. cit.*
3. There is a whole political world here. Freudian credentials are defined through membership in the International Psycho-Analytic Association and/or its largest-by-far affiliate, the American Psychoanalytic Association. The particular breaks have been made over the years with these bodies. Many of the Neo-Freudian schools have since formed their own associations—e.g., the William Alanson White Institute (Sullivanian), the Karen Horney Institute, etc.
4. See Chap. 2, note 6.
5. Karen Horney, *Neurosis and Human Growth* (New York, 1950), pp. 378, 17; See also *The Neurotic Personality of Our Time* (New York, 1937).
6. Harry Stack Sullivan, *op. cit.,* p. 295.
7. *Ibid.* pp. 214, 215.
8. Indeed the Freudian movement itself has edged toward the Neo-Freudian—while still holding onto the concept of infantile sexuality and its view of the unconscious—by developing the modification of Freud's view known as "ego psychology." Without going into detail, we can say that the ego here is in an active relation with external reality and that it enters into conflict as a force of its own along with the drives. Hence, the differences between psychoanalysis positions can be described as a matter of how much of a handicap is given to each of the players involved in psychological conflict.
9. See Erich Fromm, *Man for Himself* (New York, 1947).

Chapter 5. Jung And Analytical Psychology

1. Jung wrote a great deal and has been in turn the subject of a vast literature. The reader should peruse his *Collected Works,* especially vol. 5, *Symbols of Transformation* (New York, 1956); see also *Man and His Symbols* (London and New York, 1964) and Jolande Jacobi, *Complex, Archetype and Symbol in the Psychology of C. G. Jung* (London and New York, 1959).
2. Freud persisted in the belief, for example, that certain systems—e.g., the Oedipus complex—were innate and were laid down in human genes as a result of prehistoric experience.
3. C. G. Jung, *Analytical Psychology: Its Theory and Practice* (New York, 1968), p. 182.
4. See Philip Rieff, *op. cit.*

Chapter 6. The Existential Approach

1. May, Angel and Ellenberger, *op. cit.*
2. L. Binswanger, *Ausgewählte Vortrage and Aufsätze*, vol. 2 (Bern, 1955), p. 304, quoted in Wyss, *op. cit.*, p. 397.
3. In May, Angel and Ellenberger, *op. cit.*, pp. 237–365.
4. See Leston Havens, *Approaches to the Mind* (Boston, 1973).
5. For an unflattering view of the conceptual content of existential therapy, see Benjamin Nelson, "Phenomenological Psychiatry, Daseinanalyse and American Existential Analysis: A 'Progress' Report," *Psychoanalysis and the Psychoanalytic Review*, vol. 48, no. 4 (1961–62): 3–23.
6. E.g., Victor Frankl, *The Doctor and the Soul*, 2d ed. (New York, 1965).
7. R. D. Laing, *The Politics of Experience* (New York, 1967).
8. This was a war waged on several fronts. Along with Laing's attack from the Left, official psychiatry had to contend with the Right-libertarian critique of Thomas Szasz; see his *Law, Liberty and Psychiatry* (New York, 1963).We cannot take up the issue here except to note that despite some degree of reform, official psychiatry is holding its own quite well.
9. See Mary Barnes and Joseph Berke, *Mary Barnes, Two Accounts of a Journey Through Madness* (New York, 1972).
10. However, as Russell Jacoby has trenchantly pointed out (Jacoby *op. cit.*), Laing's effort ultimately collapses into subjectivity. This may account for its seeming inability to sustain its momentum as a body of thought.
11. See R. D. Laing, *The Divided Self* (London, 1960) and *The Politics of the Family* (New York, 1971).

Chapter 7. Rogerian Therapy

1. See Burton, ed., *op. cit.*
2. Carl Rogers, *On Becoming a Person* (Boston, 1961), pp. 90–91.
3. *Ibid.*, pp. 22, 23.

Chapter 8. Gestalt Therapy

1. Frederick Perls, *Gestalt Therapy Verbatim* (New York, 1969).
2. See Perls, Hefferline and Goodman, *op. cit.;* also Frederick Perls, *Ego, Hunger and Aggression* (New York, 1969).
3. *Gestalt Therapy Verbatim*, p. 57.
4. *Ibid.*, p. 51.

Chapter 9. Biofunctional Therapies: Wilhelm Reich And Bioenergetics

1. See Chap. 2, note 9. For the works of Reich's Marxist phase, see Lee Baxandall, ed., *Sex-Pol Essays 1929–1934, Wilhelm Reich* (New York, 1972); also Wilhelm Reich, *The Mass Psychology of Fascism*, trans. T. P. Wolfe (New York, 1946). The reader should be aware in reading Reich's work that it is in general very badly edited (an exception is *Sex-Pol Essays*). His thought underwent many changes over the years, all of which tend to get mixed up in his published work.
2. *S.E.*, vol. 9, p. 179.
3. Wilhelm Reich, *The Function of the Orgasm*, trans. T. P. Wolfe (New York, 1961). This work was first published in 1927.
4. Wilhelm Reich, *Character Analysis*, 3d ed. (New York, 1961). This, Reich's only work to remain influential in mainstream psychoanalysis, was first published in 1933.

5. They had something to do with a change in Reich's—and orgonomy's—experience with orgone energy. In brief, he began to lapse into dualism. Along with the life energy, orgone (OR), Reich claimed that, with the advent of nuclear weaponry, a deadly orgone (DOR) was making its appearance, with counter-therapeutic effects. Whatever the reasons, orgonomists rarely use the orgone accumulator in treatment nowadays.

6. Alexander Lowen, *The Betrayal of the Body* (New York, 1967).

Chapter 10. Primal Therapy

1. Arthur Janov, *The Primal Scream* (New York, 1970).
2. *Ibid.*, p. 245.
3. *Ibid.*, p. 72.
4. *Ibid.*, p. 25.
5. As with all therapies, some distinction has to be made between the way the Master laid things out and the way things eventually came to be. Primal therapy has·been around long enough already for a number of variations to appear. Obviously it is not possible to do justice to these and still remain useful. Thus what is presented here is the original, classic Janovian technique.
6. Arthur Janov, *op. cit.*, p. 246.
7. Gregory Bateson et al., "Toward a Theory of Schizophrenia," *Behavioral Science*, 1, no. 4 (1956); reprinted in Gregory Bateson, *Steps to an Ecology of the Mind* (New York, 1972).

Chapter 11. The Mysticotranscendent Approach

1. Erich Fromm and D. T. Suzuki, *Zen Buddhism and Psychoanalysis* (New York, 1960).
2. Herbert Fingarette, *The Self in Transformation* (New York, 1963).
3. Alan Watts, *Psychotherapy East and.West* (New York, 1961).
4. See Charles Tart, ed., *Altered States of Consciousness* (New York, 1969).
5. S. Freud, *Civilization and Its Discontents*, Chap. 1 (*S. E.*, vol. 21, p. 59).
6. Claudio Naranjo and Robert E. Ornstein, *On the Psychology of Meditation* (New York, 1971); see also Arthur Deikman, "Deautomatization and the Mystic Experience," *Psychiatry*, 29 (1966): 324–38; reprinted in Tart, *op. cit.*
7. R. C. Zaehner, *Zen, Drugs and Mysticism* (New York, 1972), p. 125.
8. Heinrich Zimmer, *Philosophies of India* (New York, 1951), p. 573.
9. Claudio Naranjo, *The Healing Journey: New Approaches to Consciousness* (New York, 1973).

Chapter 12. The Social Dimension: Group Approaches

1. S. Freud, *Group Psychology and the Analysis of the Ego* (*S. E.*, vol. 18, p. 67).
2. See Weston LaBarre, *The Human Animal* (Chicago, 1954).
3. See Kaplan and Sadock, *op. cit.*, for a broad survey.
4. See Jean Piaget and Bärbel Inhelder, *The Psychology of the Child* (New York, 1969). As for theories of small-group behavior, the most interesting to my mind is W. R. Bion's *Experiences in Groups* (London, 1961); see also Irvin Yalom, *The Theory and Practice of Group Psychotherapy* (New York, 1970); S. H. Foulkes, *Therapeutic Group Analysis* (London, 1964); and S. R. Slavson, *An Introduction to Group Therapy* (New York, 1943).
5. T-groups have become a growth industry, especially at places like the National Training Laboratories at Bethel, Maine. It should be plain that the line between training and therapy is not an easy one to define; and although the training centers are quite alive to the problem, the issue constantly arises. For further reading, see L. P. Bradford, J. R. Gibb and K. D. Benne, eds., *T-Group Theory and Laboratory Method* (New York, 1964).

6. See Arthur Burton, ed., *Encounter: The Theory and Practice of Encounter Groups* (San Francisco, 1969). A thoughtful essay surveying the phenomenon is Morris Parloff, "Group Therapy and the Small Group Field: An Encounter," in Sager and Kaplan, *op. cit.*, p. 174.

7. Irvin Yalom and Morton Lieberman, "A Study of Encounter Group Casualities," in Sager and Kaplan, *op. cit.*, p. 223.

8. Quoted in Marcia Seligson, "Does Werner Erhard Have the Answer?" *New Times*, October 18, 1974, p. 50.

9. *Ibid.*, p. 41.

10. See J. L. Moreno, *Who Shall Survive?* (New York, 1953); see also the chapter on psychodrama in Kaplan and Sadock, *op. cit.*

11. John M. Dusay and Claude Steiner, "Transactional Analysis in Groups," in Kaplan and Sadock, *op. cit.*; see also Eric Berne, *Transactional Analysis in Psychotherapy* (New York, 1961).

12. Claude Steiner, *TA Made Simple* (Berkeley, Calif., 1971); see also C. Steiner et al., *Readings in Radical Psychiatry* (New York, 1975).

13. Thomas Harris, *I'm OK—You're OK* (New York, 1969), pp. 18, 272.

14. For example, the Internal Revenue Service employs TA jargon in its training program. The bad taxpayer becomes the Child, while the good taxpayer—as well as the good IRS agent—behaves like the sensible Adult. Earl Klee, "Serving Time with the I.R.S.," *Social Policy* (March–April, 1975); vol. 5, pp. 43–48.

Chapter 13. Family Therapy

1. Gregory Bateson, ed., *Steps to an Ecology of Mind* (New York, 1972).

2. William Gray, Frederick J. Duhl and Nicholas D. Rizzo, *General Systems Theory and Psychiatry* (Boston, 1969).

3. See Ivan Boszormenyi-Nagy and James L. Framo, eds., *op. cit.*; also Christian Beels and Andrew Ferber, "Family Therapy: A View," *Family Process, 8* (1969): 280–332.

4. Edgar H. Auerswald, "Interdisciplinary Versus Ecological Approach," in Sager and Kaplan, eds., *op. cit.*, p. 309.

5. H. Peter Laqueur, "Mechanisms of Change in Multiple Family Therapy," in Sager and Kaplan, eds., *op. cit.*, p. 400.

6. Ross Speck and Carolyn Attneave, *Family Networks* (New York, 1973).

7. See Chap. 6, note 10.

8. See Chap. 9, note 1.

9. See Juliet Mitchell, *Woman's Estate* (New York, 1970).

Chapter 14. Behavioral-Directive Therapy

1. For some points of entry into the area, see Donald F. Klein and John M. Davis, *Diagnosis and Drug Treatment of Psychiatric Disorders* (Baltimore, 1969); Solomon Snyder, *Madness and the Brain* (New York, 1974); Lothar Kalinowsky and Paul Hoch, *Somatic Treatments in Psychiatry* (New York and London, 1961).

2. William H. Masters and Virginia E. Johnson, *Human Sexual Response* (Boston, 1964), *Human Sexual Inadequacy* (Boston, 1970); see also Helen Singer Kaplan, *The New Sex Therapy* (New York, 1974).

3. Merton Gill and Margaret Brenman, *Hypnosis and Related States* (New York, 1959); Jesse E. Gordon, ed., *Handbook of Clinical and Experimental Hypnosis* (New York, 1967); see also Ellenberger, *op. cit.*, for historical detail.

4. William Glasser, *Reality Therapy* (New York, 1965).

5. Albert Ellis, *Reason and Emotion in Psychotherapy* (New York, 1962). The titles of Ellis's work speak for themselves: *The Civilized Couples' Guide to Extramarital Adventure* (New York, 1972), *Executive Leadership: A Rational Approach* (1972), *Sex Without Guilt* (1973), etc.

6. See Chap 2, note 15; also A. A. Lazarus, ed., *Clinical Behavior Therapy* (New York, 1972).

7. Joseph Wolpe, *The Practice of Behavior Therapy* (Oxford, 1969).
8. A technique developed by Milton Erickson, in which the "reverse psychology" often employed in childrearing is applied to therapeutic purposes. See Jay Haley, *Uncommon Therapy: The Psychiatric Techniques of Milton H. Erickson, M.D.* (New York, 1973).
9. B. F. Skinner, *Science and Human Behavior* (New York, 1953).
10. Robert Paul Liberman, "Behavioral Approaches to Family and Couples Therapy," in Sager and Kaplan, eds., *op. cit.*, pp. 329–45.
11. T. Allyon and N. H. Azrin, *The Token Economy* (New York, 1968).
12. L. Birk et al., *Behavior Therapy in Psychiatry*, Task Force Report no. 5, American Psychiatric Association (Washington, 1973).
13. There have been claims that behavioral and psychoanalytic therapy are really convergent—e.g., Lee Birk and Ann W. Brinkley-Birk, "Psychoanalysis and Behavior Therapy," *American Journal of Psychiatry*, *131* (1974): 499–511. However, such studies begin by diluting the idea of repression and the unconscious. The watered-down psychoanalysis that results is indeed compatible with a reasonably sophisticated behaviorism—but it is not what Freud had in mind.
14. B. F. Skinner, *Beyond Freedom and Dignity* (New York, 1971), the arguments of which are beyond repair after Noam Chomsky gets through with them, in "Psychology and Ideology," *For Reasons of State* (New York, 1973).

Part Three. FOR THE CUSTOMER AND CITIZEN

Chapter 15. Guide For The Perplexed

1. See Chap. 14, note 1.

Chapter 16. Hysterical Misery And Common Unhappiness

1. Joseph Breuer and Sigmund Freud, *Studies in Hysteria* (*S.E.*, vol. 2, p. 305).
2. See Hendrik Ruitenbeck, ed., *Going Crazy* (New York, 1972); Jerome Agel, ed., *The Radical Therapist* (New York, 1971); Michael Glenn and Richard Kunnes, *Repression or Revolution? Therapy in the United States Today* (New York, 1973); Phil Brown, *Toward a Marxist Psychology* (New York, 1974).
3. Karl Marx, *Grundrisse: Introduction to the Critique of Political Economy*, trans. Martin Nicolaus, (Harmondsworth and Baltimore, 1973), p. 705.
4. See Chap. 9, note 1.
5. There is an interesting and as yet unworked-out relation between fetishization on the cultural scale and the sexual perversion bearing the same name, in which some material associated with the (usually female) body—e.g., hair, shoes, etc.— becomes the necessary condition for sexual arousal and—in full form—orgasm. In each case a part stands for the totality, and some materialization of fantasy is needed in order to overcome the influence of an old, and hidden, wound.
6. David Erdman, ed., *The Poetry and Prose of William Blake* (Garden City, N.Y., 1965), bk. 2, plate 40, lines 28–37; plate 41, lines 1 and 2.
7. David Erdman, *Blake: Prophet Against Empire*, 2d ed. (Garden City, N.Y., 1969), p. 472.

INDEX

ABOUT THE AUTHOR

Dr. Joel Kovel is Associate Professor of Psychiatry at Albert Einstein College of Medicine. His first book, *White Racism: A Psychohistory* (Pantheon, 1970), was nominated for the National Book Award in Philosophy and Religion. He has written and lectured widely about the social implications of psychoanalysis.